SCOTLAND'S
Nature & Wildlife

KENNY TAYLOR

Thanks to Ronan and Alice Taylor for being pleasantly wild and noticing small creatures that I'd otherwise miss; to my mother, Doris Taylor, for life-long encouragement; and to Caoline Vawdrey for typing the manuscript.

LOMOND
www.lomondbooks.com

First published in Great Britain in Hardback 2002 by
Lomond Books
13-14 Freskyn Place, East Mains Industrial Estate, Broxburn, EH52 5NF
www.lomondbooks.com
This paperback edition 2018

Copyright © Lomond Books 2018
Text copyright © Kenny Taylor 2002, 2005, 2018

Photography copyright © Colin Baxter 2018, page: back cover (bottom right), 50

Photography copyright © Peter Cairns 2018, pages: 69, 155

Photography copyright © Laurie Campbell 2018, pages: 10, 11, 17, 24, 26, 30, 33, 37, 39, 40, 43, 44, 47, 53, 54, 56, 58, 71, 75, 76, 78, 80, 82, 87, 91, 94, 97, 98, 102, 104, 109, 112, 115, 116, 119, 120, 122, 125, 127, 131, 132, 135, 137, 139, 141, 144, 145, 146, 153, 161, 165, 171, 175, 178, 181, 182, 185, 187, 195, 196, 203, 204, 209, 210, 213, 214, 219, back cover (top)

Photography copyright © Roy Glen, Windrush Photos 2018, page: 101

Photography copyright © Mark Hamblin 2018, pages: 6, 20, 23, 60, 73, 143, 150, 163, 172, 192, 200, 205

Photography copyright © Neil McIntyre 2018, pages: 1, 4, 7, 9, 13, 19, 29, 34, 63, 83, 88, 149, 157, 159, 168, back cover (bottom left & middle)

Photography copyright © David Tipling, Windrush Photos 2018, pages: 57, 93, 191

Photography copyright © Ann and Steve Toon 2018, page: front cover

Photography copyright © David Whitaker 2018, pages: 3, 14, 36, 49, 160, 217

All Maps copyright © Wendy Price Cartographic Services, North Kessock, Inverness 2018, pages: 64, 66, 84, 110, 128, 166, 176, 188, 206

Illustrations copyright © Iain Sarjeant 2018, pages: 8, 15, 27, 46, 55, 67, 81, 85, 95, 96, 103, 107, 108, 111, 117, 126, 129, 134, 138, 151, 167, 170, 177, 183, 189, 199, 201, 207, 218

All rights reserved.

No part of this book may be reproduced, stored
in a retrieval system or transmitted in any form or by any means
without the prior written permission of the publisher.

A CIP catalogue record for this book is available from the British Library.

ISBN 9781842046654

Printed in Singapore

Front cover photograph: Red Deer Stag, Golden Eagle, Pine Martin, Heath Spotted Orchid

Page 1 photograph: Red Deer Stag Page 3 photograph: Bottlenose Dolphins Page 4 photograph: Red Squirrel

Back cover photographs: Top: Thistle Centre: Red Squirrel Bottom: Puffin

SCOTLAND'S
NATURE & WILDLIFE

KENNY TAYLOR

LOMOND

SCOTLAND'S NATURE AND WILDLIFE

CONTENTS

INTRODUCTION	7
OVERVIEW	11
WATCHING SCOTTISH WILDLIFE	21
THE SEASONS	57

A REGIONAL GUIDE TO THE BEST PLACES TO SEE WILDLIFE

THE BORDERS	67
CENTRAL LOWLANDS & FIFE	85
EASTERN LOWLANDS	111
CENTRAL HIGHLANDS	129
WEST HIGHLANDS AND ARGYLL	167
NORTHERN HIGHLANDS	177
HEBRIDES	189
NORTHERN ISLES	207
USEFUL CONTACTS	220
INDEX	224

SCOTLAND'S NATURE AND WILDLIFE

INTRODUCTION

You already have the kit to help you experience Scotland's wildlife. And it comes completely free. High-resolution optics, audio inputs, touch sensors, pressure pads and taste and scent detectors, fed to a multi-channel processor so complex that we can only guess at how it works. Eyes, ears, nerve endings, nose: no lifetime guarantee on those, of course. But even if part of the sensory array of sight, hearing, touch, taste and smell is shaky or on the blink, the brain that's allowing you to interpret this page will be fine-tuning the other senses.

So to make the first move to appreciate nature, don't worry about gear and gadgetry. Home-in on what you can discover unaided, and begin in your local patch. I spent several years looking and listening to birds in fields and woods around my childhood home in Kirkintilloch, for example, before I was given a pair of binoculars. Some people would now think of that as a real hardship – how could I have been a bin-less birdwatcher? But I've been thankful for that low-tech start ever since.

The great thing about it was that it helped me to use my own senses, unaided by anything except will-power, as an aid to getting close to many birds and learning their songs and calls. Picture it: there's a small bird in a hawthorn bush, but you can't see it clearly. What do you do? Walk boldly up to the bush and it's likely to zoom off out the other side, leaving you none the wiser. Hunker down and wait, and it may hop to the outside of the bush. Or move very, very slowly and quietly and you might get close enough to see the whole bird.

It has a dull, olive-brown beak and pale

chest, washed with faint yellow. Bending, it uses its thin beak to pluck a small insect from a twig. Then it moves on to the top of the bush and sings – a glorious outpouring of sweet-sounding, rhythmical notes, but no simple melody.

You might not immediately know that it's a willow warbler. But the experience may stay in mind, something of the essence of that encounter remain. Later, if you look through a field guide to bird identification, listen to a CD of warbler songs or watch a bird identification video, you'll discover the name. But the watching and listening in that place, with that bird, at that time, came first, before the naming, before the rational sifting and filtering kicked in.

And that, to me, is the very core of what encountering wildlife is all about. You can never give a precise prediction of what birds, plants, mammal signs or insects there will be around the next corner or over the next rise. So being alert and alive to the

MOUNTAIN HARE
The mountain hare can also be called the blue hare. This is because its fur has a bluish tinge in spring and autumn. Its broad feet act like snowshoes.

GOLDEN EAGLE
(opposite)

messages of your own senses, moving like a hunter – or sometimes like possible prey – keeps you fresh to notice things that might otherwise be overlooked.

A rattlesnake reminded me about this not so long ago. I was hiking down a steep stream gully in the Shenandoah National Park in West Virginia. Pausing on a large rock in the middle of the channel, I became aware of a sound that wasn't the water, or the noise of leaves moving in the trees. Then I saw it – a timber rattler, coiled and facing me only a couple of metres ahead, shaking its rattle with a sound that now sent a chill down my spine.

Slowly, slowly, I backed off the boulder and climbed to a viewpoint high above the snake. It forgot about me and I could now watch it, unafraid. I saw how its camouflage was perfect among piles of dead leaves, how the rustle of its movement mimicked their sound. When it came to a branch shadow, it followed in the track of the shadow, becoming shadow as it had become leaves only seconds before.

The whole of the rest of that day as I hiked, it felt as if I'd been given a sensory overhaul. True, there was a slight twang of danger in mind, but the bonus was the way I now instinctively scanned every leaf pile, saw colours heightened, heard the slightest sounds in grass and trees. For a few, delicious hours, I'd rediscovered something of what our ancestors must have had up-front and everyday – the power of your senses when your instinct tells you they really matter.

Scotland is not big on venomous snakes. Most adders will retreat long before you even know they're about, and if you are unlucky enough to be bitten by one, you should live to tell the tale. Big predators were hunted out centuries ago and more. No bears, no wolves – even the medium-sized lynx has gone (though there would be a good case for bringing it back very soon). Land creatures with sharp teeth and a feisty attitude are modest in size. Wildcat and pine marten head the list, with stoats and weasels way down the scale.

But although there's no fast track to nature alertness in Scotland, courtesy of creatures which could make serious challenges to us as rulers of the roost, what we do have by the landscape load is glorious variety – of scenes, plants and creatures.

That variety is both a pleasure and a challenge. For within those varied scenes, you can be certain that there will be plenty of places, large and small, scarcely visited by anyone keen on wildlife. A wee patch of woodland, a burn gully, a stretch of shrubby ground where a factory used to stand, a stretch of wild coast kilometres from the nearest village – the possibilities are huge.

And if you make the effort to have a closer look, the beauty of wildlife is that it will be nigh impossible to be disappointed by what you find. You may have seen ladybirds countless times before, but find one on a willow-herb stem on the factory site, and you'll probably still smile at the discovery. Or the chaffinch singing in the wood, the moss by the burn gully, the spray washing the barnacles on the windy shore – fresh and refreshing, that's how it can be, if you choose to be alive to Scotland's wild variety.

Within this bigger picture, some places stand out as being so good for wildlife as to offer obvious bonuses. Whether home to scarce species or just great areas to see commoner ones, these places are true hotspots. Many are designated as reserves, under the care of a variety of conservation

Grey Heron

INTRODUCTION

bodies. By visiting such a place, you can be sure of encountering interesting wildlife, often as not in a very pleasant setting.

There may also be extra information available on or near the site, such as a leaflet, display boards or even a visitor centre, and some of the larger or more heavily used places may have seasonal or full-time ranger staff. These people will know their patch in brilliant detail, and can share their knowledge through anything from a brief chat to a full ranger-guided ramble.

Part of the purpose of this book is to help you locate some great wildlife hotspots. Within eight broad areas of Scotland, a range of places is highlighted and described in the text. The list is long, but not exhaustive. The idea is to give pointers to places which hold some of the finest wildlife the wider area hosts, and to include a wide variety of species across a number of key sites.

At some, attention may naturally focus more on one group of species than others. Caerlaverock is renowned for its wildfowl, for example, Ben Lawers for its mountain plants and Noss for its seabirds. But within these places, there is much more to encounter than the star turns. So descriptions of other species get a look-in too, with the sites for a whole region including a good sweep, from insects to mammals.

Another aim of the book is to reveal something of the varied lives of some of the many species that make Scotland their home. These featured plants and creatures include many of the ones for which the country is famous – so eagles, salmon and red deer are there – and plenty of others to give a taste of just how amazing the details of different species' lives can be. And for groups as different as whales and butterflies, there are tips on how to go about watching them.

Armed with the information in this book, you should be able to select some excellent locations, in any part of Scotland, to sample some of the nation's nature. But that could be just the beginning. For by visiting and learning in some of the hotspots, you'll be better equipped to savour the diversity on your doorstep. Croft or tenement, mansion or multi-storey, there's something of Scotland's wild heart near you, right now. It might be a starling flock over the buildings, an otter padding the shore, a spider in the bath, a honeysuckle scenting the night air and luring in a hawkmoth. The possibilities are endless, beyond anyone's imagining. And that's the real call of the wild. Once sensed, never forgotten. Enjoy the quest!

RED GROUSE
A red grouse in its element. No other bird in the world makes such substantial use of heather. The shoots provide food and the plants give cover for nests and camouflage for adults

SCOTLAND'S NATURE AND WILDLIFE

OVERVIEW

Think of Scotland, and what do you picture?

Perhaps a single bird or animal – an eagle over a mountain, an otter in a pool. Perhaps a host of creatures or plants – a group of dolphins bow-riding a boat, daisies by the thousand in a field, the purple of ling on a moor, or even a cloud of midges by a loch.

Chances are, whatever your initial thoughts and impressions, elements of landscape figure strongly both as settings and as part of the feeling associated with the wildlife. And within those landscapes, a human presence, either hinted at or up-front: lines of field boundaries or croft; the pier by the sea loch; the buildings by the park.

Nowhere in Scotland is far, by global standards, from signs of people. You would find it hard, in most areas, to travel as much as ten kilometres, even in mountain ground, without seeing some obvious human sign. Yet, intriguingly, there are plenty of places where you can experience a tingle of wild Scotland, feel challenged by the nature of the place and wonder what discoveries await as you move through the marvellous mosaic of the nation's landscapes and seascapes.

Within cities, on the hills, out on islands, along loch shores, among farms, there's a wealth of wildlife to be encountered and enjoyed. No matter that Scotland, at around 7.9 million hectares, is a small place in world terms (many individual states or provinces in North America are much, much larger, for example), it's big on variety. Part of that variety stems from human endeavour, working within the constraints of some basic national themes; part stems from those fundamental themes themselves – the foundations that underpin the richness of the wildlife.

THE TRESHNISH ISLES
Scotland has a wealth of islands to the west and north of the mainland. The Treshnish Isles sit off the Atlantic rim of Mull.

So what is different about Scotland and its wildlife? What sets it apart, and what links it to other countries in the big picture of this glorious green and blue planet? Water, weather and rock are keystones – defining elements that set the possibilities.

Sitting at the meeting of the Atlantic Ocean and the North Sea, with the nation's capital closer to the Arctic than to the Mediterranean, and Scandinavia within easy reach, Scotland is aswirl with winds and waters that come from many compass points. It is joined to places far beyond its shores, through movements of wildlife, such as migratory fish, sea mammals and birds. Yet it is also separate – a place at the very rim of Europe, where the influence of sea and ocean can be all-pervasive. The weather in the west

SCOTS PINE
The Scots pine – most widespread cone-bearing tree in the world – is one of three conifers native to Scotland. The others are juniper and yew.

SCOTLAND'S NATURE AND WILDLIFE

COMMON LIZARD
(Lacerta vivipara)

It's the only lizard that looks like one in Scotland. The other lizard – the slow-worm – keeps its lizard links under snake-like wraps. To have a chance of seeing a common lizard, the weather usually has to be warm.

These are fair-weather movers, whose cold blood needs a good warming in a sunny spot to set them up for the day. They also like a relaxing bask in the evening to keep them cosy through the night.

With this Mediterranean approach to life, it's not surprising that they hole-up for the winter in retreats such as piles of stones. Adult females are the first to retire for the season, followed by males and the youngsters. Once inactive, they use fat reserves (much stored in the tail) to see them through the months of cold.

Despite this obvious temperature challenge, common lizards are able to live in a great variety of places, from town gardens to high up on mountains. They've also managed to get to many of the islands, including the Outer Hebrides.

A lizard's ability to shed its tail (which keeps on wriggling after detachment) in an effort to distract an attacker is well known. Common lizards also have another claim to fame, through producing young which are able to move around a very short time after birth, when they emerge from very thin-shelled covers.

DID YOU KNOW?

Some of the oldest Scots pines still surviving in Scotland were young trees when Joan of Arc was alive, in the mid 1400s.

---

makes that obvious, with everything from light and breezy showers to near hurricanes hurled in on the prevailing winds from the Atlantic. But polar air comes here too, sometimes by way of the continent, bringing snows to the eastern mountains, or the chill of a sea fog or 'haar' to cast a clamminess along the North Sea shores.

You could call the climate 'oceanic', not only from the rains borne in on salty air, but also because of how the ocean keeps the west mild for a country this far north. Cross Canada at the level of Inverness, for example, and you could take in a place like Churchill, where polar bears are part of the urban wildlife scene in winter.

The North Atlantic Drift (a circulation of water linked to the Gulf Stream) helps Scotland, especially western Scotland, to walk on the mild side. So when it comes to considering the country's wildlife richness, it's perhaps not too surprising that Scotland scores high for species that like damp, wet conditions. Prominent among these, in terms of plants, are ones that many might overlook – the mosses and liverworts.

Collectively known as 'bryophytes', these plants love it in the wet. Some thrive in cool gullies within splash reach of burns and cascades, some cling to trees and rocks, sharing their perches with an abundance of lichens. It's no exaggeration to say that the variety of bryophytes and lichens in some western Scottish woodlands near the coast makes such places rank as true temperate rainforests, rich in species and with much yet to be learnt about their inhabitants.

Water – fresh or salt – is a defining feature of the look of much of Scotland. Consider the wave-washed wrapper, for a start. At 11,800 kilometres the coastline has an astonishing length for a country of Scotland's size. That's the same distance as from Aberdeen to Jakarta in south-east Asia: a long walk by anyone's standards. It's also twice the length of the entire English coast.

More than 5000 kilometres of coast surrounds the many Scottish islands, most of which sit beyond the western and northern edges of the Scottish mainland. The number of islands depends on how you count them. Include everything from wee, surge-blasted skerries where even limpets could have problems hanging on, and the figure runs to many thousands

OVERVIEW

OSPREY

After regaining a British talon-hold as a breeder by re-colonising the Highlands in the late 1950s, the osprey is also now breeding in England. Ospreys migrate to spend the winter in Africa and can make long sea crossings to get there.

(some say more than 5000, others more than 6000; perhaps it depends whether you count at high or low tide). Restrict the count to vegetated islands of slightly larger size (the proverbial 'big enough to support a grazing sheep', favoured as a definition from the time of the ancient Greeks onwards) and you get a figure of around 800.

Some, like Skye, Lewis and Harris (one land mass, but utterly different from each other in landscape character) and Orkney Mainland are leviathans; others are tiddlers of a handful of hectares. But all offer possibilities for coastal wildlife – a shore base to occupy as living space or from which to launch out to the deeps.

The freshwater picture is no less amazing. More than 90 per cent of the total amount of freshwater in the United Kingdom is held here, in over 30,000 freshwater lochs and lochans, transported in burns beyond counting, and along a bevvy of fine rivers. Mightiest of all, in terms of flow, is the River Tay, which transports more water than any other British river. Up there at the top of the freshwater league tables too sit Loch Lomond (largest surface area of any British inland water), Loch Ness (monster of them all by volume) and Loch Morar (deepest body of freshwater in Europe).

One spin-off from all this freshwater is that insects with aquatic larvae – such as stoneflies and caddis flies – or water-dwelling adult lifestyles – such as water beetles – do particularly well here. The Highland midge, in this respect, goes for a

SCOTLAND'S NATURE AND WILDLIFE

GREENSHANK

The greenshank is a scarce wading bird that still thrives in the major Scottish peatlands of Caithness, Sutherland and the Western Isles. Its name comes from the gorgeous colour of its long legs.

degree of moderation. Its larvae thrive in situations that stay damp, but fairly free of standing water; the sort of conditions that mosses which grow on bogs or by other wet areas can offer by the load.

There's no doubt that Scotland's good at doing bogs, especially the 'blanket bogs' that clamp their cold compresses of peat (produced from part-decayed moss, held in oxygen-starved limbo) and living moss (largely drawn from a broad and colourful palette of *Sphagnum* species) over huge areas of the Scottish uplands, islands and northern mainland. The big bogs of Caithness and Sutherland, in the area known as the Flow Country, are perhaps the best blanket bogs of their kind on the planet, and home to an array of scarce breeding birds.

Many of these birds, such as greenshank and black-throated diver, would be an equally natural part of communities to the north of here, in Scandinavia and farther east. Their presence in northern Scotland, together with species that can also live far to the south, illustrates another of Scotland's wildlife features, as a country where flora and fauna from north and south, and sometimes east and west, may meet.

The east-west linkage is to the fore in the pine-and-birch-clad woodlands of the Caledonian forest (where an Atlantic element is also obvious in some of the plants). Once reduced to a few beleaguered fragments, now greatly expanding thanks to new plantings of native trees, these woods give a living connection to the largest system of forest in the world. Far greater in scale than the remaining rainforests, the conifer-rich boreal forest girdles the globe from Scandinavia to the Pacific shores of Siberia, with the theme taken up again (though with different species variations) from Alaska and on across Canada.

The Caledonian pinewoods are an outpost of this global superforest, and some of their flora and fauna shows it. Plants like twinflower, birds such as crossbills, creatures like wood ants and pine martens give these international connections. A boreal element comes into other parts of the Scottish wildlife scene, adding its emphasis to the distinctively Scottish mix.

Oceanic, boreal – there's another too – Arctic alpine. The very words conjure up an idea of mountains. And Scotland is the prime place in all Britain and Ireland for those.

Don't typecast – only around 6 per cent of the land mass sits above 610 metres (2000 feet), for example. But in terms of uplands, which could be defined as land above enclosed farmland or croftland and covered in reasonably natural vegetation, Scotland has plenty.

Almost two-thirds of the whole country can be classed as upland, representing the biggest area of near-natural wildlife habitats in Britain. As pointed out by bodies that compiled such statistics of land cover, notably Scottish Natural Heritage, that's a remarkable asset for a largely urbanised nation.

More than eight out of ten Scots live in cities and large towns, and yet there are vast areas of upland within fairly easy reach of almost everyone. From deep within Glasgow, you can look across to the Campsies and the Kilpatrick Hills, with the Loch Lomond National Park not far beyond. The Pentlands rise at the edge of Edinburgh (which also has its very own uplands in the city itself, along the heights of the Salisbury Crags and Arthur's Seat).

Perth looks west to the Trossachs mountains and north-east to the Grampian peaks. Aberdeen has Bennachie as a classic upland landmark, defining part of the character of its hinterland. Inverness is less than an hour from The Cairngorms National Park and has Ben Wyvis as the presiding height overlooking the Highland capital.

Such an abundance of upland ground comes with a great array of wildlife riches. There is a greater mixture of bird species in the Scottish uplands, for example, than in any other part of Europe of similar size. Breeding waders, including the

> ### BROWN SEAWEEDS
>
> The commonest brown seaweeds in the upper and middle parts of rocky shores, which are not too exposed to the waves, are called 'wracks'. Different species of wracks tend to grow in different parts of the shore and, in a place like a sheltered sea loch at low tide, you can follow a fairly predictable sequence of them from high tide mark to the waterline.
>
> Typically, the brown seaweed farthest up the shore is chanelled wrack (*Pelvetica canaliculata*) a fairly small weed, with the colour of pale fudge. Its fronds are curled to form a channel up one side, so helping to retain water when the plant is high and dry. Close by, but not quite so able to resist drying-out, could be spiral wrack (*Fucus spiralis*), with a twist to its fronds.
>
> Hit the middle shore and bladder wrack (*Fucus vesiculosus*) – the one with the little air bladders that tempt children, and some adults, to give them a quick pop – can be quite abundant. Serrated wrack (*Fucus serratus*), with saw-tooth frond rims is usually also present, with the chance of finding some egg wrack (*Ascophyllum nodosum*), which has big bladders along each frond, on sheltered shores. If you hit the kelp beds you're subtidal. Time to head back up the beach!

dapper-plumaged dotterel, are among those high-fliers, plus others including ptarmigan, ravens and a range of birds of prey, with the golden eagle soaring as the symbol of the whole upland scene.

The variety and abundance of mountain-dwelling plants here is excellent, with mountains in the southern Highlands (where the rocks are lime-rich) particular hotspots for this aspect of biological diversity. Scarce Arctic-alpine plants are part of this 'biodiversity' picture, but so too are swathes of much more extensive vegetation –

Corncrake

SCOTLAND'S NATURE AND WILDLIFE

> ### SEA EAGLE
> ### (Haliaeetus albicilla)
>
> Get close to an adult sea eagle, or white-tailed eagle as it is also known, and there are many things that impress. The sheer size, for one thing. This is one of the largest flying birds in the world. So when a sea eagle is soaring overhead, it can look as if a chunk of barn door is defying gravity.
>
> On the ground, it can come a good way up the height of a fence post when it's standing upright. The white tail (only gained in full snowiness in adulthood at the age of five or six) is striking; the huge bill even more so. Then there's the brightness of the yellow eyes, the inspiration for one glorious Gaelic name for the bird – *Iolair Suill na Greine* – 'eagle with the sunlit eye'.
>
> Things weren't sunny for Scottish sea eagles early last century. The last pair in the country was shot in 1916. In 1975, after an earlier short-lived attempt on Fair Isle, young sea eagles were taken from Arctic Norway to the island of Rum to start a reintroduction programme. Now the big birds have slowly reoccupied some of their former range, gradually increasing the numbers of fledged chicks to more than ten per year.

eye for wildlife across less travelled hills, ridges and peaks. From those heights, you can also get an idea of some of the monumental scale and complexity of the rocks that are the framework for the whole country – the foundation stones, weather-workers, soil-shapers, water-channellers. Look at a satellite picture that distinguishes high ground and low, or a map that picks out hills or shows underlying rocks, and a three-way split in the Scottish mainland becomes obvious. Highlands, Central Lowlands, Southern Uplands – these familiar terms reflect fundamental differences in geology, whatever other comparisons they conjure.

Rounded hills with smooth slopes, cut by narrow steep-sided valleys in the Southern Uplands; a plain punctuated by volcano-spawned hills in the centre, where the bulk of Scotland's 5.1 million people dwell; mountains with cliffs and corries stretching across the Highlands like waves in a sea of rock dipping to troughs of glens: those are broad-brush aspects of that three-fold division. But the major geological faults – those zones of meeting and realignment of huge chunks of country and continent – add further divisions, giving at least a five-fold split in the Scottish mainland.

moss-and-lichen-rich heaths high on the mountains, carpets of blaeberry, sweeps of heather in the middle ground, squelches of bog in upland hollows, high in the hills or down in the glens.

More than 90 per cent of the mountain area (the land above 610 metres) in Britain is here, and almost all the land over 915 metres (3000 feet). Top of the lot is Ben Nevis, peaking at 1347 metres, but the pleasures and possibilities offered by the other mountains are legion. Those over 915 metres are classed as 'Munros' (after Sir Hugh Thomas Munro, a founder member of the Scottish Mountaineering Club, who first listed them) and are a honeypot for hillwalkers.

You can see some excellent wildlife on Munro ground, as described in parts of this book, but there's also a great deal to be gained by stravaiging with an

The major divisions in rock types and geological history are reflected fairly strongly in the mainland regions described in this book, all of which sit principally in one, or partly in two of these. Most of Scotland's uplands are composed of ancient rocks. Oldest of them all is the Lewisian gneiss that is prominent in the north-west and the Hebrides, to the west of the fault called the Moine Thrust.

Three other major faults, also roughly aligned on a broad south-west-

> ### DID YOU KNOW?
>
> *Freshwater pearl mussels, now rare, can live for well over a century if undisturbed. This means that some have lived in the same stretch of river since the time of Queen Victoria.*

OVERVIEW

LAMMERMUIR HILLS
The rolling hills of Scotland's Southern Uplands, such as Berwickshire's Lammermuirs, are carved from sediments laid down in a vanished ocean.

to-north-east axis, lie between here and the border with England. The Great Glen Fault, the Highland Boundary Fault, the Southern Upland Fault, like the Moine Thrust, each marks the boundary between different geological mega-blocks, each of which reveals something of the story of wild Scotland over tens of millions – and sometimes thousands of millions – of years.

Moving south-eastwards from the Lewisian foreland (legacy of a long-vanished super-continent called Laurentia, in which Scotland was once linked to North America, and an ocean away from the rest of Britain), the underlying rock – the 'bedrock' – gets younger, in the journey to the sedimentary rocks of the Southern Uplands. Many hill areas in central Scotland hold younger, volcanic rocks, with the youngest of all in the volcanic outpourings locked in stone in places such as the Cuillins of Skye and Rum, and at Ardnamurchan.

The history of these rocks is complex – punctuated by world-changing events such as continental collision, mountain building and disappearance of oceans – but ultimately shaped by the much more recent action of glacial ice. Whatever the transformations, folds and faults held in layers of rock as evidence of distant eras and vanished lands, the face of present-day Scotland has been chiselled and shaped, more than any other factor, by recent ice ages.

The contours of the hills, whether

DID YOU KNOW?

One tiny species of moth (a so-called 'micro-moth') has been recorded only from inside whisky distilleries.

SCOTLAND'S NATURE AND WILDLIFE

> ### MOUNTAIN HARE
> ### *(Lepus timidus)*
>
> Also known as the blue hare, and a host of other names besides within its huge world range, the mountain hare is widespread in Scottish uplands and islands. Some island populations of both mountain hares and brown hares are the result of introductions by people keen to boost the variety of furry fauna, which they could then go out and shoot. Success of introductions varied from place to place, as demonstrated by brown hare fortunes after the local Member of Parliament, Samuel Laing, took them to both Orkney and Shetland around 1830. The Shetland browns lasted until 1937, since when there have been no records. On Orkney they are restricted to Mainland and Rousay.
>
> Mountain hares have fared rather better on Shetland. They were introduced to an island called Vaila, off west Mainland, in 1900, and to the Kergord estate in about 1907. Now they are widespread on Mainland and still surviving on Vaila.
>
> On Orkney, mountain hares were already present on Hoy – still the only part of the group where they live – as long ago as 1529, when John Bellenden recorded them as 'white hares'. This name is highly appropriate to their winter coat. Its camouflage qualities might not be too good on islands, where snow lie is patchy and unpredictable – perhaps that's why Irish mountain hares don't have a seasonal colour change. But in the North Isles, that drawback seems to be offset by the heat-retaining qualities of the snowy winter coat – not what you'd expect at first glance, but the structure and arrangement of hairs make the coat a good thermal jacket.

CAPERCAILLIE
The cock capercaillie, as big as a turkey, is the world's largest grouse. Pine needles are the principal food that powers caper cocks and hens.

curved or sharply cut, from corries to sheer cliffs; the basins that hold lochs; the gravels heaped in drumlin hillocks or scattered wide; the fjord-like sea lochs, some 80 of which poke salty fingers deep inland along the western seaboard; all those and many more features have their origins in the grinding, shunting, smoothing, flattening and dumping power of ice. And from these features spring possibilities and constraints for life – opportunities for plants and creatures to colonise and thrive, or to perish if conditions don't suit them – in an ancient land that emerged, as if new-minted, when the weight of the ice-age glaciers was taken off its rocky shoulders.

Across 10,000 years and more, Scotland has been the home of many, many species. Some have vanished, and some of the places they once inhabited have shrunk to a shadow of their former spread. But what remains is still one of the finest arrays of wildlife in the whole of Europe.

Mudflat and mountain, forest and park, farm and heath, loch and river: those and many other places, plus the host of plants, birds and animals that can use them, are just part of the legacy from water, weather and rock. Watching wildlife in these places can reveal layer after layer of living variety, give a new sense of natural communities, in, around and beyond our own communities, all tackling the challenges of life at Europe's sea-swept edge: Scotland the Wild, a nation of possibilities.

OVERVIEW

SCOTLAND'S NATURE AND WILDLIFE

Watching Scottish Wildlife

According to the most recent figures, Scotland is home to approximately 90,000 species of birds, animals, plants and microbes. That won't be the end of it, for as people look closely at different places, fresh discoveries await. You can bet your walking boots, for example, that there are insects not yet known to science living right now in the Scottish mountains and on some of the islands.

New species have been found in such places in the last 25 years, including a type of fly collected by a member of an expedition that I took part in to the remote island of Boreray, northernmost of the St Kilda group. Scotland still holds plenty of unknowns, plenty of challenges, for anyone with an interest in wildlife.

Among the tens of thousands of wild Scottish residents, nearly half are so small as to be invisible without the aid of a microscope. These single-celled organisms, including viruses, bacteria and things like those walking miracles of unicellular travel, amoebas, play hugely important roles, often for better, sometimes for worse, in the lives of the many-celled beings (including us) around them.

Using the specialist kit of a pair of binoculars or a single-lens microscope – even one that you could hook up to a computer – you might get the bug for ogling such microfauna (though viruses would still be beyond your ken). But for practical purposes, wildlife for most people will mean the other 45,500 or so species that we at least have a chance to register on our human sensory radar.

Fungi, algae, mosses, ferns; flowering plants, trees; slugs, snails, sea molluscs, insects, spiders; fish, amphibians, reptiles, birds, mammals: those are some of the broad groupings of species that live in and around Scotland. Look at that list, and you'll likely find that the last few words could suggest more names to you than much of the rest (flowering plants, trees and fish apart perhaps).

Familiarity Breeds Discovery

Frogs, lizards, ospreys, deer, dandelions and herring tend to be more familiar than, say, banded snails and buckler ferns. You can use your knowledge of one group – or even one species – to improve your ability to find others. Sifting the dandelions from the buttercups is child's play to many – but it's also a step towards knowing that those other yellow flowers, over there by the road verge, or up the mountain scree, are different. And through that perception, you can begin to home-in on recognising a species you'd

TAWNY OWL
The facial disc of owls, like this Tawny, helps to collect and focus sounds (such as mouse rustlings) from small prey.

SCOTLAND'S NATURE AND WILDLIFE

WHITE WATER LILY
(Nymphaea alba)

There's something breathtaking about the beauty of water lilies in a Hebridean or West Highland setting. It's not just the paleness of petals that does it, but the further layers of contrast: white flower on peat-dark water; golden heart of flaring stamens; the crispness of line in the lotus-like blossom against a wildness of lochan edge beyond.

The massive, rounded leaves are solar collectors and energy stores, waxed on the upper surface to keep them dry. This is also where the water lily's tiny breathing pores – stomata – are positioned, unlike most other plants which have stomata on undersides of leaves.

Air pockets in stems and leaves act as flotation chambers, and the whole structure is anchored by a stout rhizome to the bottom silt. It adds up to an impressive show, also functioning as a platform which frogs, water snails and insects such as moths which have semi-aquatic caterpillars can use.

DID YOU KNOW?

Scotland is the best place in the world for actively growing 'blanket' bog, thanks to a combination of rainfall and the luxuriant growth of different kinds of bog mosses.

perhaps not noticed before.

It's a basic principle, but if you learn to cultivate curiosity about the colours, forms, scents and sounds of nature, you'll never be short of fresh pointers to expanded knowledge. Some groups will tend to remain too obscure, too finicky to tackle, for many folk. This is one reason why so much remains to be discovered about a host of Scottish insects, spiders, algae and fungi. But you can still find great pleasure in getting at least a nodding acquaintance with some of that number.

The sections that follow won't make you an expert on beetles or any other group. But they will give you pointers to help you watch and discover more about Scottish wildlife. Beyond those pointers, there's a nation of possibilities. Some general principles (beyond that all-important curiosity and faith in your own senses) apply to all groups. Top priority should be that the welfare of the creatures and plants that interest you, and the places where they live, should be paramount. So treat both species and their habitats with respect.

Move as if you were a guest, not an owner, and you'll be on the right lines. Whether trying to get closer to a starling in a bush, a butterfly on a flower or a hare on the hill, the idea is the same and the same rewards will stem from it: wildlife that you can appreciate without harming or frightening unduly; creatures that can stay put or return to their daily business soon after you've moved on.

Don't Be a Rustler

Wearing the right gear can help you to get closer to mammals and birds; though you've a fair amount of flexibility in gardens and parks (where many of the creatures are pretty street-wise and not readily shocked by the latest fashion trend). Brightly coloured rainwear made of noisy, scrunchy fabrics will turn you into a walking alarm bell on many estuaries, hills and in the woods. If you want to dress wildlife-savvy, dull down and hush up. Muted greens, browns, charcoals – you know the kind of thing – with fabrics like weather-proofed cotton (soft cotton is ideal, as is supple waxed cotton) are just the job.

Since Scotland is big on water – falling from the sky, swelling bogs, splashing shores, filling lochs – a pair of wellies should be high on the list for many keen to ramble in search of wildlife. Weather-waxed hiking boots and gaiters (including those expensive, crazily named, but very efficient super-

WATCHING SCOTTISH WILDLIFE

gaiters called 'yetis') are another option.

In the optical department, don't go crazy over the latest German designer binoculars until you're sure what suits your wildlife-watching style, and your budget. High magnification may sound good, but don't be lured by anything more than x10 magnification, and go for as wide a front glass diameter as you find comfortable. That diameter is revealed in the second number of the specification of a pair of binoculars. A pair of 8x40 binoculars magnifies eight times, for example, with a front glass width of 40 millimetres, and so has more light-gathering power than a pair of 8x30 binoculars.

Monoculars – often sold as quite compact, single-tube affairs – are an under-used resource among wildlife watchers. Their great benefits are that they are very portable (you can slip one into a top pocket), reasonably priced (think £50.00 and you won't be too far wrong) and focus very close. This last feature is a boon for watching dragonflies, damselflies, day-flying moths, butterflies and even some beetles.

Small is Spectacular

Take the close-up idea a stage further, and a 'hand lens' – a small, quality magnifier sold by optical supply shops – is an even more compact piece of kit. A x8 hand lens can be about the size of an adult's thumb and reveal amazing details of

COMMON (OR HARBOUR) SEAL

Common seals often use sandbanks as haul-outs and summer pupping sites. So a newborn youngster needs to be able to swim as soon as the tide comes in.

SCOTLAND'S NATURE AND WILDLIFE

PUSS MOTH – LARVA
Invest in a hand lens and you could get up close and intimate with some amazing mini wildlife, such as this puss moth caterpillar. But don't get too close – a puss moth larva can release formic acid as a defence.

pattern and structure – a must for moss appreciation, but also good for looking at everything from rock patterns to the heads of obliging ants.

Recording some observations in a notebook can be an aid to memory, a help in sussing-out species identification at a later date, fun to re-read and even a way of checking for changes in things like migrant arrival dates over a long spread of years. Don't feel hide-bound by formality if you make notes. Some people write wildlife notes and diaries as if they were a police constable reporting events and statements at the scene of a crime. Fine if that's how you really want to do it, but otherwise an unnecessary cramping of style. So let the real you get some breathing space if you're writing and sketching notes and impressions of wildlife. A list of species seen might figure and be valuable, but so too might your ideas on the scent of the bog myrtle, the shape of that high-flying bird, the way the wind felt in the oakwood.

Photographs can also be a good addition to notes, so a tip here is to use ring-binder pages for storing your notes and diary jottings. That way, you can add photographs at a later date to writing or sketching entries, but still keep them in the correct place.

There are many books on identification of different wildlife groups. Birdwatchers are best served by these, with many good 'field guides' available. Other field guides covering everything from fungi to sea mammals are available, specialising in clear illustrations and text to let you discover the identity of different species.

This book is not a substitute for field guides (although the many pictures should be a help in identifying a good swatch of different species). Rather, it's a way of giving an introduction to watching and studying different groups, and of choosing a range of places where you can hone your skills. For starters, let's dive in at the deep end and think big; very big.

Sea Mammals

The massive tail fluke, wide as a small dinghy is long, is held poised, almost motionless. Then it slips beneath the sea surface, with only a patch of flat-looking water remaining to show where the ocean giant has dived.

That's the image many people have of whale watching. It's based on countless still pictures and TV documentaries of classic whale performers, especially humpbacked whales. More than most of their fellow cetaceans (a group that includes whales, dolphins and porpoises), humpbacks seem able to play to a gallery of human observers, making their moves in slow-mo, allowing people to savour the moments and press shutters as the action unfolds.

Whale-watching in Scottish waters isn't usually like that. True, you can be lucky to see a humpback off Shetland on a fairly regular basis. Other marine megafauna swim far offshore, including the mother of them all – the blue whale. The largest creatures ever to have swum the seas, and a match in size for the land-shaking dinosaurs, blue whales run deep off the islands of the St Kilda group. But their presence can only be detected from high-tech underwater listening devices – the gadgetry of defence systems turned to peaceful scientific use.

Watch the Minke

For the most part, watching larger whales around Scotland focuses on one species – the minke whale. Known, sadly, as the animal still hunted for meat by Norwegian whalers, the minke also presents some challenges for those who simply wish to watch it. The principal of these is that minkes don't hang about at the surface for long.

This means that if you're with a party of would-be whale oglers on a boat, and someone else sees a minke surface, the animal may have dived before you swing your gaze to the place where it's just been – but isn't any more. The solution is to stay alert yourself, scanning the sea surface for signs of anything large rising. If a whale does show, the size and position of the dorsal fin (on the back) gives clues to species, as does the behaviour at the surface and the shape of the steamy blows it makes to breathe out. Getting the hang of the many variations on this fin/back/breath theme is worth doing for anyone serious about watching whales on a regular basis or in different countries. But for many people, remembering that the minke has a very small dorsal fin and that it scarcely pauses for breath before diving

---

PIPISTRELLE BATS
(*Pipistrellus spp.*)

Not so long ago, it would have been easy to say that the commonest bat in Scotland was the pipistrelle. Things got more complicated in 1999, when it was discovered that you can often distinguish – on the basis of tone of echolocation calls – two different widespread species of pipistrelle in Britain. This difference has now been confirmed by studies of bat DNA.

So where does that leave the Scottish 'pip' picture? It's still a wee bit confusing, since the species now widely known as the 'common pipistrelle' (*Pipistrellus pipistrellus*) (which dings-in at 45khz on the bat detector, bat lovers) seems to be less common in many parts of Scotland than the 'soprano pipistrelle' (*P. pygmaeus*) (which broadcasts at 55khz). And to add further intrigue, there's a third species, Nathusius' pipistrelle (*P. nathusii*) which seems likely to be more widely recorded in Scotland in future, as expert bat observers set out to seek it.

But for most of us the message is – don't panic! If you see a small bat (pipistrelles are Britain's smallest) making fast, jerky flights to pursue insects near buildings and trees, there's a high chance it will be a pipistrelle. Beyond that, you pays your money and selects your echo station.

SCOTLAND'S NATURE AND WILDLIFE

MINKE WHALE
The minke is the commonest whale in Scottish waters. But because it seldom spends long at the surface, it can be hard to point out to other people.

again can be sufficient for watching in Scotland.

Organised whale-watching trips are on offer around the Hebrides and in Shetland, where expert guides can help with ID challenges. But you can also enjoy good success from the decks of passenger ferries. Particularly good routes are those from Ullapool to and from Stornoway in Lewis, from Tarbert in Harris to Uig in Skye and from Aberdeen to Lerwick in Shetland.

An important tip for ferry-based watchers is to get out on deck as soon as you can after departure. This is because there can often be good concentrations of small fish (such as sand eels that minke whales and various dolphins relish) near the divide where shallow, inshore waters drop away to the greater depths of the open sea. Linger too long over an on-board beverage to celebrate anchors-aweigh, and you could miss some of the best cetacean action, whether a sight of some porpoises close to shore, or chunkier creatures farther out.

For both larger whales and their dolphin relatives, you can also have some success in land-based watching. A headland overlooking a sea-mammal-rich sea area can be ideal, and Scotland has several classic places of this kind, such as the Eye Peninsula on the east coast of Lewis, Ardnamurchan Point in the West Highlands or Sumburgh Head at the southern tip of Shetland (and many others which you could explore by picking out big promontories on a map). These can take a bit of travel effort to reach, so be sure to choose calm weather, and be prepared for a long wait. Cetacean watching takes patience, but the rewards, in terms of the thrill of seeing large sea creatures in their element, are huge.

Dolphins for Landlubbers
Classic locations for dolphin-watching are the narrows of the Inner Moray Firth near Inverness (near Ardersier, Fortrose and at the Kessock Channel beside the city) and also around Aberdeen Harbour, all favoured by bottlenose dolphins.

If you choose to go on a whale- or a dolphin-watching tour boat, make sure you choose one that is accredited through a scheme such as the 'Dolphin

Space Programme' operated in the Moray Firth, or listed by the Whale and Dolphin Conservation Society. That way, the quality of your trip will be enhanced by hearing information from knowledgeable crews, and you'll know that the captains will be alert to the animals' welfare when sailing among the creatures you've travelled to watch.

Outside the breeding season, both common and grey seals can be easier to watch in the water than at haul-out sites, where they tend to be jumpy about people approaching. In both Orkney and Shetland, though, you can sometimes get near non-breeding common seals simply by crawling – very slowly – along the beach towards them. You need to do this from downwind (i.e. with the air blowing from the seals towards you) and hunkered so as not to show above the skyline.

This type of approach is also something you can use with some land mammals, especially deer, so a little bit of quiet seal stalking (stopping well before you feel that you might spook the beach party) could stand you in good stead for later forays far inland. If you do get in range for a good view, you'll see how each animal has its own coat pattern, marking it out as an individual.

Once in the water, seals are often curious about movements onshore, so they may come closer to get a better look. This inquisitiveness could also explain why they can sometimes be attracted by someone playing a penny whistle, flute, fiddle or other instrument; the strangest piece of seal charming I've witnessed was when a friend gave a saxophone concert to an audience of seemingly appreciative seals beside a village on Islay.

Land Mammals

Small may be beautiful, but it can also be downright elusive when it comes to mammal-watching. Many parts of Scotland are home to abundant 'wee, tim'rous, cooring' beasties in Burns's description (perhaps used for a long-tailed field mouse, but gloriously descriptive of the behaviour of many other small rodents when confronted by a person).

From the moose aboot the hoose, to shrews in the shrubbery and voles on the moor, the country holds small mammals by the million. Owls know it, buzzards and foxes know it and local cats know it down to the last nuance of age, sex and abundance of neighbourhood species.

But to get in on any of this action, you need pre-planning. Dedicated observers have been known to spend hours sitting quietly by scattered grain in a wood in the hopes of watching mice by the light of a red-filtered torchbeam (less bothersome to animals than white light). Another, simpler (but still not easy) way is to make a mammal feeding table that can be viewed from indoors. You can do this by attaching a wooden box with one side

Golden Eagle

> DID YOU KNOW?
>
> *The male dotterel is less brightly coloured than the female and takes the main responsibility for incubating eggs and rearing the young, while his mate flies off in search of another partner or to the North African winter quarters.*

SCOTLAND'S NATURE AND WILDLIFE

GARDEN SPIDER
(Araneus diadematus)

It can often take a breath of autumn mistiness to reveal the webs of different kinds of spiders in a neighbourhood. The garden spider – sometimes called the garden cross because of a distinctive white cross on its back – is a maker of classic orb webs.

These near-vertical constructions, with strands spiralling out from a central hub and the whole structure slung and tautened by web lines attached to surrounding vegetation, can use some 10 metres of spider silk. This material is amazingly strong – much stronger, weight for weight, than steel – and represents a big investment of bodily resources for the maker.

When its web gets dry, torn and dusty, a garden spider does some prudent recycling. First, it rolls up the old silk, makes it soupy with its digestive juices, then laps it up. Later, the proteins from the silk are transferred to glands towards its rear, ready to play their part in a new web. Each web is first spun with non-stick silk. Silk with prey-trapping droplets is incorporated later in the outer spiral.

missing to the outside of a house window. Then run a small-diameter pipe from the box to a patch of cover in the garden, such as the bottom of a hedge.

Mousetime Caledonia

Put food inside the box, with some in the pipe and around the entrance (peanut butter is a must-experience taste for some small rodents, and other nuts, grains or crumbled granola biscuits can go down well). Then, if small mammals crawl up to the takeaway after dark, you might be able to watch gh the window of a dimly lit room beyond the box.

For the truly besotted, home closed-circuit TV installations can also be used to monitor garden wildlife. Adverts for these are usually pitched at people who want to install a nest-cam in something like a blue tit box. But you can also use the same gear to transmit live pictures from, say, a part of the garden where you've put out some night-time nibbles for the local woodmice, or, if you're in one of the increasing number of western and northern areas now blessed with pine martens, something jammy for sweet-toothed night-time visitors.

Bat-watching might seem like a tall order, given the nocturnal habits, small size and fast movements of these creatures. But there are many rural areas of Scotland with healthy bat populations, especially pipistrelles and brown long-eared bats. By picking your time and place with care, and perhaps using some simple equipment, you can enjoy some success in experiencing their aerobatics.

Bats are particularly active in summer (although the occasional winter flier can surprise people as far north as Caithness), and emerge from roosts and nurseries around dusk. Old buildings, large or small, can offer lots of space for them to hang out by day, and sheltered areas near tall vegetation – such as down a woodland ride or edge, along a big hedge or windbreak plantation of native trees – give good feeding areas. If you go for a dusk walk along a woodland trail on a still, warm evening in late June, for example, in an area with scattered houses, you might well see some bats flitting overhead if you keep glancing up at the dimming sky.

Watching the Detected

Some people set great store by 'bat detectors' – transistorised devices that pick up and modify ultrasonic bat calls. These transform the calls into a series of

WATCHING SCOTTISH WILDLIFE

clicks and swishing sounds that you can hear, and can even help expert ears to distinguish between species. Part of the fun of a bat detector can be when it picks up the changes in signals as a bat homes in on possible prey. But like many aspects of wildlife-watching, it's a good idea to hone your bat detecting skills using your own senses, and then, if you choose to, have a bat detector as a back-up or bonus, rather than relying on the gadgetry as your basic tool.

There's a good network of 'bat groups' across Scotland, which allow enthusiasts to meet, carry out joint projects and help with bat conservation. These groups are also a means by which you could become a licensed bat worker, able to advise householders on bats in their loft and to visit roosts and nurseries, which are otherwise out of bounds to the unlicensed under UK wildlife conservation law.

Everyone knows what a rabbit looks like. Whether your taste developed with early Peter and Benjamin tales, courtesy of Beatrix Potter, or runs more to Bugs, Roger, or Watership Down bunnies, the rabbit shape is familiar, even if the stories often tell us more about human behaviour than the lives of the twitchy nosed furry kind. To get acquainted with the real McRabbit, first find a good warren. After that (and this may sound funny for watching such a common creature), a good bet is to gradually move a hide to a position from where you can watch the animals without them seeing you.

Common sense and courtesy dictate that you should ask permission from the relevant landowner if you're doing this away from your home patch. But if you get a hide installed, the benefit is that you can watch how rabbits socialise when they're not worried about a nearby human. Otherwise, finding a hidden vantage point from which you can watch through binoculars will help in both rabbit- and hare-watching.

Things to watch for include: scent marking (male rabbits use a gland under their chin), courtship chases, territorial disputes and males spraying females with urine (in rabbit terms a real token of being impressed by a chosen mate).

Hares are much less common than rabbits, whether the brown hares

RABBIT

Rabbits are common and widespread. So if you want to hone wildlife-watching skills, they can offer great opportunities for observing the behaviour of free-living creatures.

29

SCOTLAND'S NATURE AND WILDLIFE

RED FOX
Get your nose trained to recognise the pungent scent of red fox and you'll detect more signs of their presence than you will do by sight.

whose numbers have been significantly reduced in lowland farming areas in recent decades, or mountain hares that live mainly on heathy hillsides in the uplands. Both species really do get pretty self-absorbed in the 'madness' of their breeding antics. So for would-be hare-watchers, timing is of the essence, with the period between February and April offering the best chances of seeing brown hares boxing and chasing in fields, before crops have grown high, or white-coated mountain hares moving among winter-browned heather and grasses. Choosing the right time of day to watch also helps, since both rabbits and hares can be more active at dawn and dusk.

Going Nuts

Some of the best chances to watch squirrels come in city parks, where grey squirrels have not only settled in, but have become part of the reason for park visits for a sub-culture of dedicated squirrel feeders. Some people dislike them, seeing the greys as a tribe that may have ousted the native reds from many woodlands, or as pushy food scroungers. But others enjoy their perky presence in park or garden, or actively encourage them with hand-outs of nuts. Watch a squirrel move, over the ground or up a tree, and few could be unimpressed by the flow and smoothness of its muscular control.

To see a native red squirrel in action is more difficult, but if you know you're

WATCHING SCOTTISH WILDLIFE

in an area which still holds breeding reds, than a good tip is to put out bait – such as nuts, seeds or grains – on a tree stump or branch within an area used by them. You can check for squirrel signs in places with coniferous trees by looking for cones nibbled down to the central stalk. The best time to put out the bait is in the early morning before dawn (not last thing at night, or mice and voles may muscle in). You could do this for several days before staying to watch. Then, as ever with mammal-watching, sit hidden, stay quiet and wait.

Tea with Tarka

Scotland is a great place for otters. Amazingly, signs of otters have been recorded over much of the country, even large distances away from obvious otter haunts such as clean, fish-rich rivers, wild coasts with offshore kelp forests and reedy marshlands. An otter can range over many kilometres in the course of a single night. Few people will glimpse these nocturnal ramblings, but you can get evidence of them by staying alert for otter droppings, called 'spraints'.

These are often deposited in a prominent position, such as a streamside boulder, or the middle of a path. Dark-coloured and stuffed with prey remains, such as frog bones and fish scales, otter spraint has a completely characteristic smell. Closest description for me is that it has the aroma of jasmine tea; so much so that if you've never inhaled that bouquet and are an aspiring otter watcher, brewing a pot of jasmine tea to 'get your nose in' for otter spraint should be taken seriously as a warm-up exercise! In contrast, mink droppings simply stink.

To watch otters by day, your chances will be upped by going to the west Highland coast, western and northern isles. Here, the sea-feeding otters can be quite busy with crabbing and fishing in the seaweed beds at turns of the tide. The most distinctive feature of a feeding otter is the way it dives: head first, a slow curve of wet back, the tail following, often vertical, before the animal vanishes from view.

If you see an otter dive, think fast. You should have a good 20 seconds before it will resurface. So if you want to get closer, make your move to the shelter of a boulder or tussock as soon as it dives. Keep a low profile, then

> **RED FOX**
> *(Vulpes vulpes)*
>
> The fox is the most widespread and abundant wild carnivore in the world. Its distribution is vast, stretching from Ireland to the Pacific coast of Siberia and Japan, south to the Nile Valley and India, and across North America from Alaska to Texas. In Australia, an introduced population has now spread across much of the continent.
>
> In Scotland, some people still think of the fox as a kind of agricultural pest – a killer of lambs – and spend time and effort killing it on farmland. Scientific evidence from studies of fox diet suggests that such persecution is largely unnecessary and also ineffective. Only a minority of foxes can be proved to be lamb killers. The rest make use of carrion (including dead sheep, old or young) when they can.
>
> Rabbits and field voles, both of which can have an impact on the growth of young trees, are also staple fox foods. So targeting all foxes because of fears about lamb killing, as well as being unjustified, could have a knock-on impact on forestry schemes. This was pointed out decades ago by the great Scottish ecologist, Sir Frank Fraser Darling, but is still widely ignored. One day, perhaps, we'll be able to have systems of land use where predators can be accepted as a valuable part of natural systems. But for now, enjoy those foxes you may come across.

> **DID YOU KNOW?**
>
> *A female birch shieldbug is an attentive mother. She sits over her batch of eggs to protect them from parasites until they hatch.*

SCOTLAND'S NATURE AND WILDLIFE

OTTER
(Lutra lutra)

Together with the North Isles, the western Scottish mainland and the Hebridean islands hold higher densities of otters than the rest of Britain. Otter numbers slumped in many places away from these northern and western strongholds for a few decades after the late 1950s. Thanks to better pollution control and measures to restore more natural riverside vegetation, these sinuous swimmers are now returning to some of their old mainland haunts.

The Highlands and Islands still have an edge for otter watching. Keep alert for signs of movement a few metres offshore (where kelp beds often begin) as you walk a stretch of coast, and you could be lucky. Better still, sit quietly beside a beach-side rock that hides your outline, looking out to sea in the early morning or in the evening, and you might be rewarded with a really close view of an otter.

Signs to point you to some likely viewing areas include prints of webbed paws in damp sand and 'spraints' (small, dark droppings often containing fish bones and with the scent of jasmine tea) on rocks and grass tussocks.

squat or lie down so that your outline doesn't show above the horizon. Then stop, wait and scan the water. With luck, you'll get a sight of the same animal resurfacing and going about its business (which may take it gradually out of sight as it works the inshore and moves on).

Brock Solid

More books have been published about badger-watching than about any other aspect of British mammal study. One reason is that watching badgers at a sett gives the opportunity for repeated sightings of different individuals, helping to build up a picture of the various characters involved. Another is the appeal of being able to watch behaviour such as nest-material gathering or cub play at close quarters, heightened by the tingle of doing this late in the evening in a woodland – a time when few folk would otherwise venture out among the trees.

With all the words that have been written, there's no shortage of advice about badger-watching. But the simplest tip of all is to go straight to the experts to find out what to do in your own area. There are 'badger groups' in many parts of the country, dedicated to the study, conservation and welfare of their local brocks. By joining such a group, you'll get the benefit of a good deal of sensible advice and should be able to go out and watch a sett in the company of experts.

The foremost of the points to remember if you do decide to try and watch a sett is that the badgers' welfare is paramount, A few sad and misguided individuals still persecute badgers in some areas, so anything that draws undue attention to a sett (such as flattening vegetation, making an obvious new route towards it, or even talking too freely about its whereabouts) should be avoided. That said, if there is a sett that you reckon you could watch from time to time, think of the following: can you overlook the holes from a bank or tree a reasonable distance away, so as not to disturb the animals? Are the holes close enough together and reasonably free of screening vegetation that you can see several at once? (If not, a night visit could amount to little more than catching the occasional glimpse of badgers in motion). If you can answer 'yes' to these questions, it could be worth paying the occasional visit, either alone or with a very small number of other people you can trust to stay quiet

WATCHING SCOTTISH WILDLIFE

on site.

Badgers often emerge an hour or so after sunset, so you need to be in position a good while before that and be prepared for a long wait. Leave only when the badgers have moved off or you are confident that you won't frighten them away.

Dropping Hints

Badger-watching, for all its potential rewards, is a pursuit for the really dedicated brockaholic. But you can get a good deal of information about badger movements by looking for obvious signs, such as tufts of hair caught on a low strand of barbed wire fence, pawprints in mud or snow that look like something made by a small bear, with prominent pads and big clawmarks, and 'latrines'. These are specially dug holes, about 10 centimetres deep, where the badger deposits droppings that are left uncovered – often near a sett or beside a track.

Droppings, fur on fence wires, footprints and scent are also great clues to fox activity. Fox droppings can often be placed in prominent places (such as on boulders) to draw attention to them as part of fox territorial behaviour (but beware – some domestic dogs have a nasty habit of doing this too). A spiral twist to them, pointed end and distinctive musky scent can give extra signs that a fox has left a trail marker on its nightly round. In some urban areas, especially in central Scotland, you've a

OTTER

Otter droppings can be black and may contain crab shell and fish bones in coastal areas or fish, frog and toad parts inland. The scent of fresh otter spraint is a bit like the aroma of jasmine tea.

SCOTLAND'S NATURE AND WILDLIFE

RED DEER – STAG
The 'rut' of red deer, when stags bellow and compete to mate with hinds, can be a noisy part of the autumn scene in the Scottish hills. Each stag tries to control a harem of females.

chance of seeing foxes that pay night visits to gardens and may be less wary of people than their country cousins.

Not surprisingly for creatures that have been hunted for meat since way back when, most wild deer like to keep their distance from people, bounding away into woodland cover or over a mountain ridge at the first hint of close approach. Stalking red deer on the open hill is a craft and art in its own right – a blend of reading local conditions (including wind direction and cover available between watcher and watched) with intuition about the flightiness of the animals.

Luckily, there are some places where you can get good views of deer by using a vehicle as a hide. If the animals are used to coming down near a road (perhaps for winter feed or to avoid the extremes of weather on the high tops), they may also be more used to the proximity of vehicles, giving you a chance to watch from a comfortable position. The Drumochter Pass on the A9 (where there are major lay-bys) is one place where deer regularly come down close to the highway in winter, as is the minor road between Braemar and Mar Lodge in Deeside.

Get Out for the Rut

Autumn is a time when you can appreciate hill deer without even needing to get close to them. Bellows of rutting red deer stags resound and echo in the glens, especially in October.

In more and more places, the calls of introduced sika deer (now widely interbreeding with the native reds) may give you a bit of a surprise – they sound like a turbo-charged hybrid between a whistle and a squeaky gate. Although red and sika deer can be very much at home in woodland, the principal woodland deer in Scotland is the roe deer. The roes' rut is in July and August, when bucks may chase does around prominent features like a tree, large rock or even a big clump of heather.

These sexual athletics, which include mating as part of the chase sequence, produce circles or figure-of-eight patterns of flattened vegetation, known as 'roe deer rings'. These rings, together with scrapes made by bucks at the base of trees, before and during the rut, are good late summer signs of roe deer activity in a woodland. The best vantage point for roe-watching is above deer height overlooking a clearing where you've seen evidence of deer use, taking up your position very early in the morning or well before sunset.

For many people, perching up a tree to do this will be impractical, unless you've got access to a purpose-built tree house or other high seat. So to up your chances of at least catching some glimpses of woodland deer, the best bet is to walk very slowly among the verticals of tree trunks and bushes, and to look for horizontal lines among the trees that may be deer.

Birds

The enormous popularity of birds gives an instant familiarity to some types, especially a range of garden birds and a handful of others that seem to rank as celebrity species among the wider feathered throng. Eagles, owls and puffins fall into the second category, as species, or groups of species whose images would be as recognisable to many people as the garden robin or the tits on the peanut dispenser.

This acquaintance with the look of some species can give you a head start in pushing an interest in birds a little bit further. The number of species breeding in Scotland is fairly modest, at 242 breeders. Within that tally, you can subdivide into a much smaller number of different groups.

The blackbird looking for worms on the grass is a member of the thrush family, for example – and two other thrushes, the song thrush and mistle thrush, are widespread breeders in Scotland. Noting not only the general size and shape of that blackbird, but

---

ADDER
(Vipera berus)

Yes, it's poisonous – an unusual situation for a creature that lives in Scotland. But it is not dangerous if you're careful. The markings are gorgeous – a dark zig-zag down the back, set against a background that varies according to the sex of the wearer. Males, which emerge from winter hibernation in underground lairs a bit earlier than females in spring, ready to challenge other males, tend to be paler, even silvery, with black zig-zags. Females are duller, majoring on brown and yellow tones and are a few centimetres longer, with orange eyes (males' eyes are red).

Likely spots to look for adders include large stones and sunny banks in moorland during summer, where they can catch some morning sunlight to warm them into action. In the unlikely event of being bitten, stay calm and seek medical help. But since an adder will usually be keen to give you a wide berth, the challenge is often how to see one, rather than how to avoid one.

DID YOU KNOW?

The Scottish crossbill is the only species of bird unique to Scotland. It uses its crossed mandibles to prise open pine cones and extract seeds.

DUNLIN

The dunlin is a small wading bird that breeds in particularly dense concentrations in some of the machair grasslands of the Hebrides. A large part of the world population of one dunlin race lives in Scotland.

also the way it moves – hopping with both legs as if in a sack race – gives a pointer to what birdwatchers term the 'jizz' of the species and its near relatives.

Jizz is an overall sense of the character of a bird – not just the wing shape, say, but the way the wings are flapped; not just movement from branch to branch, but the speed of movement, and whether the bird calls much as it does it. Homing-in on jizz means repeated watching of a particular type of bird.

Okay, so you know that it's one of the park blackbirds. But have you ever spent even as much as a whole minute just watching a blackbird, focusing only on that one individual and being alert to the subtleties of its behaviour? If you haven't – whether with watching a blackbird, blue tit, robin, sparrow, chaffinch or another very common and widespread bird – then you'd be well advised to pay them some close attention before you go off in search of birds much further afield. It's just common sense, because these widespread birds give you enormous opportunities to hone skills that will stand you in good stead in a host of other situations.

Vive la Différence
Suss-out the blackbirds, and you'll be better prepared to recognise migrant fieldfares and redwings (also members of the thrush family) when they sweep across from Scandinavia in the autumn (or even on a rare occasion when you might find one in summer in some Highland glen). Know your chaffinches, and siskins (also finches) should stand out more when you find some. Recognise the way blue tits behave, and the coal tits in the conifers will be more obvious, not only because of their similarities, but also because of their differences.

Those differences extend to calls and songs. Birds can be highly vocal creatures, although a few, such as puffins, don't seem to say very much that registers to human watchers. The details of those calls and songs can vary hugely between even very closely related species. A song thrush, which likes to sing in bursts of repeated, short phrases and mimic other birds and sounds (including telephone ringing tones), sounds nothing like the fruity, melodic blackbird. Willow warblers and chiffchaffs – two summer visiting warblers – look so alike as to be sometimes indistinguishable by eye at a distance. But when the males open their beaks to sing, they're chalk and cheese – the chiffchaff making staccato and monotonous repetition of its own name, the willow warbler a high-pitched, sweet and jazzy cascade of notes.

You can begin to get your ear in by watching and listening carefully to your local feathered team, associating a bird with a particular call or song. But there are also some excellent aids to bird sound learning now available. A compact disc can be especially

WATCHING SCOTTISH WILDLIFE

useful, the beauty being that you can immediately jump to different tracks to hear an example of a particular species, without having to get finger and ear fatigue in an effort to find the correct place – a drawback of analogue audio-tape.

Going birdwatching with someone well-versed in jizz and song features, as with approaches to other types of wildlife, is a great way to learn the ropes. Here, would-be bird-buffs are particularly favoured in comparison to people who might, say, have a sudden hankering for deep knowledge of parasitic wasps. The popularity of birdwatching means that various bird clubs and societies are on the go throughout much of Scotland, offering the chance for members (or people interested in finding out more about them) to come along on field trips and to hear indoor talks about birds.

Go Clubbing

From Shetland Bird Club events to meetings of the Scottish Ornithologists' Club and RSPB in towns near the Solway, there are many opportunities to join in, learn from others and discover the pleasures of good birdwatching locations (including many described in this book). In some places, a general 'natural history society' (such as Curracag, the Western Isles Natural History Society) will have bird-related trips as part of its schedule, but also offers chances to learn more about many other kinds of wildlife. The same applies to the local groups of the Scottish Wildlife Trust.

Once you've begun to get really tuned-in to birds near to home, met some other enthusiasts nearby and discovered some good birding locations within reach, you can continue to develop and refine your skills as you choose. Some get particularly excited by rarities, others find more pleasure in awareness of the details of the lives and fortunes of common birds.

A good field guide to British birds is a vital part of a birdwatcher's kit. But beware of ones that have a huge geographical scope. You may like the look of the Caucasian snowcock or wonder how to pronounce Cretzschmar's Bunting, but the chances of seeing either within 1000

RED KITE

Long wings and a deeply forked tail (that can be turned to make fine adjustments to the bird's position) are obvious red kite flight features. The red kite is a scavenger, closely related to vultures.

SMALL TORTOISESHELL
(Aglais urticae)

Gorgeous and hardy – that's the small tortoiseshell. On the basis of its abundance and the spread of places where it feeds, it's the most successful butterfly in Scotland. Open moorland, grassland on coast or mountain, gardens, city centre parks – it can use all of these as feeding areas.

And if there's a nettle patch handy, the small tortoiseshell can breed there. Nettles are the only plant eaten by small tortoiseshell caterpillars, after they hatch from eggs laid in a batch on the underside of a nettle leaf. So if you want to help your local small tortoiseshells (and the less common peacock butterflies, or the migrant red admirals that might come your way), keep nettles in a wildlife garden plant mix.

Small tortoiseshells hibernate in buildings and other sheltered places, but an unseasonal blast of winter warmth can sometimes rouse them too soon from torpor. That's why you might sometimes come across one fluttering around at a loft skylight or in a garden shed at a time of year when there's no sign of any other butterflies.

Those that wait to read the more reliable heat cues of spring correctly can take flight again as early as March. Their brood takes to the air later in the summer, to be joined in late August and September by migrant small tortoiseshells from southern Britain in a final flurry of autumnal fluttering before survivors settle down for the big winter sleep.

---

kilometres of Auchtermuchty are about nil. So go for a book with clear illustrations that is geared to this part of North-West Europe.

For binoculars, a pair in the range from 8x30 to 10x50 are ideal for birdwatching, while some compacts and monoculars are handy for carrying in a top pocket. Remember, though, that the compact size will give you a narrower field of vision and cut the light-gathering power. So a monocular, while useful for insect-watching, might cramp your style with birds.

If you get really serious about birdwatching along estuaries, at big freshwater areas or by the coast, a telescope can revolutionise the way you see wildfowl, waders and seabirds (and come in handy for ogling seals). As with binoculars, a wide front glass that lets in plenty of light can be a major plus-point for a telescope destined for use under skies that may not always be Mediterranean blue. A tripod is the best aid to stop 'scope-shudder' (and helps if you want to share that close-up view with others), but you can also get good results using a monopod.

Reptiles and Amphibians

When you think of what reptiles need to be active – frequent top-ups of solar power and fills of energy-rich food – it's a wonder that Scotland has any at all. But the common or 'viviparous' (meaning 'live-bearing') lizard, slow-worm (a legless creature that makes like a snake in appearance) and adder manage to make a go of it, even surviving the challenges of Highland winters to walk, wiggle and slither again the following spring.

Sunshine in spring can coax them back above ground from the places they've holed-up through the cold months. What a reptile loves is a place where it can catch some of those rays, and through basking, build up body heat to go off in search of food or for others of its kind (if the mating mood is on it). Rocks that catch the light from the south or sunny, sheltered banks are ideal. But features like these are legion, so the likelihood of being alert to every basking reptile possibility is slim.

One way to boost chances of lizard-watching (no guarantees, but worth a try) is to leave a pile of big stones in a garden as a reptile solarium and hideaway. Resist the urge to tidy the rocks away or use them elsewhere and one or two viviparous lizards might move in. If they don't, at least the rubble should be popular with woodlice, earwigs and other beasties that relish a bit of under-stone snuggling.

Both adders and slow-worms do well in heathy places, so be on the look-out for their sinuous shapes by scanning the track ahead or watching patches of shorter vegetation on moorland walks. Boulders down at sea level, often found on Jura, can also shelter adders.

Most encounters with amphibians in Scotland involve frogs and toads, and the bulk of these take place around or near ponds. From schoolchildren to pensioners, the fascination of watching spawn transform to tadpole and then to grown frog or toad is something which can keep its allure year after year – both symbolic of seasonal shifts and amazing in the sheer extent of the transformations.

COMMON LIZARD
The common lizard is one of only a handful of reptiles hardy enough to cope with the rigours of a Scottish winter. Piles of stones can be handy places for lizards to warm up in summer.

Night Moves
Daytime checking of ponds, ditches and other flooded ruts for signs of spawn is fun, but a night hunt in mild, damp, spring weather can be a revelation. Go armed with a torch in March and April and check that wet area you thought you knew. You might manage to see the mass coupling of frogs or toads in full swing – males trying to hold tight to slippery female bodies (often several males for one female) in a glistening orgy of mating and spawning. For the rare natterjack toad, which has a claw-hold here only in the inner Solway, the only experience you're likely to get of courtship is the sound of a distant, croaking chorus.

The result of the night moves will be clumps of frogspawn or strings of toadspawn. Newts also produce spawn in strings. The commonest species in Scotland is the palmate, which sports webbing between its fingers and has a drab brown colour scheme. Much more flamboyant is the multi-coloured great crested newt – a real little dragon of still freshwater – now rare but still clinging on in some hotspots such as wetlands around Glasgow.

If you've got use of garden ground,

SCOTLAND'S NATURE AND WILDLIFE

COMMON FROG
Some common frogs (usually males) can hibernate in mud at the bottom of ponds, emerging at the end of winter to mate.

whether your own patch or a communal area, you can be near-certain of upping your amphibian-watching by making a pond. Instructions for wildlife pond designs are now widespread in books and on the Internet, but one extra feature is worth considering to give additional pond pondering pleasure. By fitting a piece of plate glass in one side of the pond, sunk down below ground level to keep it ice-free and with a viewing chamber dug beside it, you could get a whole new perspective on everything from tadpoles to water beetles. Perhaps you might even see eye-to-eye with a mini pond dragon if some newts come on the scene.

Small Wonders – Invertebrates and Insects

Complex creatures without backbones, known as 'invertebrates', make up a huge part of Scotland's store of biodiversity. With around 25,000 different species here, getting to grips with this major group may seem daunting.

But don't despair; some of the living variety could come to you, not just in the form of midge bites, but in the beasties that include your house and neighbourhood in their travels. Just the other day, I was sitting at my kitchen table beside a bright window when a winged insect whirred in and landed on the inside window pane. Going quietly towards it, I could see it was something out of the ordinary. Slowly and gently, I placed a glass beaker over it, then carefully slid a postcard between the beaker and pane. That way, I could lift the insect off the window, look closely at it through the glass, then release it.

She (and I could see it was a she from the long egg-laying tube at the end of her body) was almost entirely black, with a very narrow waist and a glossy sheen. Peering through a hand lens I could see how, using forelegs, she stood and preened, as if spreading body oil over her sleek surface. The head features were chiselled and fierce-looking, the bearing confident, the body coating almost sensuous – like a Grace Jones of the insect world.

She flew off, and only later could I get a good idea, using a range of insect guides, of her identity. Her name was *Lampronata setosas* (there's no common tag, just the Latin) and she was a large ichneumon. That meant she was a parasite on other insects, intent on laying her eggs in the body of the larva of another species.

But there was more. This particular ichneumon is very choosy, seeking only the grubs of the goat moth as hosts for her flesh-eating brood. Goat moth larvae are big (9 cm long or so), smell strongly of goat, and tend to live in particular trees favoured by their own mothers as 'goat moth trees'. They are also, surprisingly, almost certainly overlooked in many places where they live.

Surprising Chic

So not only had the coolly chic *Lampronata* been a revelation in herself, she'd also given an indicaton that another interesting insect, and perhaps a tree favoured by several of its kin, was living nearby. I still haven't seen any goat moths hereabouts, but the idea that they could be around has changed my perception of the local area.

Insects are like that. Look closely, learn more and they seem to unfold a parallel reality – of this world, but so surprising in many ways as to seem a world apart. To take an interest in them further, the old glass-and-postcard-on-the-window routine is a genuinely good way to look closer and a humane way to transport them back to the great outdoors.

A hand lens is very useful both at home and away. So is a 'bug-box' – a perspex container with a hinged or removable magnifying lid, combining some of the benefits of both hand lens and insect-friendly container in one device. These are now becoming more widely available through companies that specialise in nature products.

Specialists on medium- and small-sized insects still tend to be collectors, often capturing and killing some of the creatures they study to be sure of identification. That's because the details that separate one species from another can sometimes only be visible under a microscope. But for practical purposes, there are plenty of larger insects around (the same applies to spiders and harvestmen) that you can watch, appreciate and record without harming them, using unaided eyesight or simple optics. For photographers, a dedicated 'macro' lens can help you to record close-up details (though you may need supplementary flash equipment to get the lighting correct), while close-up lenses, which screw in like filters at the

> **GOLDEN-RINGED DRAGONFLY**
> (*Cordulegaster boltonii*)
>
> Dragonflies and damselflies, collectively known as 'Odonata' to those who study them, have an ancestry on earth that stretches back more than 250 million years. In that huge span of time, they've taken flight control to astonishingly high levels of sophistication.
>
> A dragonfly, for example, has two sets of wings that it can move in different directions. When the front ones go up, the back ones go down. Acceleration is superb – up to 100 body lengths forward per second, or three body lengths backward.
>
> Hovering, stalls, sudden changes of direction, all are achieved with a mastery of air. But Odonata live much of their lives as creatures of water in the form of free-swimming larvae that prey on other insects. The golden-ringed is the largest of all Scotland's dragonflies. Unusually its larvae grow up in running water, such as small hill burns (most other dragons and damsels choose still water), before taking to the air to grab prey as large as wasps.

> *DID YOU KNOW?*
>
> *The small blue is the smallest butterfly in Scotland. Despite the name, the main colour in both sexes is a dark brown, with a blue gloss in the male. Small blues live in colonies, mostly at a scattering of coastal places where there is good growth of kidney vetch – the small blue caterpillar's food plant.*

COMMON LIMPET
(Patella vulgata)

Limpets are among the easiest hard-shelled creatures to see on rocks around the middle zone of a rocky shore. They are a type of 'gastropod' (a name that means 'belly foot') – a group that includes both sea snails (like limpets, and the periwinkles, whelks and topshells you might find along a beach) and land snails.

By using a powerful horse-shoe of muscle, these cone-shelled molluscs are amazingly good at clinging to their home rock. They need to be, not only because of predators such as oystercatchers, but especially because of the sheer force of waves they have to withstand. Limpets feed when the tide is in, grazing on the thin film of young seaweed on stones.

Each limpet has its own 'home scar' on a particular rock – a place where it can clamp down its shell precisely. It does this either by grinding down a notch in soft rock or by altering its shell shape to make a perfect fit with a hard rock. In soft-rock places such as sandstone coasts at low tide, you can sometimes see the ghostly outlines of dead limpets, in the form of empty home scars which are the exact shape of the limpet that once lived there.

---

front of a normal lens, are a low-cost option.

Think like a Hoverfly

Thinking about what helps to keep some insects going during the day can also help you to locate them. That type of notion applies as a general rule to other groups, for it makes sense to try and imagine what aspects of the environment are going to be useful to a particular creature if you're trying to choose places to look for it. Given the weirdness of invertebrate ways, that may seem like a tall order when applied to insects. But you can focus-in by considering some basic needs, especially for flying insects. A boost from sunlight can help them to get on the move, and pollen and nectar give them fuel for flying. So patches of bare ground that warm up quickly can be good basking areas for flying insects – as well as hunting grounds for insects such as visually guided predatory beetles that like to launch rapid attacks on other insects.

Flies can also gather on tree trunks that catch morning sunshine, so move slowly from the opposite side (taking care not to let your shadow fall on the sunny side of the trunk) to have a look. Plants such as clover provide classic nectar sources for bees. But if, for example, you're trying to get your eye in for hoverflies, other types of plants can be worth a close look. Different species of 'umbelliferous' flowering plants – often white and bearing their blooms in clusters that look like an opened umbrella – are particularly popular. Hogweeds, cow parsley (common along verges) and wild carrot all fall into this category.

Butterflies

The most familiar of any group of insects to many people, butterflies and moths seem almost synonymous with a type of natural richness and variety. The butterflies over the meadow, the moths circling the outside light, or even the bedside lamp, these are insects that make a big impression on people.

Butterflies have good colour vision. So if you really want to get acquainted, approach them as you might stalk a larger creature – move slowly and quietly, keeping a low profile. Don't, whatever you do, cast your shadow over them on a sunny day or they'll flutter away. But, since butterflies and day-flying moths need to warmup for flight, seeking them out on a dull day could reap dividends. In overcast conditions butterflies may be grounded, so look for them under flowerheads or perched on stems and leaves. If you're really keen on butterflies, you could boost your watching possibilities by planting nectar-rich flowers, such as buddleia, in a garden, or smaller nectar providers, such as stonecrops, in a window box, gravel bed or on a balcony.

Moths

Most moths are night-fliers, although there are some striking exceptions in Scotland. These include the emperor moth – a large day-flier over moorland areas and the only British member of a family that includes silk moths. Burnet moths – a group that has some species that are widespread in Scotland and others that are rare and found in only a few places – are other bonny fly-by-days.

To get a close impression of some of the many moths that are more active by night, try going out after dark with a red torch; you can tape a piece of red tracing paper over the lens of a regular torch, or use coloured gel or cellophane to alter the colour.

Moths don't see red, but will fly off if you go near them with an ordinary white torch beam. So the red beam gives you a type of moth friendly night-sight. Some kinds of nectar-rich flowers that have blooms open at night can be popular with certain moths. Honeysuckle is a classic moth flower in this respect, with its heady scent in warm evening air and trumpets of flowers that can lure in hawkmoths. Night-scented stocks and evening primrose are other good moth lures, so you might consider planting these close to home to add interest to midnight rambles by the light of a reddened torch beam.

Painting a sugary solution on a tree trunk or post could also pull in moths, which can then be delicately moved to a bug box for closer inspection. The standard recipe is a mixture of brown sugar and black treacle laced with rum – almost sounds too tempting to slosh outside. Be prepared to be bedazzled and bamboozled, not by the sugary mix, but by the sheer variety of Scottish moths. Camouflage meets abstract intricacy of lacework in the patterning of their wings. So even if you can't identify a species with precision, you can still be impressed by it before releasing it back to the wild – do this before dawn, so as not to turn your mothy objects of wonder into a fast snack breakfast for the local birds.

Dragonflies and Damselflies

As eyesight-guided aerial attack specialists, with a successful record of many tens of millions of years for their kind, it makes sense to be very careful

SMALL PEARL-BORDERED FRITILLARY
You need to move slowly and quietly to get a close view of a butterfly like this small pearl-bordered fritillary (the commonest and most widespread fritillary in Scotland).

DID YOU KNOW?

Some fish in the wrasse family change sex as a normal part of growing up. All cuckoo wrasse begin life as golden-coloured females. After a few years, they shift to a blue and yellow scheme of scale colours and become male.

43

SCOTLAND'S NATURE AND WILDLIFE

WOOD ANTS
Several species of wood ant live in Scotland. They are the country's largest ants, construct large nests from conifer needles and can get special 'honeydew' food from aphids.

DID YOU KNOW?
Dozens of kinds of lichen were once used for dyeing wool and cloth. To colour Harris tweed in a traditional way, lichen, wool and human urine would be left to steep together. This process could give the resulting coloured tweed a very characteristic aroma in hot weather or in a warm room.

about how you move in an area where you think dragonflies and damselflies may live, Not that you're at any personal risk from these small hunters – although I did once get a strong nip from a dragonfly larva in a West Highland lochan. It's just that they can be acutely aware of your movements.

Since they are particularly sensitive to movement across their field of vision, it makes sense if you see one of the objects of your desire to choose a line of approach, then stick to it, while moving slowly to get nearer.

As with butterflies, cooler weather isn't always a complete drawback with dragonfly- and damselfly-watching. The cold may ground them, and breezy days also make flying difficult for them. When it's breezy, you may find that an area just downwind of a wetland breeding area is worth a close look – not for flying dragonflies, but for ones clinging to vegetation until the weather improves. And in case you're wondering, a simple way to tell a dragonfly from a damselfly is that dragons rest with their wings open, whereas damsels rest with their wings shut. Dragonflies also tend to have larger bodies, with Highland burns a good habitat for one of the largest British breeding dragonflies of all – the gold-ringed.

Spiders and Harvestmen

Spider and web; the words go together like horse and carriage, even though some of these eight-legged, many-eyed wonders, like the wolf spiders that make quick dashes to grab prey, don't make them. When morning dew picks out the webs along a line of bushes, you may wonder how you'd overlooked such festooning before. There could be hundreds where you'd only noticed a handful. All web-making spiders tend to do their stuff at night, so if you want to get an idea of the action as it unfolds, go spider spotting by torchlight – if a torch has a reddened beam, this can double as a moth hunt too.

If local feeding conditions are good, an individual spider may use the same general location for many weeks or even months. So you might have scope to develop a personal acquaintance with several spiders in a garden. Some, like the garden cross spider, are chunky bodied creatures, so you should also have a chance of quiet watching, sitting near a web, by day. For a closer look at spiders and harvestmen, a quick sweep with a long-handled net made from white material (such as old shirt cloth) in a simple frame (such as a reshaped coat hanger) can scoop up some beasties that you can transfer to a bug box before releasing them back on their home turf.

Land-based Slugs and Snails

Slugs love damp conditions, so much of Scotland is a good place for them. Even so, both these and land snails tend to stay holed up by day, hidden in moist places and out of sight of predators. Under stones and logs, at the base of walls, within cracks in tree bark could all be daytime slug and snail havens. A careful peek into such places could be rewarded with a view of a sheltering mollusc.

On wet days, some species such as the *Limax*, a large black slug, venture widely on slimeabout. A walk along a woodland track could be worth it if you've an appetite for slugging in the rain.

At night, an old wall favoured by land snails, such as the garden snail, can be transformed with a studding of slow-moving crawlers. To get to know them better, a small spot of waterproof marker on a shell could allow you to recognise an individual on a future night out on the brickwork.

Sea Molluscs, Crabs and Fish – the Pull of Pools

A classic mollusc-watching place is, of course, a coastal rock pool. Scotland has no shortage of rocky shores, especially along the west coast and around many islands. As ever with wildlife-watching, the gung-ho approach to a rock pool won't pay dividends. So although repeated sweeps with a pond-dipping net may trap some of the rock pool inhabitants, such as a small fish or prawn, it will scare the inhabitants and make it harder to observe them in action.

While a gentle brush with a small hand-net over some weed can persuade a crab to move from hiding, or get a prawn to swim, a good way to appreciate rock pool life is simply to kneel at the edge and watch. Since we're talking rocks here, be careful not to let your knees seize up in the process. A pair of kneepads is a good investment if you plan to do much of this.

To destroy any semblance of designer beachwear effect, but to get a window into the depths of the pool, put on a mask and snorkel. That way, you can gently peer beneath the surface and see the pool inhabitants with great clarity, untroubled by the reflective or wind-ruffled water surface.

Tides are mainly controlled by the movement of the moon around the Earth. Therefore, good shore-

---

SCOTS PRIMROSE
(*Primula scotica*)

Look at the average postcard image of the Scots primrose and you could be forgiven for thinking that it's as large as the primroses you see on woodland slopes and clifftops, or the cultivated varieties in gardens. Yet part of the splendour of this species (which grows nowhere else in the world except the north Scottish mainland and Orkney) is its small size. On a flower stalk about the size of an adult's little finger, with a mauve flower that could sit on a fingernail, the Scottish primrose is a stunner – five centimetres of pure floral magic.

There are usually between two and eight flowers per plant, and two periods when you've a chance of seeing some of the plants within a colony blooming. The first flush of flowering is between late April and early June. After a short break, there's a second flowering season between the end of June and the first half of July – although some plants may flower as late as October.

Scots primroses are well suited to conditions of flying salt-spray and strong winds in the clifftop maritime heaths where they still thrive, but are poor at competing with more vigorous, taller-growing plants. So short turf, grazed in winter but left free of livestock in late spring and summer, can help it to keep a root-hold in the only country it calls home.

watching can be enhanced by good moon-watching, since the moon has such a big influence on everything living on a rocky shore. Twice a day, as the moon orbits the Earth, the pull of its gravity on our planet's seas strengthens then relaxes. Twice a day, pulled upwards by the moon's invisible force, the tide rises to a high point on the shore, then ebbs to a low point as the force fades. Twice a month, when the moon is new and the moon is full, the tide rises extra high and falls extra low in the so-called 'spring tides'. At the halfway between these moon phases, the tidal rise and fall is least, and 'neap tides' slosh around the middle part of the shore.

Wildcat

Beach Rhythms

The upshot of all this lunar-linked rhythm is that if you want to go rock-pooling, the state of the tide matters. Low tide can give access to pools down the shore only visible twice a day; a low-water spring tide reveals things that may only be accessible a couple of times a month.

Fortunately, tide timetables that give the times of high and low tides are often available in newsagents in coastal areas, or published in a local newspaper. Scanning these in detail could help you to plan a pool-watching trip to coincide with a low tide; don't dismiss high tides though, because they can send a pulse of salty refreshment into upper shore pools, reinvigorating inhabitants such as brine shrimps and tiny snails.

As with all forays along coasts, be very aware of the possible dangers of getting caught by an incoming tide. This applies at any time, and is doubly important if you choose to go down to a rock pool at night – highly recommended as a time when rock pool creatures can be very active, but also requiring careful planning, such as checking the route to and from pools by day. An underwater torch is a good piece of night-pooling kit, and quite an eye-opener when you peer beneath the surface of your chosen pool during low tide after dark.

The possibilities for fish, mollusc, crustacean and anemone-watching in this way are excellent. Gobies, blennies or sticklebacks could be on the move, while beadlet anemones wave their many arms nearby; winkles and limpets make tracks for feeding places and crabs scuttle over different-coloured seaweeds. You may find it hard to move away, but remember that the tide will return, however engrossed you become.

Plants

The great thing about plants is that they won't get wind of you first, uproot and run for it when you approach. You can appreciate them at your leisure, study details, inhale scent from those that have it and generally take things at an easy pace.

That's the good news. Slightly more daunting is the knowledge that there are 1117 species of flowering plants in Scotland – more if you add in the several hundred tiny variations on the theme of hawkbits and dandelions, a group that seems to revel in genetic diversity. Then there are thousands of algae and fungi, including lichens (something like 9000 of the latter at the last estimate). It could be easy to get swamped by all this richness. Getting to grips with trickier groups, such as lichens, can be fast-tracked if you go out in the company of experts. So if you have a desire to be a fount of fungal knowledge – a skill which would be much valued as an aid to conservation of Scottish plants – then going on a beginners' course run by the Scottish Field Studies Council could be a good way of testing the water.

If the notion still seems sound, you could join a specialist society to pursue your passion further. The same approach would be equally advisable for boosting knowledge of many other plant groups, including the mosses and liverworts with which Scotland is particularly blessed.

Simple Finds

But if, like many people, you simply want to take an interest in wild plants, just a few steps further than the most basic knowledge, you could begin by concentrating on your home patch. A garden can be a great place to get a feel for some of the big differences that can exist between plant communities, even in a small area. By looking at those garden habitats in detail you can prepare yourself for recognising some of the themes you might encounter in much wilder situations. Habitats are, at a fairly fundamental level, communities of plants. And if you zoom in on the plants – botanists are forever peering down at the ground or looking at other surfaces at close range – you'll recognise lots more subtle communities and habitat variations within the larger habitat scene.

Here's a realistic scenario for a garden, or allotment fringe, where some wild plants still thrive: an old brick wall gives some pointers to mountain cliffs; there's a greening of two kinds of moss along the top; clinging to some crevices in the lime-rich mortar is a small fern (wall rue), while a flowering plant (the ivy-leaved toadflax) is draped as if from a hanging basket at another part.

The lawn is obviously a type of grassland; mown last week, but now sprouting well, it holds a spangling of

SHORE CRAB

The common shore crab is well named, for in Scotland, that's exactly what it is – the commonest crab around our shores. Its colours can vary to include different amounts of green, yellow, red, brown and black to camouflage it amongst seaweed.

DID YOU KNOW?

The feathers on a ptarmigan's legs and feet help to insulate it from cold and to spread its weight, acting as snowshoes.

SCOTLAND'S NATURE AND WILDLIFE

> **ROWAN**
> (*Sorbus aucuparia*)
>
> Modest in size, but bonny in blossom, leaf and berry, the rowan is closely linked in lore to people. Many is the Highland house that still has a rowan near to ward off witches, and you can often spot an old upland house site from its rowans before you see the ruin of its stones.
>
> 'Rowan tree and red threid gaur the witches guid speed' ran one rhyme. But there's no magic to the way rowans can sprout in tricky looking situations, such as a crack in a boulder (with no other trees around) or a crook of a tree on another tree. The berries are good food for birds, martens and people alike. So a dollop of droppings from either of the first two could easily sow the seed for a new tree in a place that might otherwise look inaccessible.

RED-THROATED DIVER
Red-throated divers can breed on fairly small pools and lochans. But they feed on larger lochs or at sea. The closely related (and rarer) black-throated diver both feeds and breeds in large lochs.

DID YOU KNOW?
Roaring is one way that red deer stags try to deter rival males and attract females ('hinds') to their harem. Both sexes assess the quality of the vocal performances to help them make choices about mating or picking a fight.

daisies, and the cobalt-blue flowers of common speedwell; under the hedge, which mimics some of the features of a woodland edge, red campion and hedge mustard have survived beyond the cut of the lawnmower.

A patch of gravel, left over from a building project, acts like a shingle beach or sparse mountain top; one clump of thrift, or sea pink, has seeded here from an ornamental source deeper into the garden; by the side of the recently resurfaced driveway, the verges are like mini clearings, created by fire in a woodland or local flooding in a river; spikes of rosebay willow-herb, or 'fireweed', are sprouting here, with foxgloves adding other shades of shocking pink close by; in the pond, spearwort has colonised, its yellow buttercup-style flowers showing well against the dark water.

Steps to Variety

All this variety could be encompassed in a walk of a couple of minutes or less, across only a few tens of metres of ground – I know because my own garden has almost all the plant variety just described. Many opportunities for plant study could be close to the doorstep, if you choose to look closely.

Out 'in the field', beyond your home patch, a few other aids can come in handy. Photographs or sketches can be a real boon to help later identification, or simply help you savour some of your discoveries at a later date. A hand lens will also be a portal to some excellent close-up views of colour and pattern, revealing aspects of even the most familiar plants that you may never have noticed before.

And if you develop a nose for those subtle variations of habitat that could lead to differences in plant communities, your walks may never be the same again. The only trouble could be that your companions might wish you could hurry up a bit and stop staring at your feet.

WATCHING SCOTTISH WILDLIFE

49

SCOTLAND'S NATURE AND WILDLIFE

THE SEASONS

January

The light levels can be low, the days short, the nights cold. But even January storms can fling some interest ashore, by piling seaweed debris along strandlines, including big fronds of kelp that might not otherwise be accessible. Rummage among the beached weed and you should be able to find some of the hangers-on that use the big marine algae as their base of operations.

Bryozoans – 'moss animals' that make tiny mat-like colonies on fronds – are widespread. The lattice of root-like anchorage at the base of a big kelp stem could shelter a small freshwater sponge, or that jewel of the inshore, the blue-rayed limpet – a small seaweed-munching mollusc whose shell is streaked with electric-blue lines.

Along muddy and sandy shores, wader flocks will be feeding and roosting in strength. Inland, hedgehogs will still be in hibernation mode, inert among leaf piles and other cosy nooks. Foxes are still in mating mood, their calls ringing out at night (not just in country areas, but around the many urban places where they live) with females set to get pregnant during the next few weeks.

In pine woods, many crossbills will be pairing or even sitting on eggs, their breeding timed to take advantage of cone crops to come. These and other woods may be sheltering woodcock, which leave cover at dusk to fly out into the fields and feed on the soft earth.

This is a time to appreciate details of structure in plants that might otherwise be hidden behind leaves. The patterns of branch and crown can be distinctive in different tree species, so try telling your oaks from your ash trees, the sycamores from the birches this month, and you'll really get a feel for the contrasting shapes and forms.

Dry stalks and flower heads can look amazing in the depths of winter, especially against a backdrop of snow. The spiky heads of treasel (used in the past for carding wool) are a winter classic, but even a browned stem of dock, the tiniest details of seed and shrivelled leaf visible, takes on a certain beauty at this time. Ivy, meanwhile, has kept its green leaves, and its berries may give a meal for birds, including the occasional blackcap in central and southern areas.

February

The grip of cold can be more severe in February than in any other month, but spells of sunshine are enough to get some resident birds on song. A tinkle of robin song (switching from minor key winter melody to something more upbeat) and a wren trill can be heard all winter, but now others such as thrushes are joining in. Most weatherproof of the lot is the mistle thrush or 'stormcock' which can stay in fine voice from a treetop even in a February squall. On lochs and offshore, many ducks are courting – mergansers and goosanders go in for splashing

SILVER BIRCH TREE
Silver by name and silvered by natural elements, a frosted birch tree shows why some people call this species 'Queen of the Woods'.
In the past, birch timber was widely used to make things such as bobbins for spinning and weaving.

SCOTLAND'S NATURE AND WILDLIFE

PINE MARTEN
(Martes martes)

This hunter of the woods is a smoothie with attitude, with a sleek coat to die for – as many martens did in times past. Marten fur is amazingly soft and insulating. A close relative, the sable, native to Asia, has perhaps the finest, warmest coat, weight for weight, of any mammal.

Both the hunt for fur and persecution by game-rearing interests had restricted Scottish martens to a few areas of the west coast by the 1920s. Helped by conservation efforts and by the spread of new forestry, which gave it cover from those out to get it, the numbers of martens has increased dramatically in the last 80 years.

Now they've built up a healthy population across much of the Highland mainland and in the Eastern Lowlands, with many more people now reporting visits from them to gardens. Nocturnal in their habits, and thinly scattered, even in areas that are considered to be strongholds, martens are hard to see. But the chances are getting better by the year.

rushes, goldeneye are bobbing and head-flicking and eider ducks chest-puffing and cooing. Badger cubs are being born in the shelter of their setts. In the mountains, young ravens are being fed in their crag-clamped nests, benefiting from carrion picked from carcasses of sheep, deer and mountain hares. Some of these will be near the reindeer that roam over part of the Cairngorms. Reindeer are casting their antlers now, the females having kept theirs through the winter as an aid to scraping snow from the ground.

Adult wildcats usually keep to themselves for much of the year, but this month and next, males and females will be contacting each other. They do this through an impressive range of caterwauling and screeching and by sending scent messages in urine spray.

Especially in gardens and milder urban areas, some early-year flowers, such as snowdrops and winter aconites, can poke through. Beyond them, the big, knobbly-looking heads of butterbur are one of the earliest flowers to appear in the wider countryside, along ditch-sides and damp verges.

Mixed flocks of tits, goldcrests and other small birds still flock together in the woods, ready to freeze if an alarm call sounds the alert for a low-flying sparrowhawk. Early dusk boosts the chance of seeing these bird catchers in action, since the time around sundown (and the early morning) is a favourite period for their hunting forays.

March

Yellow is the colour of the early spring bloom. Hazel catkins dangling like lambs' tails catch the breeze and spread their yellow pollen; pale yellow primroses start to show on sunny banks; the bolder yellow of lesser celandine appears in damp areas under woodland trees and on old grasslands. Woodmice are on the move, getting a protein boost by nibbling the centres of newly emerging flowers. Some also keep their teeth in trim by nibbling on antlers cast by red and sika deer, now growing new headgear beneath velvet-coloured skull bumps.

The dawn chorus of residents is powerfully on song, but the residents won't have it all their own way for long. By late March, early migrants such as chiffchaffs add their notes to the woodland songscape. On the hills, wheatears are among the first bird migrants back from Africa, while ospreys should have returned to their breeding places by the end of the month. On cliffs and islands, seabirds such as guillemots, razorbills, shags and gulls are getting settled in (some shags could even have laid eggs).

With more nectar and pollen sources on offer by the day, watch out for some of the first bumble-bees and hoverflies on the move. Some small tortoiseshell butterflies may also be on the wing.

In patches of water large and small, March can be a time of great activity for frogs and toads as they gather to mate and spawn. Toadspawn (and newtspawn) is laid in strings, frogspawn in wobbly clumps. Another frenzy of sexual competition is happening out on fields still fortunate enough to hold breeding groups of brown hares. The March 'madness' of hares is famous – a reflection of their high-energy 'boxing' (which can leave males' ears quite battered).

Male badgers are on the move in search of new mates.

April

As the days warm, so the possibilities for insects to get on the move increase. Ladybirds that lay low in dead stems and among seedheads in the winter can now be obvious as they range over fresh shoots to mop up some of the year's first batch of greenfly.

On sunny, sandy tracks and banks in upland areas, green tiger beetles are getting active, making short-hop flights and glistening like small emeralds of colour from the ground. Bees, wasps and hoverflies, now abundant, are able to capitalise on the increasing variety of flowers now on show.

One of these is lady's smock, a pastel-flowered plant of marshy and damp areas, also known as 'cuckoo flower' for its appearance at this season. You'll likely have heard many of the migrant birds singing before the first cuckoo registers, but there's still a special magic to that simple, but mellow cuckoo call.

For resident birds, and some quick-off-the-mark migrants, April is a time of egg-laying. Some, like thrushes, may pack in more than one brood over the breeding season. Tits, in contrast, put all their eggs in one basket, varying the clutch size to suit the likely feeding conditions in the weeks to come.

SEA THRIFT

Flowers exploding from a cushion of short stems, sea thrift is like a burst of floral fireworks among the crags where it thrives. By far the earliest Scottish mountain plant to bloom, it can weather the worst of arctic-like conditions.

SCOTLAND'S NATURE AND WILDLIFE

WHOOPER SWANS
Whooper swans fly to Scotland each autumn from breeding grounds in Iceland. Families may stay together through the winter (the young birds still have a large amount of brownish-grey feathers in their first winter). Courtship can happen in winter flocks and involves a head-bobbing greeting and head turning.

Whooper swans are on their way back to Iceland, and geese, such as pinkfeet, greylags and barnacle geese, are returning to breeding places from Greenland to Spitzbergen. Over ponds and loch fringes, along woody rides and shrubby wood edges, where pussy willows of several kinds are showing, bats are on the wing in the evening.

May

Pond life is in full tilt, with large numbers of tadpoles now free-swimming. To appreciate these and some other pond dwellers, including water beetles, pond skaters and water boatmen, try looking after dark as well as during the day (many pond creatures can be very active by night).

May is the classic month when bluebells (or wild hyacinth as some call them) carpet well lit woodland floors. Mix their colour wash with the onion smell of ramsons (or wild garlic) as sensuous appetiser, before continuing with the sound of a swathe of songbirds. Wood warblers, tree pipits and redstarts are back in western oak woods and in Caledonian forest areas, while newly arrived swifts scream high overhead. The young of many resident birds can be noisy in their nests now – a real come-on for predators such as weasels, stoats and martens (meaning that they too may be more visible by day this month).

In a handful of wild upland locations, the song of greenshank will be trilling and red-throated and black-throated divers keening their strange calls, while dotterel settle to breed on some of the highest mountain plateaux. Red-purple flowers of mountain azalea will be putting on a show at just above ground level to rival the dotterel's colours.

Downslope from the high fell fields, several other members of the heather family are blooming: mat-forming bearberry, the leathery leaved crowberry with its bell-shaped pinkish-white flowers; and blaeberry – a widespread plant, both among the ling, bell heather and heath bushes on the hills and above their normal reach – with puffy-looking, red-green flowers on stalks that sprout where the leaves join with the stems.

In Caithness, Sutherland and

Orkney, late May is a time to look for Scots primrose blooms – a beauty of maritime heaths which has two flowering periods. In lowland areas, the hawthorn blossom – 'Flowers of May' – that shares its name with the month, can be late in putting in an appearance, depending on the weather. So perhaps heed the old saying and 'Ne'er cast a cloot till May is oot' by keeping your thermal undies until the hawthorn scents the hedges.

June

This is a month for youngsters. Red deer are beginning to calve in sheltered places among hills and upland woods and roe have fawns in woods high or low. Some of the rabbits born earlier in the year could already be producing their own offspring, and hares are still giving birth.

Common seals are taking up positions on sandbanks, ready to pup within the next week (while some males, out of sight, roar to proclaim underwater territories nearby). Male and female bats moved to separate summer roosts last month, and now the females are ready to give birth in the nursery roosts late this month and into next. Hedgehogs will also be ready to produce litters of four or five blind, bumpy-skinned babies (white spines sprout quickly afterwards, with dark spines coming within a fortnight, when the hoglets open their eyes).

Wildfowl broods make visits to everywhere from town duck ponds to rivers and lochs offering great possibilities for watching ducklings getting into the swing of things. Broods of garden birds, such as great and blue tits, may be on the move and noisily begging for parental beak-outs of food. Along coasts and on islands, seabird young, such as the triple-chick broods of gulls and (later in the month) the single chicks of guillemots, razorbills and puffins will be endlessly demanding food from adults.

Late June is a great period for flowers in grassland areas, with none better than the machair regions of the Inner and Outer Hebrides. Between now and early July is the best time for seeing a variety of wild orchids in Scotland, with grasslands, moors and marshlands all offering good orchid chances.

Variey of flowers is also linked to variety of flying insects. Painted ladies will be up from Africa, red admirals in from

> ### PUFFIN
> *(Fratercula arctica)*
>
> Familiar through a host of pictures, logos and soft toys and perhaps most popular of all northern seabirds, the puffin has its British and Irish breeding capital in the Hebrides. But the hundreds of thousands of pairs that breed here are mostly concentrated in a handful of places, including St Kilda, the largest and most famous puffinry of all.
>
> Encountering puffins away from these mega-colonies is a matter of looking for small groups on sea or land at the sprinkling of places in both inner and outer isles where they visit between April and mid August. If you get close enough to a puffin group onshore to see details of the multi-coloured beaks, look for signs that can help you distinguish young birds from older ones.
>
> As puffins grow, their bills develop grooves – furrowed lines that run vertically down the red-orange part of the mandibles. A puffin with less than two grooves is almost certainly a youngster of less than five years.

Cormorant

SCOTLAND'S NATURE AND WILDLIFE

SCOTCH ARGUS BUTTERFLY

The Scotch argus is still fairly widespread in Scotland, but has declined in several other European countries, including England. It lives in tall grassland in upland areas, including damp areas at the edge of bogs. Its caterpillars relish access to plenty of purple moor grass, thought to be the main larval food in Scotland.

Europe, while some of the native small tortoiseshells that emerged in spring will be looking a bit care-worn and bird-frayed by now.

Warm weather can help wood ants to redouble their efforts to build up nests in pine woods, using old needles, twigs and grass to raise colony domes half a metre or more above the woodland floor.

July

Feeding time at seabird colonies still means much of daylight time this month. This is a huge chunk of any 24-hour period over most of the country. But the light lingers especially long in northern areas, where an afterglow can keep the wee sma' hours softly lit in the fairly short span between sundown and sunrise.

A classic attraction among this seabird action in July is the sight of adult puffins ferrying beakloads of small fry to their young which are hidden down burrows. Puffins only carry fish this way when they're fulfilling their parental duties, and July is prime time for watching them do it. In the second half of the month, young guillemots and razorbills leave the ledges and crevices where they hatched. They usually do this in late evening and some have to jump tens of metres to join an adult in the sea below.

Bottlenose dolphins pursue fish shoals (and sometimes chase porpoises) in the inner Moray Firth and around some of the islands, where minke whales are also much more in evidence both this month and next. In the Minches, look out for white-beaked, white-sided and Risso's dolphins, as well as minkes and the occasional orca. Around the Small Isles and Skye, watch for big groups of common dolphins and gatherings of manx shearwaters on the sea surface.

July is a great month for thistle flowers. The spear thistle has emblematic Scottish links, but there are other common species here too, so look for creeping thistles in fields and verges and marsh thistles in wetland areas, including damp grassland. Thistles attract a lot of hangers-on in the form of flies and months whose larvae live in thistle heads, stems and leaves, and beetles and bugs that live on the outside of flowers. Add the usefulness of thistles as nectar source to hoverflies and butterflies and you can see why it's worth giving this national symbol a second glance.

The early floral spectacular continues on a roll, with blowsy, pollen-fragrant meadowsweet. This icon of summer is joined by the white flower heads of many kinds of umbel-forming plants (such as cow parsley) and a big range of other hedgerow plants. In acid soils and boggy places, blue-flowered butterworts are flowering.

THE SEASONS

Striking Lepidoptera in July include different kinds of day-flying burnet moths, hawkmoths that visit nectar-rich flowers such as honeysuckle by night, and butterflies on the go during daylight hours anywhere from the coast (look out for graylings) to the mountains (where Scotch argus will emerge at the trigger of some July sunshine). Some caterpillars are getting obvious too, including the larvae of cabbage whites hard at work in gardens.

August

August is a month of ripening and harvest. The flurry of summer action is over for many birds, and song is at an annual low point. Residents are working to feed and build up stores of fat to see them through the winter. Migrants are already on the move, including waders from beyond Scotland now starting to call in on estuaries, while flocks of home-grown lapwings on the move are a sure sign of the changing season.

Late in the month, broods of swallows and martins (still not averse to a food boost from parents) limber up in groups to prepare for the long haul to Africa that lies ahead. But some later breeding ospreys will still be carrying talon-loads of fish to their young. Other birds that rely on a bit of extra-nest help after fledging include the many buzzard chicks now on the wing.

The roe deer rut which began last month is still on the go. Look out for telltale rings of flattened vegetation around trees and prominent boulders – a sign that a roe buck has been prancing his stuff. Stags of red deer, sika deer (and the fallow deer on some islands and in parks) have completed the growth of new antlers.

Much smaller mammals are at their peak population level now. Squeaks from the grass clumps are often all there is to show that shrews or voles are nearby. But bats can be more in evidence, especially on warm, still August nights when you might even get some high-speed courtship chases around houses within bat feeding areas.

Plant colours are striking different notes from summer, with purples, blues and reds as prominent tones. Cross-leaved heath and bell heather can be past their best in some places

PUFFIN
An Atlantic puffin has rather small wings in relation to the size and weight of its body. This makes it easier for the bird to dive in pursuit of prey such as sandeels. But it means that the puffin often has to beat its wings fast to stay airborne.

SCOTLAND'S NATURE AND WILDLIFE

RED GROUSE
A red grouse looks out warily across its native heath. The red wattles above a male's eyes are particularly prominent in spring. They use these to good effect in close range courtship communication to impress females.

by August, but the purple of ling often looks in peak condition from around the start of the grouse shooting season (12th of August) through the next few weeks into early September. Harebells along road verges and in grasslands, and poppies on waste ground, give splashes of blue and red, with the richer reds of rowan berries now colouring well. Beneath the trees, autumn fungi of many kinds are poking their fruiting bodies above leaf mould, rotting wood and warm soil.

There can still be tadpoles in ponds this month, but faster developing froglets and toadlets will already be leaving water where they've completed their change of body shape and lifestyle. Watch for viviparous lizards – young and old – basking on stones, and for dragonflies and damselflies getting a heat boost from sunny rocks to help them get airborne.

September
The coolness of September mornings, when the ground retains some warmth and the air is still, makes spiders webs show up like tent cities in bushes, grass clumps and rushy patches. With every stride of a walk along a path you could pass a dozen obvious webs, whitened with misty droplets. Look very closely, and you might see some of the web builders themselves. This is a great month for spider activity, whether in houses or out on the hills. And if you do pause to look at a bush with many

webs, you might also see some arachnid courtship – the male approaches, waving his legs in semaphore and strumming the web lines to show he means no harm. The female replies in kind before they meet and he transfers packages of sperm for later use as she sees fit.

By the second half of the month, some red and sika stags will already be roaring (or whistling in the sika's case) to announce the start of their autumn rut. But the hills around them will be fairly quiet now. Many birds, such as meadow pipits and upland breeding waders have already moved down to lowland areas or over to coasts, leaving the hardy residents, such as red grouse and ptarmigan (both of which will be securing territories now) to soldier on through the upland winter.

A feast of berries for birds and others around and beyond the upland heaths includes blaeberry, crowberry and bearberry (would that Scotland still had some bruins to enjoy them!). These and rowan berries have great appeal for pine martens, so watch for colourful, berry-stuffed droppings along trails in the Highlands.

Woodland fungi are getting to a peak of showiness now, with many kinds of Russula brittle caps giving a big palette of fungal colour, including red, yellow, purple and charcoal. Look at fungal heads to see signs of nibbling by mice and voles and for the smaller chompings from fungus eating insects.

Mid September onwards is a time of arrival for flocks of grey geese in from Iceland, so look up to check skies for v-formation skeins and listen at night for wild cries of flocks on the move.

> **THISTLE**
> *(Cirsium spp.)*
>
> What's your take on this national emblem? Prickly customer; hard to grasp; fiercely armed; stylish but no push-over? Somehow the last phrase seems to chime in with current ideas. But whatever the messages here, there's no denying that something about the thistle does fit the bill for some aspects of the Scottish character.
>
> The plant with this burden of symbolism to bear is the spear thistle *(Cirsium vulgare)*. It's widespread on grassland and rough ground, and where conditions suit it, can soar to 1.5 metres or more higher. Both stem and hairy leaves are spiky. It shares this feature with two other common thistles. The creeping thistle *(Cirsium arvense)* has many, rather small flowers compared with spear thistle's fewer, larger ones. The marsh thistle *(Cirsium palustre)* grows in marshes and damp grassland and has small flowers in clusters.

Some other migrants begin to pile in too (as the tail-ends of summer-visiting swallows, martins and even some long-stay warblers leave), with the first fieldfares and redwings and the possibility of more exotic and rare vagrants (such as yellow-browed warblers) clocked at places such as Fair Isle, North Ronaldsay and the Isle of May.

October

The autumn deer rut is in full throat now, as red, sika and fallow stags seek to gather and defend harems of females against competing males. Even roe bucks, which had their principal rut in mid-summer, can have another short burst of sexual activity this month in a less intense, so-called 'false' rut that gives another chance to mate with females that could be ready for pregnancy at the end of the year.

If the feeding has been good this

> *DID YOU KNOW?*
>
> *The red squirrel is a typical part of the fauna of the great forests of the northern world. Dominated by coniferous trees such as pines, spruces and firs, boreal forest covers a far greater area of the planet than any other type of forest. Martens and crossbills are other widespread boreal forest inhabitants.*

SCOTLAND'S NATURE AND WILDLIFE

year, with abundant rabbits, smaller mammals and birds on offer, some wildcats can have a third litter of four or more young this month. Meanwhile, hedgehogs young and old are seeking cosy places to make winter nests.

Grey seals are hauling ashore at the beaches and islands where they breed. Each female will give birth to a single white-coated pup. At the same time, grey seal bulls are defending territorial space both ashore and in the water and seeking to mate with the females now gathered at the breeding sites.

October is the finest month for autumn colour. Frosty nights spark the leaf magic, heightening the range and intensity of red, golden and tawny tones. If the month is windy, this display can be torn from the trees before you've much time to appreciate it. But a calm October can bring a tonal bonanza to city parks and Highland glens alike. Sycamores and other members of the maple family can be quick off the mark with high intensity colour changes. Cherries are others to watch for sheer brilliance, while birches can specialise in a long, slow glow of gold and saffron, best seen in the low sunlight of a fair October afternoon.

Down at heather height, blaeberries are also giving their autumn colour show before their leaves fall, while out on the open hill grasslands and heaths, the orange-brown stems of deer grass (a type of sedge) give starbursts of strong colour to many uplands. Look closely too at the leaves of brambles (if you can divert your gaze from those plump, ripe berries) – each one a gorgeous mix of colours, often scribbled with the signature of leaf-mining insect larvae.

Autumn arrival of bird visitors is in full tilt, with flocks of thrushes piling in from Scandinavia and the yelping, honking hordes of whooper swans, Bewick swans, barnacle geese and Greenland white-fronted geese fresh in from the far north of the wider world at places such as Islay, Montrose and the Solway.

November

When broad-leaved trees shed their leaves, it's easier to see birds among the lattice-work of branches. Some small woodland birds stick together for safety and feeding efficiency through much of the winter. So roving bands of long-tailed tits that make themselves obvious as they flit across woodland paths could point to other species in train with them, such as coal tits and great tits, goldcrests and (clamped to tree trunks and branches) treecreepers.

Great spotted woodpeckers can also join in this kind of moveable feasting and mutual defence ensemble, since they are also at risk from predators – especially sparrowhawks – that could nail a woodland bird as a meal. Along coasts, some merlins and peregrines from upland breeding areas have moved in to benefit from the flocks of wading birds and ducks now thronging estuaries, while out on some islands, Manx shearwaters, storm petrels and Leach's petrels can still be feeding young this month.

With the general reduction in colour and cover in deciduous trees and bushes, this is a good time to notice other plant colours and shapes, including the many tones and patterns of lichens that cover rocks and tree

GREAT SPOTTED WOODPECKER
The great spotted woodpecker is widespread in Scottish woods, but it occupies large territories and so only occurs in small numbers. The female (shown here) is completely black on the back of her head. The male has a patch of sealing-wax red on his nape.

DID YOU KNOW?

Like many trees, birches rely on the wind to carry pollen and fertilise other birches. Each tree has both male and female catkins. The male catkins have hundreds of tiny flowers and can produce more than 5 million pollen grains. That adds up to billions of pollen grains formed on each tree.

SCOTLAND'S NATURE AND WILDLIFE

faces in areas of low air pollution, ferns in damp hollows and mosses and liverworts on walls and woodland floors.

Some very striking orange lichens live on coastal rocks above the high tide mark. At this time of year, both these and the glistening toffee and treacle colours of seaweed cast up on the strandline or exposed at low tide can give a different range of colours (though still big on browns) to those you encounter inland.

Along rocky shores, watch for purple sandpipers and turnstones, now in from the Arctic. It's also breeding time for limpets (spurred to spawning by falling temperatures and the extra force of waves) from now through the middle part of winter. Out on sandy and muddy shores (where wader flocks may major on dunlin, knot, plovers, curlews, oystercatchers and redshank), look down to notice the wiggly casts of burrowing worms. Lugworms could provide part of the food for foraging waders, but top priority for them in November, in addition to avoiding those probing bills, is breeding. Males shed their sperm together, which then drifts to fertilise eggs within the females' burrows.

The autumn and winter sequence of fungi is still progressing, with species that like damper conditions now putting in an appearance. So don't assume that because you had a good look at the fly agarics and russulas in autumn, you've seen all that could be on offer in your local woods and grasslands. Milkcaps, inkcaps and blewits are some of the bigger fungi still very much in evidence, while the leathery-looking spheres of puffballs by paths and on other bare patches of ground are now primed to puff at a paw-brush, hoof nudge, or even a gentle prod from yourself.

December

As the old year winds down to the shortest day, it can be hard to find the time to range far afield in search of wildlife. So providing food for local birds, either on a garden bird table or from feeders mounted at a balcony or window, can be a boon to both birds and wildlife watchers alike.

This is a time to get to know in detail the behaviour of the different bird species that make use of food handouts. A robin that reckons the area near a feeder is part of its territory, for example, will often try to guard a bird table or the ground beneath it from others – effective with other robins, chaffinches and some tits, but a no-hoper with a gang of greenfinches.

Watch how tits can hang by one foot from a feeder, like tiny feathered monkeys, and how they interact with each other. If your area is visited by siskins, you'll discover that they can be surprisingly tolerant of your presence if you move very slowly towards them. You might also get to recognize a great tit or two by the breadth and shape of the dark stripe down its chest. This varies a little bit between individuals, and in general, males have broader stripes than females.

Remember too, that although the midwinter months are key times for bird feeding, current scientific advice is that it's a good idea to keep providing food all year round. So don't

---

DID YOU KNOW?

Female frogs are choosy about which males they allow to mate with them in a crowded pond and can dive, twist and splash to reject unwanted suitors. If a male is welcomed aboard, he uses special 'nuptial pads' on the thumbs of his fore-limbs to cling tight in an embrace that can last for several days.

cut off supplies in a few months' time when summer eases in. Away from the feeding stations, rose hips (on both wild roses and cultivated varieties) can be popular with seed-eating finches at this stage of winter. And if you've a cotoneaster bush nearby, you might be lucky to get a visit from a bunch of waxwings, breeders in the boreal forests far to the east. They come over here if a failure of food supplies in Scandinavia and Siberia has swept them in on an 'invasion'.

In the hills, mountain hares are now white-coated. This is good camouflage in snow, but a potential liability in mild weather, so perhaps that's why the mountain hares on Shetland don't hold with this winter whitening routine. Stoats are in their snowy furry ermine too, but unless you're very lucky, the most you'll experience of them is a squeal from a rabbit being dispatched by this expert predator's needle-point teeth. Badgers are pretty inactive by now, snug in their setts, and with females (like roe deer does) beginning pregnancies this month. Foxes are much more in evidence. The grab-the-back-of-the-nostrils reek that hangs on the chill air in places where a fox has sprayed urine to scent-mark a territory is perhaps the most frequent sign for those with a nose for it.

Then there's the scream of the vixen as she tries to call in a mate, and a range of yips and low barks as these night movers make long range contact. On a clear night, when the ground sparkles with frost and the winter constellation of Orion the Hunter (his dog at heel) is rising in the southern sky, those fox calls seem to catch some of the essence of the end of the year. Cold and hair-tingling, but with the promise of new life beyond the months of dark.

MOUNTAIN HARE

Mountain hares thrive in parts of the Scottish uplands and islands where there is good growth of heather. Seasonal changes of coat colour partly help to hide them from predators such as golden eagles.

Scotland's Nature and Wildlife

REGIONAL GUIDE

A REGIONAL GUIDE TO THE BEST PLACES TO SEE WILDLIFE

THE BORDERS	66–83
Border Country	68
Solway	75

CENTRAL LOWLANDS & FIFE	84–109
The Clyde	86
Loch Lomond	94
Fife and Kinross	99
Lothians and Berwick	104

EASTERN LOWLANDS	110–127
Inner Moray Firth	112
Troup to Cruden	116
Ythan to Dee	119
Howe of the Mearns to Arbroath	124

CENTRAL HIGHLANDS	128–165
Tay Country – Wild West	130
Tay Country – Wood & Water	136
Upper Deeside	140
Cairngorms West – Spey Wetlands	145
Cairngorms North West – Forest	147
Cairngorms East – Caenlochan	154
Creag Meagaidh	156
Near Loch Ness – Woods & Water	158
West of Loch Ness – Wooded Glens	162

WEST HIGHLANDS AND ARGYLL	166–175

NORTHERN HIGHLANDS	176–187

HEBRIDES	188–205

NORTHERN ISLES	206–224
Orkney	208
Shetland	214

CARE FOR SCOTLAND'S COUNTRYSIDE

When enjoying Scotland's wildlife, please show awareness and respect for:

- the natural heritage
- those living in and managing the countryside
- others enjoying the countryside for recreation

in particular:

- protect wildlife, plants and trees
- keep your dogs under close control
- make no unnecessary noise
- help keep all water clean
- leave gates as you find them
- take your litter home

SCOTLAND'S NATURE AND WILDLIFE

THE BORDERS

REGIONAL GUIDE

There's no simple way to encompass the scale and variety of scene within the great sweep of Scotland that runs from the rim of the Irish Sea across to the North Sea. Mudflats that glisten like burnished copper as the sun sinks to the west of the Solway; a broad river with a fly-fisher thigh-deep in dark waters; rounded grassy hills where the raven calls echo from the rocks in a steep-sided dale; a froth of flowers – yellow, pink, blue, white – clinging to a cliff edge above a grey shore – these are some of the images from within the lands that sit between the border with England and Scotland's central plain.

Here, even more than most places, you can see how rivers, large and small, have run through the lives of local folk for countless generations and set the pattern of settlement and society. Nowhere is this clearer than with the cluster of towns along the Tweed, Teviot and Jed Water at the heart of the Borders.

So many dales are picked out on the Borders map – the word an echo of Norse occupation, the name ringing with associations in later ballads and history – Lauderdale, Teviotdale, Annandale, Nithsdale, Eskdale and many more. These clefts in the hills and water courses across low ground point to many possibilities for seeking wildlife. For there's something very satisfying about the natural divisions that rivers carve within a landscape – both separating and connecting different areas and giving ready-made routes to explore. And Border Country is blessed with many rivers to follow.

Hills in these lands that feed the Tweed (the river that plays such an important part in the life of the central, southern and eastern parts of the area) are on average 200 metres high or more, with snow lying later on the Tweedsmuir Hills than in any other area south of the Highlands. The Lammermuir, Moorfoot and Langholm Hills all have good heather moors on their free-draining slopes, and are used by red grouse and birds of prey, with breeding waders such as dunlin in the wider uplands. In the rivers that run through the long, deep valleys that cut through the hills, otters are doing well, eels are widespread, and populations of salmon and trout can be outstanding.

Hen Harrier

Dumfries and Galloway and southern Ayrshire have a different character from the lands to the east. The Solway Firth is a major influence here, drawing rivers south to merge with its salt water. Inland, some of the largest blocks of forestry in Scotland cloak hill and glen, and numerous lochs give important refuges for wildlife. The network of roads and tracks through the forests is excellent, giving many opportunities for access to the core of the woods and to nearby uplands such as Cairnsmore of Fleet.

The gathering of winter geese, ducks and waders in the Inner Solway is famous, and a must-see, but there's so much more to enjoy about Dumfries and Galloway's wildlife. A healthy population of red squirrels in the forests, red deer and wild goats roaming the Galloway Hills, wildfowl using lochs as roosts and superb shows of bluebells and other spring and summer flowers in native woods of oak, ash and elm are all part of what the wider Borderlands can offer the wildlife seeker.

67

SCOTLAND'S NATURE AND WILDLIFE

BORDER COUNTRY

The country linked to the River Tweed and its tributaries takes in a great sweep of rounded uplands, burn-cut valleys, dales and broader plains west from the Moffat Hills above Annandale and across to the North Sea. People are thinly scattered here, with towns and villages snuggled on the low ground, beyond grassy slopes and tops left largely to sheep.

The quiet of much of this area belies a turbulent past, shot-through with the red of battles, blood feuds and cross-border raids and spiced with the mystery of links to wizards such as Merlin and Michael Scott. This history and the many ballads that have sprung from it can give an extra sparkle to walks on the windy heights, or down in some wooded den. Only a handful of hotspots for wildlife enthusiasts figure in the wider perception of the area. But beyond these, a huge territory of now peaceful hills and the waters that spill from them rewards wider exploration.

GREY MARE'S TAIL

The Moffat Hills are at the divide between the waters that flow eastward and those that flow south to the Solway Firth. Rising beyond the town of Moffat, they have some classic ice-cut features, one of which is the hanging valley through which flows the Grey Mare's Tail waterfall (NTS).

The valley here was scoured by glaciers, leaving the outlet burn from Loch Skene to drop down a sheer rock face. Accessible from a car park by the A708, 16 kilometres north-east of Moffat, the 61 metre main fall is one of the highest in Scotland and worth visiting for the water spectacle alone. A series of cascades of varying size splash over rocks which jut into the flow and plummet into plunge pools, so the place has plenty of splash and ozone.

But a good range of plants also grows here and in parts of the hills beyond, thanks to a mixture of lime-bearing rocks and the exposure of rock ledges and high tops (just the thing for some hardy Arctic-alpines). The winding path to the south-west of the Tail Burn and its waterfall has plants such as goldenrod, dog's mercury, wood sage and rosewort growing nearby. A high path on the other side of the burn leads to Loch Skene, where alpine lady's mantle grows in the scree. Feral goats range across this part of the hills, where ravens and peregrines breed. A small NTS reception centre beside the A708 has a CCTV link to a peregrine eyrie in summer and views of the hills, allowing people of all abilities to sample something of the nearby wilds (the walk by the waterfall is steep and requires great care).

CARRIFRAN

A few hundred metres nearer to the south-west of the Tail-Burn and also flanking the A708, Carrifran (Borders Forest Trust) is a deep, u-shaped valley. Here, Firthhope Burn also flows down in a series of falls – not so spectacular as their famous neighbour, but no less attractive. This joins other wee streams to feed the Carrifran Burn. Once cloaked in varied natural tree cover, Carrifran, like much of the Borders hills, has lost the bulk of its trees to sheep grazing over many centuries. Long before that, a yew

---

DID YOU KNOW?

The St Kilda house mouse (a so-called 'sub-species' of the type of house mouse common in much of Scotland) was first described to science in the late 1800s. Less than half a century later, it was extinct. Its downfall probably came with the evacuation of villagers from St Kilda, which allowed St Kildan field mice (also a sub-species) to move into the abandoned cottages and oust the house mice.

REGIONAL GUIDE

hunting bow used by a local hunter broke and was thrown away. Found in peat bog 6000 years later by a hillwalker in 1990, this 'Rotten Bottom Bow' – named for the part of Carrifran drained by Games Gill – is the oldest ever discovered in Scotland.

Now the Wildwood Group of the Borders Forest Trust is working to change the treeless nature of the bowman's old place, using a long-term programme of planting to restore some of the richness that has been lost. The group's vision is to recreate 'an extensive tract of mainly forested wilderness with most of the rich diversity of native species present in the area before human activities became dominant'. The woodland that develops here will not be exploited commercially, but be allowed to take its natural course.

This is one to watch and to visit over the decades and see a new chapter in Borders history unfold. For now, you can see some hardy surviving trees and bushes (some ash, birch, willow and hazel, plus hawthorn, dog rose and burnet rose) along steep burn sides, and new saplings beyond. The general area has some interesting ferns, including parsley fern on areas of scree. Globeflower grows in at least one place and there are clumps of sea campion on ledges beside Games Gill.

GORDON MOSS

Just to the south of the A6105 between Gordon and Earlston, 1.5 kilometres from Gordon village and close to the remains of Greenknowe Tower, sits Gordon Moss

PEREGRINE FALCON

Peregrine falcons are famous for their high-speed attack dives on prey such as pigeons. In such a 'stoop', a peregrine folds its wings back and plummets to grab its next meal using powerful talons.

BROWN TROUT
(Salmo trutta)

There's a glorious variety in the appearance of brown trout – an appreciated and sought-after fish in many of its home waters, including Borders rivers and lochs. The background colour gets darker with age, tending towards brownish-yellow or nearly black. But it's the spots that make each individual trout distinct. Even within one population, there are countless combinations of large and small spots, some red, some black, some ringed with lighter haloes.

Some trout migrate to mature and spend part of their life in estuaries or at sea (where feeding can be good) while others never leave freshwater. What prompts these lifestyle choices is poorly understood, although in some areas, three times more females than males go to sea.

Large 'sea trout' that have spent several winters at sea come back to fresh water in spring and early summer and (like salmon) most travel in late autumn to burns where they themselves were hatched. Males are first back on the spawning grounds, with movements upstream from a main river or loch stimulated by rising water levels after autumn rains. Unlike salmon, some of the breeding trout (mainly females) survive to spawn again in some other years.

(SWT). This is the surviving remnant of a once much larger raised bog, formed when vegetation gradually piled up in the basin of a 600 hectare loch.

Peat cut from the Moss was an important source of fuel for local people for centuries until a railway was built across it in 1860, bringing coal from outside the area. The railway is now abandoned, but the course of its track runs across the heart of the old bog, forming a route that can be reached from a side track beginning at a car park near the A6105.

Birch and willow have taken root on the peat land over many years, further drying the surface and changing parts of the place to woodland. Today, this mix of vegetation – from bog moss to trees – gives Gordon Moss great value for a wide range of creatures, especially the many kinds of insects that live here. Over 200 different species of moth and ten species of butterfly have been recorded, including pearl-bordered fritillaries and ringlets.

Tree trunks are rich in lichens, with a mixture of sphagnum bog mosses, grasses and ferns below and beyond. Coralroot and five other orchid species grow here. Clearings along the old railway line are sometimes used by basking adders. These open spaces are being kept clear of trees as a benefit to the insects, plants and reptiles that use them.

RIVER TWEED

There are various places along the course of the River Tweed where you can go on a riverbank walk to see local wildlife. Rings on the water surface from a salmon, sea trout or brown trout rising may be all you'll see of the river's three most important economic assets. This is one of Scotland's major rivers for fishing these species – a reflection of its fairly undisturbed waters.

The character of the river changes along its length, from fast-flowing upper reaches above Peebles, to less frenetic waters in the middle sections to Kelso, to deep and slow-moving parts, down to the estuary at Berwick-on-Tweed. You can find shifts like this along other major rivers, but thanks to the fairly natural channel of the Tweed, these transitions are particularly marked, making it well worth having a look at its waters at different places between headwaters and sea.

Plants give clear indications of the changes in river flow and gradual increase in available food. Mosses and liverworts

REGIONAL GUIDE

– those primitive damp-loving plants without internal veins – are the main vegetation both in the river, and on rocks and banksides in the fast upper stretches. Middle reaches have more food for plants, birds and animals in the water (reflected in the growth of reed canary grass and bur-reed by the banks). Downstream from Peebles, pondweeds, milfoil and water crowfoot can be abundant. The crowfoot, which puts on a fine show of white flowers in summer, is more extensive in the Tweed than anywhere else in Scotland.

Breeding birds include dippers and grey wagtails on faster sections, plus the common sandpiper, oystercatcher, mallard, mute swan and occasional goosander. Otters live in low numbers throughout the river system.

One place to sample the delights of the Tweed's banks is between St Boswells and Newton St Boswells. A public footpath leads through woodland, giving the chance of seeing both wetland plants, such as marsh marigold, water avens and moisture-seeking butterbur, and woodland ones, such as wood stitchwort, primrose and wild garlic. Parking is available in both towns, and there is also a small car park where the B6404 crosses the river south-east of St Boswells at Mertoun Bridge.

THE HIRSEL COUNTRY PARK

By the A697, 3.2 kilometres north-west of Coldstream (where the Tweed forms the border between Scotland and England

RIVER TWEED

The River Tweed at Scott's View in Lauderdale, looking across to the Eildon hills and named in honour of the great 19th-century writer, Sir Walter Scott. He loved this area, and once wrote that he could stand on Eildon and 'point out 43 places famous in war and verse'.

GUILLEMOT

A common guillemot in full summer finery of chocolate brown head feathers and white chest. In some individuals, the line behind the eye is white. The proportion of these 'bridled' guillemots increases the further north you go.

from here down to the sea) is The Hirsel Country Park. The estate here has been the residence of the Earls of Home since the seventeenth century. These include the late Sir Alec Douglas-Home, who gave up his title in 1963 to become Prime Minister, before retiring to the Hirsel later in the decade. The parkland here is open to the public (there is a modest entry fee for cars) and has a variety of colour-coded walks which are worth exploring for the range of native wildlife and ornamental plants. The bird fauna is especially rich, with 160 different species recorded. A visitor centre gives an idea of what wildlife can be seen here.

Centrepiece is the Hirsel Lake, one of the largest stretches of open fresh water in the Borders. Dug from wet mossland in the late 1700s, the lake now stretches over 17 hectares, fringed by reeds at the north and woods at the south. Sedge warbler and reed bunting nest in the reeds, and a large variety of waterfowl use the open water as a feeding and roosting site. This includes numerous mallard and coot, plus moorhen, little grebe, heron, mute swan, shoveler, tufted duck and pochard. In winter, the lake is also used by whooper swans and goosander and numbers of other duck (especially mallard) can be swelled by birds from other areas. Water rails are also most frequently seen in winter. A hide by the lake overlooks some of this action.

Dundock Wood, south of the lake, is famous for its collection of rhododendrons and azaleas, whose planting began in the late 1800s. But a walk through the wood also has much to offer birdwatchers. In Scottish terms, the wood is exceptional as a place where you could have a chance of seeing both marsh tit and hawfinch – neither of which have much of a clawhold in the rest of the country. Other breeding birds in the wood include the great spotted woodpecker, redstart, garden

---

REGIONAL HIGHLIGHT: ST ABB'S NATIONAL NATURE RESERVE

DESIGNATION:
National Nature Reserve (NTS, SWT, SNH).

LANDSCAPE:
Sea cliffs, coastal paths, plus scrubland and trees around the Mire Loch.

HIGHLIGHTS:
Thousands of guillemots and kittiwakes along the cliffs, and lesser numbers of shags, puffins, fulmars and razorbills; also flycatchers, goldcrest and common warblers. Plant highlights include Scots lovage, spring sandwort, kidney vetch and sea campion, along with an interesting variety of butterflies and moths such as the northern brown argus and six-spot burnet moths.

BEST TIME:
Early summer for guilllemots, spring and autumn for small migrant birds.

FACILITIES:
Nature centre (Easter–Oct) with exhibition and camera link to nesting birds; car park and café.

ADMISSION:
Small car parking charge.

DIRECTIONS:
Two miles N of Coldingham, off A1107.

CONTACT:
Ranger's Cottage, Northfield,
St Abb's, Eyemouth,
Borders TD14 5QF

Tel: 01890 771443
www.nts.org.uk

www.nnr-scotland.org.uk

REGIONAL GUIDE

SCOTLAND'S NATURE AND WILDLIFE

> ### FLY AGARIC
> #### (Amanita muscaria)
>
> With its bright red cap flecked with freckles of torn veil and its strikingly white stem, the fly agaric is one of the few fungi many people recognise, even if they don't know what it's called. The name comes from its traditional use as a fly killer, an indication of the poisons contained in the fly agaric's otherwise rather appealing natural packaging.
>
> The chemicals in the fungus are poisonous to humans, but it has long been used by humans in northern tribes (after special preparations to reduce potency) to induce hallucinations that suggest contact with spirits. Much more down-to-earth is the fly agaric's association with trees. Like many fungi, its network of underground threads (the mycelium) interweaves with plant roots.
>
> In Scotland, the fly agaric has a particularly close relationship with birch and pine; (worldwide it has associations with at least 23 species of birches, pines, beech and willow trees). This subterranean hook-up allows the fungus to get sugars, produced by photosynthesis, from the tree, while the tree benefits from uptake of minerals channelled by the fungus. Both tree and fungus benefit, but the exact balance of resource sharing is still a hot topic of scientific research.

warbler and both pied and spotted flycatchers.

The Leet Water, which runs through the Hirsel down to Coldstream and on to meet the Tweed, adds further variety to the area. Grey wagtail, dipper and common sandpiper breed along it, and you might get the odd glimpse of a kingfisher. Mixed woods nearby are used by green woodpecker, jay and pied flycatcher and give further chances of seeing a hawfinch.

ST ABB'S HEAD NNR

The coast north of Eyemouth is craggy and spectacular, riddled with caves once used by smugglers and guarded by offshore reefs and skerries. Centrepiece of this rugged Borders fringe is the headland that juts into the North Sea from the fishing village of St Abb's. The St Abb's Head National Nature Reserve (NTS and SWT) blends the attractions of a major seabird colony with variety of cliff and inland habitats that make it valuable for a wide range of vegetation and insects.

Access is off the A1107 at Coldingham (just under 5 kilometres from Eyemouth), taking the B6438 to a car park beside an exhibition centre and tea room at Northfield Farm. From here, you can follow paths along the coast and back close to the Mire Loch. Plants along the path to the clifftop include primrose in early summer, and thrift, early purple orchid and purple milk vetch.

Kittiwakes and guillemots steal the show along the cliffs. Nationally important populations breed along the Berwickshire coast, with St Abb's the principal stronghold. Tens of thousands of both species can be seen at fairly close range within the National Nature Reserve, thanks to the deep inlets that bite into the cliffline, giving vantages to seabird nests and ledges across the divide. Best views are of birds on cliffs and stacks north-west of St Abb's lighthouse. Kidney vetch, spring sandwort and common rockrose grow beside the lighthouse path. Best time for guillemot watching is early summer (the chicks jump from their nests in the middle of July), but the kittiwakes are part of the scene for longer.

Razorbills, fulmars, shags and some puffins also breed along this coast. Thick growths of common scurvygrass, thrift and sea campion drape parts of the red felsite rocks, together with Scots lovage in places. Inland, the trees and scrub around the artificial Mire Loch are attractive to small migrant birds. Goldcrest, common warblers and flycatchers can pause here before moving on in spring and autumn, and the area has also turned up rarities such as the yellow-browed warbler and red-breasted flycatcher.

The reserve can attract migrant insects, such as the Camberwell beauty butterfly and the death's head hawkmoth, named for the skull-like markings on its upper body – appropriate livery for a coast with a history of skullduggery. Breeding insects you might see here include small copper, common blue, northern brown argus and grayling butterflies and six-spot burnet moths.

ST ABB'S & EYEMOUTH

The stretch of coast between Pettico Wick (east of the major headland of St Abb's) back past the headland on down to Eyemouth (between the coast features known intriguingly as Hairy Ness and Buss Craig) is a voluntary nature reserve. This St Abb's and Eyemouth Marine Reserve is the first underwater sanctuary designated in Scotland. Clear waters, swept by cold currents from the north and warmer water from the south give the area a mix of both cold and warmer water creatures. Wolf fish and lumpfish are amongst the chill-out fauna here at around the southern limit of their ranges. Edible crabs prefer to walk on the milder side. Thick kelp forests, plus anemones,

SOLWAY

soft corals, hydroids and brittle stars on rocks exposed to pounding sea plus some

beautiful underwater scenery, make this area a mecca for divers with an eye for wildlife.

The lands that run west from Annandale and the M74, across to the shores where the Irish Sea meets the Clyde, are linked to the Solway. This enormous firth prises Scotland and England apart, but once it marked the meeting of continents.

Time was, the lands to the north of the firth (and north of what is still the border between nations running across to Berwick-on-Tweed) were further apart from Cumbria to the south than Britain now is from North America. The great Iapetus Ocean divided them. But

FULMAR

In the early 1800s, the only fulmars in Scotland were on St Kilda. Now they breed around many mainland and island coasts. The distinctive tube at the top of a fulmar's beak shows that it is part of the same family as albatrosses.

SCOTLAND'S NATURE AND WILDLIFE

CAERLAVEROCK

The autumn and winter variety of wildfowl at Caerlaverock, not far south of Dumfries, is superb. Unusually for Scotland, this includes some Bewick's swans, which come here from Siberia.

continents drifted and met and the lands joined. In the process, Iapetus vanished, closed off 460 million years ago by the meeting of rocks, like the shutting of some spooky trap in an adventure yarn.

Caledonian mountains were spawned to the north in molten heat by that collision. Stumps of them still remain in the Scottish hills. But of Iapetus, only the line of the Solway marks the spot of epic meeting, now cooled and smoothed by some of the largest mudflats in Britain.

The Scottish side of the Solway coast has two aspects. The inner firth, from around Gretna and out to around Kippford, is fairly sheltered, with great expanses of sandflats and mudflats, locally known as 'merse'.

The tidal range is great here – a possible trap for the unwary venturing too far on the flats at low tide, for things can change fast after the tide has turned. Further west, and out to the Rhinns of Galloway the coast outcrops again and again, with many cliffs and raised beaches, but also broad sandy or shingle-covered bays.

CAERLAVEROCK NATIONAL NATURE RESERVE

At the fringe of the inner Solway, just south of Dumfries, Caerlaverock National Nature Reserve (SNH/ WWT) is one of the only breeding sites in the country for the rare natterjack toad. Reached on the B725 Glencaple road, there are car parking and picnic areas within the wider reserve. But

REGIONAL GUIDE

REGIONAL HIGHLIGHT: CAERLAVEROCK NNR

DESIGNATION:
National Nature Reserve (WWT, SNH).

LANDSCAPE:
Salt marsh and mudflats.

HIGHLIGHTS:
Attracts huge huge numbers of barnacle geese, plus whooper and Bewick's swans, pink-footed and greylag geese, along with smaller wildfowl such as teal, pintail and shovelers. Wading birds include curlew, golden plover and redshank. The reserve is also famous for its population of breeding natterjack toads.

BEST TIME:
Late September through spring for migrant wildfowl and wading birds.

FACILITIES:
Visitor centre (open all year round), with car park, picnic area and café. Wildfowl viewing facilities at East Park Farm.

ADMISSION:
Fee charged.

DIRECTIONS:
Off B725, 10 miles SE of Dumfries.

CONTACT:
WWT Caerlaverock, Eastpark Farm, Caerlaverock, Dumfries DG1 4RS
Tel 01387 770200
www.wwt.org.uk
www.nnt-scotland.org.uk

---

the main focus for many visitors is the Wildfowl and Wetland Trust's visitor centre and viewing facilities at East Park Farm, reached from a signed turn-off the B725, 1.6 kilometres south of Bankend. Here, there are several observation towers, 20 hides and a 'wild swan observatory', linked by screened walkways and nature trails. Caerlaverock is a great place to see wildfowl and wading birds at any time of the year, but it comes in to its own as something truly exceptional from late September and early October through the winter.

This is when the barnacle geese – thousands upon thousands of them – arrive. The entire breeding population of barnacle geese from the Svalbard (or Spitsbergen) group in the high Arctic winters here. It's a real success story, built on the firm foundation of a sanctuary provided at Caerlaverock since the establishment of the National Nature Reserve in 1957. Careful control of wildfowl shooting in the Inner Solway, coupled with productive breeding in the Arctic, has led to growth in this population from a few hundred before the reserve was established to some 25,000 now.

Hundreds of whooper swans, from Iceland, also winter here, together with some Bewick's swans. Smaller than whoopers, the Bewick's home in on the Solway from nesting areas in Siberia. The gathering at Caerlaverock is the largest in Scotland. Pink-footed and greylag geese (which roost on the merse) make up the winter complement of larger wildfowl. Add hundreds of shelduck and flocks of wigeon, teal, mallard and pintail, plus some shovelers and gadwall and it's clear why Caerlaverock is a must see for Scottish wildfowl enthusiasts.

The duck and goose spectacle has some rivalry from the big concentration of wading birds that feed on the mudflats and roost on the merse. In early winter,

---

DID YOU KNOW?

In the bird world, only the male tends to sing. But both male and female robins sing in autumn and winter, helping to stake a claim to their territory. The bluethroat (a widespread breeder in Scandinavia, but very rare in Scotland) is a close relative of the robin, and also has females that can sing.

SCOTLAND'S NATURE AND WILDLIFE

EARLY PURPLE ORCHIDS
Despite its beauty, the early purple orchid (early because it flowers in spring) has a trick up its petals. The loose spike of flowers often smells of tom cats. Early purple orchid grows in grassland, on mountain ledges and in sunny woodland and does particularly well in parts of western Scotland.

rush. Noisy during the mating season, but quiet at other times, the natterjack toads live in pools in sandpits dug for the construction of coastal flood defence banks. It's good to know that the toads are there. But hearing a chorus on a spring night is about as close as you're likely to get to these scarce amphibians, which are completely protected from disturbance by UK wildlife law.

MERSEHEAD

Off the A710 near Kirkbean, the RSPB's recently established Mersehead reserve covers a large area of farmland, wet meadows, merse and mudflats. In addition to its use by wintering geese, an exciting feature of the new reserve is management to encourage lapwing, curlew, redshank and other waders to breed, and the creation of a reedbed.

SOUTHWICK COAST

Two unusual rock features, sculpted by the sea but now high and dry in the merse, give a pointer to the position of the Southwick Coast reserve (SWT).

The first is the Needle's Eye, a natural rock arch that sits seaward of a car parking area by the A710 towards Sandyhills, 9 kilometres south-east of Dalbeattie. The other is Lot's Wife, a dramatic rock pillar, named for the biblical character who didn't heed divine advice about keeping her eyes averted from the destruction of Sodom and Gomorra, and was turned to a pillar of salt for her oversight.

The reason for these stranded geological curiosities is also rather dramatic, reflecting the massive change

these can include many thousands of oystercatcher, dunlin and curlew, followed by huge gatherings of golden plover in January and smaller numbers of grey plover, knot and redshank. With such a variety of possible prey, large and small, it's not surprising that hen harrier, sparrowhawk, peregrine and merlin all hunt over the salt marsh in winter (while barn owls look out for rodents around the reserve).

Typical plants on the salt marsh are red fescue grass and sea aster, with salt marsh flat sedge and salt marsh in sea levels since after the end of the last ice age, when waves pounded and eroded both these rock features and the sections of cliff behind. In turn, those cliffs are composed of granite founded in the heat of long extinct volcanoes. These rocks are rich in minerals including arsenic, bismuth, lead and even uranium.

Southwick combines a narrow strip of wooded cliffs rising to over 40 metres, running near the road, with an expanse of salt marsh flanked by reedbeds and fen at the cliff foot. The woodland is an ancient oakwood, Heughwood, whose trees have weathered many a gale from the west. Beneath the canopy, holly and honeysuckle grow well and the ground flora includes early purple orchid, dog violet, bluebells and woodruff.

On the steeper parts of the cliffs there are some areas of more open lime-rich grassland (benefiting from rocks laid down on sea sediments hundreds of millions of years ago). A highlight of these banks in June is common rockrose, whose small yellow flowers only open fully in bright sunshine. Bloody cranesbill – with flowers such a vibrant shade of deep pink as to seem to sing with colour even on the greyest of days – also grows here.

Beneath the cliffs, sea lavender and sea club rush grow in the merse, which is used as a feeding ground (as you might expect along this part of the Solway) by some of the area's wintering pinkfeet, greylags and barnacle geese. The reserve is a good place for moths and butterflies, with over 70 species recorded, including pearl-bordered fritillary.

> ## CHAFFINCH
> *(Fringilla coelebs)*
>
> Pick a wood – any wood. Now take a walk there, anytime between March and June. Chances are, if you've an ear for the lusty lyrics of a chaffinch male proclaiming his worth to the world, you'll hear some chaffinch song at least once during the walk.
>
> The chaffinch is widespread and numerous throughout mainland Scotland and much of the Inner Hebrides, with smaller numbers in the Outer Hebrides and Orkney. Gardens, farmland with hedges and parkland are all part of the chaffinch territory portfolio, but it's in woods of many kinds where they really come on song in terms of numbers.
>
> A cock chaffinch is a magnificent confection of colours, at their most vibrant during the breeding season when he'll be aiming to impress more than one of the local chaffinch hens if he can. Come autumn, and he dulls down a bit, though he still stands out against the background much more than the females do in their standard issue camouflage drab (a defence against nest-seekers and aerial attackers, such as sparrowhawks).
>
> Look closely at groups of chaffinches you might come across in late autumn and through the winter. If you see a flash of white rump, you're in luck – there's a brambling among the chaffinches. It will have come in from the Continent to flock with these close relatives in Scotland before heading back across the sea when the time for a song comes around again.

LOCH KEN

The Loch Ken – Dee Marshes (part RSPB) and Threave Wildlife Refuge (NTS) form a long system of loch and river, flanked by swamp, fen, woodland and grassland. They run for some 16 kilometres from near the A75 west of Castle Douglas in the south to the A712 at New Galloway in the north. The Threave refuge is open during the winter from November, with access from a car park at Kelton Mains farm off the A75, some 2.4 kilometres from Castle Douglas. Several hides, including on a disused railway line and by the river, give a vantage over marshes

> *DID YOU KNOW?*
>
> *The male starling is an expert mimic, adding phrases picked up from other birds to his song. Listen and you might identify some of the starling's neighbours in his song, such as the blackbird, curlew and buzzard.*

SCOTLAND'S NATURE AND WILDLIFE

BLUEBELL WOODS

Even hidden under screening trees, a bluebell carpet can reveal itself by scent, rich in tones of leafy summer. Over the floor of woodlands, especially in southern Scotland, the massed blooms of these 'wild hyacinths', as botanists call them, lap at trunks like waters of some tropical sea, becalmed beneath northern branches.

used by greylag geese, wigeon, mallard and teal and goosanders in the river.

The RSPB reserve includes both wetland and woodland areas, and in the winter is used by the largest flock of Greenland white-fronted geese on the Scottish mainland. Access is from a car park from a minor road which runs northwards from the B795 at Glenlochar before curving back south-west to join the A762 near Lauriston.

The Galloway Red Kite Trail that encircles much of the wildlife-rich ground between Castle Douglas and New Galloway is worth visiting at any time of the year. Winter wildfowl, summer oakwood birds and breeding waders in wet meadows add plenty of allure beyond the resident kites. So, too, do the

willow tits from what is reckoned to be Scotland's largest breeding population. Red squirrels and otters both use the area.

CARSTRAMON WOOD

Just over 3 kilometres north of Gatehouse-of-Fleet, with access from a minor road branching from the B796, Carstramon Wood (SWT) is the largest of four oakwoods in the valley of the River Fleet. This is a long-established wood, which survived in part because it was long used for timber production. Areas of Carstramon have been 'coppiced' by cutting back stems and allowing the stumps of hazel and other trees to sprout fresh, straight growths, since at least the 1600s. Wood cut in this way was used both for charcoal production and for turnery to make bobbins; (Carstramon supplied a local bobbin mill until the 1930s).

The wood is well known for its late spring show of bluebells under an attractive mixture of trees such as sessile oaks and bushy hazels with ash, alder, and wych elm along watercourse, and some birch. Other vegetation includes a wide range of mosses and liverworts and flowers such as primrose, dog's mercury, wood violet and wood sorrel. One plant in the wood – climbing corydalis, a small yellow-flower scrambler – is the food of choice for Carstramon's most unusual wee beastie. This is a rare weevil found only in Britain and known only by its scientific name of *Procas granulicollis*. Once thought to be extinct, it was rediscovered at Carstramon in 1996 and is now known from a handful of places, all in Dumfries and Galloway.

Other interesting invertebrates at Carstramon include longhorn beetles that benefit from dead wood in the reserve. A number of good paths provide circular routes, from which you might see a red squirrel or hear some of the fine woodland breeding bird community such as a wood warbler, pied flycatcher, redstart or green and great spotted woodpeckers.

GALLOWAY FOREST PARK

Inland from Gatehouse-of-Fleet and Newton Stewart, a huge area of forested glens, lochs and grassy uplands stretches away to the north and into south Ayrshire. Thousands of hectares of this ground is within the Galloway Forest Park (FC). Robert the Bruce was raised in these parts, and had a soft spot for Loch Doon, in the heart of the Forest Park. His foes would not have shared that liking, since it was from this area that the Bruce (also Earl of Carrick) launched a counter-offensive to re-conquer his kingdom, ambushing and routing an English force in Glen Trool in 1307.

Much has changed in the area since Robert the Bruce's day, when he hunted deer and flew trained falcons in a landscape which would still have had many woods of sessile oaks and other trees. Plantations of introduced conifers now dominate great swathes of high and low ground here, but these are generally being restructured as trees mature and are felled in commercial forestry.

Skylark

The forest park is blessed with a superb network of trails. You can walk, cycle or go on horseback along hundreds of kilometres of routes here, or drive on roads that take transects through the park. The Southern Upland Way long distance footpath, which runs from the Irish Sea coast at Portpatrick across to the North Sea at Cockburnspath, also runs through the Park. Best access point is via the A714 north of Newton Stewart to Glentrool village, then along a minor road to the FC's Glen Trool visitor centre beside the River Minnoch.

CLATTERINGSHAWS

In Glen Trool, a 7.2 kilometre trail goes around Loch Trool. Birds to watch out for include wood warbler, redstart, tree

DID YOU KNOW?

Both golden eagles and sea eagles go in for some impressive aerial displays on fine winter days. It's part of the run-up to mating and nesting. In the most flamboyant sea eagle move, male and female lock talons and then cartwheel downwards, calling loudly, before releasing their grip close to the ground or sea.

SCOTLAND'S NATURE AND WILDLIFE

EMPEROR MOTH
The emperor moth is an impressively large, day-flying moorland dweller. Large spots on its wings are an anti-predator device. A quick flash of these eye-like markings could scare a would-be attacker. The caterpillar is large, green and hairy, with prominent pale pink spots.

pipit and pied flycatcher in summer (benefiting from some remnants of native oak and birch in the area) and hen harrier, peregrine, siskin and crossbill throughout the year. Another FC visitor centre at Clatteringshaws (on the shore of Clatteringshaws Loch) sits between the hills of the Rhinns of Kells and the Merrick (at 844 metres the highest peak in southern Scotland). These hills, and those at Cairnsmore of Fleet National Nature Reserve are the largest unafforested areas within the park. These granite massifs have extensive bogs, acidic grasslands and wet upland heaths, grazed by sheep, red deer and wild goats and hunted by merlin, hen harrier, peregrine and the occasional golden eagle. Ravens also breed in these hills.

CAIRNSMORE OF FLEET

The Cairnsmore of Fleet reserve is a working farm, managed by Scottish Natural Heritage. Here, a flock of several hundred blackface sheep is being used to graze the heather and upland vegetation in a controlled way for the benefit of native plants and other wildlife. The FC's Kirroughtree visitor centre, left off the A75 just south of Newton Stewart, beside Palnure is nearby. From here, a trail leads along the valley of the Palnure Burn which is used by dipper and grey wagtail, and where free-ranging golden pheasant are among the breeding birds.

WOOD OF CREE

Along the valley of the River Cree within the Forest Park, an ambitious project run by the Cree Valley Community Woodlands Trust is extending and linking oakwoods to form a corridor of native tree cover from the source of the river to the sea.

There is a network of paths, including boardwalk and paths for wheelchair access, leading through and beyond these woods the best known wood within this Cree complex is the Wood of Cree (RSPB), some 6 kilometres north of Newton Stewart via Minnigaff on the east bank of the river.

Wood warbler, pied flycatcher, redstart, tree pipit and willow tit are among the resident breeders in the wood, while the adjacent wet meadows are used by teal, mallard, oystercatcher, snipe and water rail and hunted by barn owls. Bluebells, primroses, ramsons, cow-wheat and woodruff flower in the wood, which is used by Scotch argus and purple hairstreak butterflies. Otters use the rivers, lochs and other wetland areas across the Forest Park. Within the conifer areas, there are also small numbers of pine martens, descendants of animals released here in 1982.

WIGTOWN BAY

South beyond the park, where the Cree flows into the Solway, Wigtown Bay (around and opposite the town from which it takes its name) is the largest Local Nature Reserve in Britain. Three of the rarest fish in Britain – the allis shad, twaite shad and the sparling (or smelt) – have all been recorded in the estuary of the Cree. Sparling is a relative of salmon and is sometimes called the 'cucumber fish' because of its distinctive smell. There is a great deal of grazed merse around the bay, with abundant sea pink, sea milkwort and sea aster, plus another local rarity, lax-flowered sea lavender. The bay is a roosting and feeding ground for many wintering wildfowl and waders, including flocks of pink-footed geese.

MERLIN

The merlin is a dashing little falcon that hunts small birds, such as meadow pipits, over moorland areas. This includes heathery ground within large tracts of blanket bog. The brown female, here perched on an old stump, is a bit larger than the male, which is slate-blue above and only the size of a thrush.

SCOTLAND'S NATURE AND WILDLIFE

Central Lowlands & Fife

The bulk of the Scottish population is concentrated in the low ground that runs south-west to north-east between north Ayrshire and the Firth of Tay. But there's a surprising amount of greenery between and beyond the buildings of the main urban centres.

Two major rivers – the Clyde and the Forth – and a bevvy of waters that feed them, traverse through the heart of the cities that grew up along their banks. Towards the sea, their firths hold mudflats that feed hordes of wading birds and wildfowl, with the islands in the Forth giving breeding space for a great variety of seabirds, plus an excellent grey seal colony on the Isle of May.

Inland, the river systems are rich in woodlands, both planted and native-style, with the gorges of the Clyde holding superb old woods of ash and elm – home to many kinds of scarce insects and great places to see and hear a wide variety of woodland birds. To the east, wooded dens – the short, steep-sided burn valleys that run down to the coast – can give small patches of strong wildlife contrast within the wider farmland scene all around.

In the heart of urban areas, the number of parks means an expanse of greenspace is only usually just a modest walk away. Add to that the green of gardens, the corridors along canals and railway lines (used and abandoned), the vacant land where buildings once stood and may one day stand again, and the scope for seeing different kinds of plants, insects and birds within city limits is immense.

A plot of land newly cleared of buildings can seem an unpromising location for wildlife-watching, but look closer and it can be amazing to see how quickly different species start to move in. Plants such as rosebay willowherb, dandelions and poppies are great opportunists, able to make speedy use of the possibilities presented by a patch of recently exposed soil. Home-in on the first two of these flowers, and you could have a chance of seeing several insects, including ladybirds that might use the willowherb as a winter refuge, or hoverflies and bees that benefit from the dandelions.

St John's Wort

Elsewhere, the abandoned debris of former industrial activity, such as coal bings and other spoil heaps left undisturbed for decades, forms a distinctive part of the Central Lowland scene in some areas. Vegetation on these post-industrial sites can include good growths of willows, birches and other trees, providing cover for warblers, and other breeding birds, with the occasional surprise nearer the ground, such as a scarce orchid. Lanarkshire, the Lothians and Fife have many such human-linked habitat creations, such as bings, old quarries and flooded gravel workings, which are often overlooked by people going in search of wildlife.

For something breezily different, the coasts of Central Scotland are a good contrast. The shores of Fife, for example, offer a superb range of muddy, sandy and rocky stretches. From the reedbeds along the Tay to the islands towards the Forth Road Bridge, there is plenty of natural variety to blow away any mental cobwebs that have taken hold in town.

SCOTLAND'S NATURE AND WILDLIFE

THE CLYDE

A mention of the River Clyde can stir deep feelings in many Scots. This is the living ribbon that threads to the heart of Glasgow. It saw the building and launch of many world-famous ships and sent the products from what was once the manufacturing hub of the world out along its estuary to many continents beyond.

A major chunk of the Scottish population lives in Glasgow and its surrounding large towns. Many of these people live within easy reach of the main river, the estuary, or one of the rivers that feed the Clyde supersystem. So the Clyde is part of home for millions now and millions before.

But this river that runs through the life and landscapes of the nation's lowland core rises far from the city. Its source is at the edge of the Southern Upland, in the quiet moorland of the Lowther Hills, 121 kilometres from the weir at the upper tidal limit in Glasgow city centre. It crosses the divide to the Lowlands at Roberton, moving over the line of the boundary fault at the southern edge of the great rift valley that splits the country from west to east.

Turning north-east along a broad valley under the shapely, isolated hill of Tinto, the young river comes within a whisker (in flood and flow terms) of the River Tweed. The divide between them is the watershed of the county, with waters on the Clyde side flowing to the Atlantic and waters on the Tweed side flowing to the North Sea. Yet, as noted by Professor Geikie in the nineteenth century, only the broad, flat valley of Biggar – not much above the level of the Clyde – divides the Clyde from the Tweed at this point, so that 'it would not cost much labour to send the river into the Tweed'. How different

DID YOU KNOW?
The beaver – now set for a comeback in Scotland after an absence of several centuries – was once hunted to extinction here. Highly valued for its fur, it also provided an oily substance called 'castoreum' that was used as a pain killer.

REGIONAL HIGHLIGHT: **FALLS OF CLYDE**

DESIGNATION:
SWT reserve.

LANDSCAPE:
Broadleaved and mixed woodland run along both sides of the river.

HIGHLIGHTS:
A huge variety of wildlife including badgers, otters, butterflies and fish such as trout, pike and minnow. Birds feature prominently, and visitors can see peregrine falcons, sparrowhawks, warblers, tits, herons, grey wagtails and dippers.

BEST TIME:
Organised walks and activities run from April to September, including bat and badger evening events, and peregrine walks from April to June. Spring brings a good show of bluebells and wood anemone.

FACILITIES:
Visitor centre (open all year round), exhibition, shop and car park.

ADMISSION:
Free.

DIRECTIONS:
Through New Lanark, signposted from all major routes.

CONTACT:
www.swt.org.uk

CENTRAL LOWLANDS & FIFE

the history of the nation might have been if that had been the case, with the coalfields and mineral workings of the western lowlands severed from their artery.

Where the Clyde reaches New Lanark, further downstream, there's no doubt about its direction and strength. Here, the river runs through a steep-sided gorge, cut by glacial meltwater, beside the World Heritage Site of New Lanark – where the cotton mills of early factories were once powered by its waters.

THE FALLS OF CLYDE

The Falls of Clyde reserve (SWT) can be reached through New Lanark, which is signposted from all major routes in the area, including the A72 or A744 from Glasgow, A743 from Edinburgh and A70 from junction 12 of the M74 travelling from Ayrshire and the south.

A good entry point to the reserve is at the Scottish Wildlife Trust visitor centre in the old dyeworks. From here, the reserve stretches along both sides of the gorge upriver, offering walks through the broadleaved and mixed woodland, with good vantages of three of the waterfalls which give the site its name. Dundaff Linn (3 metres), close to the village and once a power source for the New Lanark mills, is one of these. The others – Cora Linn (at 28 metres the largest of the falls) and Bonnington Linn (11 metres) – are part of Scotland's first public hydroelectric scheme.

Established in 1927, this diverts water from a weir at Bonnington to a power station at Cora Linn. Intriguing though this industrial history may be, it still seems sad that the hydro process robs the Clyde of a major part of its waterfall grandeur for much of the year, greatly reducing the flow over Bonnington and Cora, except on special days when the pipes are shut. This happens about five times each year between April and October. Details about 'Waterfall Days' are available from the Falls of Clyde Centre.

Long-established woods here are rich in oak, birch and ash. Over many years, forestry work linked to nature conservation has been gradually expanding such native tree cover and reducing conifer plantations. Plants

HEDGEHOG

Hedgehogs are excellent creatures to have in gardens in mainland areas (but not on islands, where they are a menace to ground-nesting birds), since they can eat plenty of slugs and snails that might be keen to share the garden produce. The badger is a hedgehog predator and is strong enough to prise a rolled-up hedgehog open to eat it.

SCOTLAND'S NATURE AND WILDLIFE

ROE DEER
Winter can be a peaceful time for a female roe deer, like this one, so long as she finds food and shelter. The frenzy of late summer courtship chases is over and her kids will not be born until late the following spring or into the next summer.

under broadleaved trees include bluebells and wood anemones in spring, and wood vetch and common cow-wheat. Spray-splashed cliffs near the river are good for mosses, liverworts, and ferns, with butterwort and purple saxifrage on ledges. Minnow, trout, grayling, pike and lamprey all live in the river.

Many kinds of birds feed and breed at the Falls of Clyde. Herons, dippers and grey wagtails use the river, which is also a haunt for otters. Five species of tits, including the willow tit, use the woods together with several warbler species, spotted flycatcher, great spotted woodpecker and tawny owl. Birds of prey include breeding sparrowhawks and peregrine falcons.

A hide open to the public directly opposite the falcon's nest gives good opportunities for watching peregrines in summer.

Badgers are another star turn at the reserve, with organised badger-watching possible through advanced booking with the SWT ranger service (Tel/Fax 01555 665262). The badgers are watched at dusk from a seated area overlooking a sett. Invertebrate life is also varied, with abundant ground beetles and 12 species of butterfly. These butterflies include breeding meadow brown, ringlet, green-veined white and orange tip and a small colony of small heath.

CLYDE VALLEY WOODLANDS

Other important woodlands lie within the Clyde Valley Woodlands National Nature Reserve. This comprises three different woodlands, all of which are important for wildlife and together hold the largest areas of ash-elm woodland in any Scottish river valley. Public footpaths lead into and through the woods. Cleghorn Glen and Cartland Crags are on the outskirts of Lanark and Jock's Gill Wood at the edge of Carluke. Alder, hazel, rowan and birch form an understorey below the taller ash, wych elm and oak trees, with a mixture of ferns, rushes, bushy plants (such as raspberry and bramble) and other flora carpeting the ground. Spring and early summer flowers include wood anemone, wild garlic, dog's mercury, wood sorrel, bluebell and primrose, with less common species such as wood fescue, herb paris and pendulous sedge.

Wet slopes on gorge sides above Jock's Burn and the Mouse Water hold alternate-leaved golden saxifrage and rough horsetail. The gorges have protected the woods from felling and agricultural grazing in the past, and dead wood has been left in place. This standing and fallen dead timber supports many kinds of insects and fungi and helps to provide food and nest holes for breeding birds, including redstart, great spotted woodpecker and tawny owl. Wood warblers also breed here and mammals include badger and roe deer.

BADGER
(Meles meles)

The black-and-white-striped headgear is instantly recognisable, even if you've never seen the animal up close on its home ground. Badgers are much less numerous in Scotland than in England and Wales, and are more widespread in lowland areas than in the Highlands.

A large mustelid family relative of the weasel, stoat, pine marten and polecat (very large – a badger can weigh-in as heavy as 12 kilograms in autumn), the badger is nocturnal. So signs of badger activity are often more noticeable than the animals themselves. Tufts of coarse badger hairs on low strands of barbed-wire fences, medium-sized, bear-like footprints on soft ground, and a musky odour are all clues to suggest local badger activity.

If you're lucky enough to have the chance to join in an organised watch at a sett – best done through a local badger group – you're also likely to hear a surprisingly wide variety of noises from brocks young and old. 'Churr', 'purr' and 'kecker' are some of the terms used by those in the know to describe sounds produced by adult badgers; 'chirp', 'cluck', 'coo' and 'squeak' – as you might guess – are cub noises.

POSSIL MARSH

Glasgow is blessed with some excellent greenspace within its city limits. This includes many parks, the Kelvin walkway, which runs from the heart of the city near the University out to Kirkintilloch, and wildlife areas on former industrial sites. One of the green gems is Possil Marsh (SWT, Glasgow City Council), which has been a favourite stomping ground for urban naturalists for the best part of two centuries. 'Every Glasgow naturalist is baptised in Possil Marsh', wrote Sir William Hooker, a Professor of Botany at Glasgow in the early 1800s. The area was first declared a private nature reserve in 1930 when several of the city's natural history societies joined forces to protect it.

On the outskirts of Lambhill, close to Bishopbriggs and east of the A879 after it crosses the Lambhill Bridge over the Forth and Clyde Canal, Possil Marsh holds both a shallow loch rich in plant food, and fringing damp grassland, dry meadow and birch and willow scrub. An extensive fen at the southern end of the marsh has large stands of great reed mace, bulrush (or common reed mace), bogbean, which grows in deeper water spaces, bottle sedge and water sedge, with greater spearwort, marsh cinquefoil and common cottongrass flowering in summer.

The loch is important for wildfowl, including mute swan, tufted duck, coot, teal and breeding great crested grebes. Reed buntings use the willow scrub to the north, south and west of the loch, which also gives cover for migrants such as warblers. A huge number of invertebrates have been recorded here. Some of the more obvious ones include small tortoiseshell butterflies on the wing in summer and a variety of water beetles, spiders and harvestmen.

HOGGANFIELD PARK

Another good wetland within Glasgow is at Hogganfield Park, off the A80 between Provanmill and Milloston. A path around the loch of the same name gives a circular walk of nearly 2 kilometres and good views of both loch and grassland. The bird list here is currently 115 species, including over 30 species of ducks, geese and other waterfowl. These include records of the rare black-necked grebe and a good flock of wintering goosander (sometimes numbering more than a hundred).

Amphibious bistort is abundant in the loch and the long-established grassland has goat's beard and pignut, with lady's smock in damper places. Wildflower meadows have been actively developed at Hogganfield to promote summer flowers and provide a food source for many kinds of bees, butterflies and other insects.

POLLOCK COUNTRY PARK

Pollock Country Park and Estate (Glasgow City Council) is accessible from several places between Pollock and Shawlands, including entrances off Dumbreck Road and Pollockshaws Road. One way to get there is to follow signs for the Burrell Collection off the M77. This is the largest 'Site of Importance for Nature Conservation' within the city. Although well known for its museums – one housing the world-famous Burrell Collection and Pollock House (NTS) which holds a fine collection of paintings, silver and ceramics – Pollock also includes many different habitats within its massive 481 hectare spread.

The waters of the White Cart are fished by kingfisher, otter and mink. Foxes and roe deer live in the park woodlands. Most of the mature broadleaved woods here are a mix of sycamore, horse chestnut, beech, elm and large-leaved lime, with older remnant oaks in the North Wood. Unusual plants in the woods include toothwort (parasitic on hazel and elm), moschatel (also known as 'Town Hall Clock' because of the arrangement of its flowers) and broad-leaved helleborine.

DID YOU KNOW?

Giant hogweed, with its huge, rounded clusters of multiple flowers, is an introduced plant with a bad reputation. Its juice can cause burns on skin exposed to sunlight. But the same also applies to its much commoner, native relatives – common hogweed and wild parsnip.

CENTRAL LOWLANDS & FIFE

This orchid – scarce elsewhere – has become something of a Glasgow speciality, occurring in parks, gardens and wooded-over industrial sites.

Spring flowers include ramsons in the woods and along the riverbanks (where butterbur can be the first flower of all to appear), with bluebells and pink purslane in later spring and early summer.

LOCHWINNOCH

West of Glasgow, on the A760 between Largs and Paisley, Lochwinnoch (RSPB) has two short nature trails suitable for wheelchairs and pushchairs, and a visitor centre with a viewing tower and hides. Aird Meadow – a stretch of shallow water surrounded by marshland – lies to the north of the centre (29 kilometres from the city). Once part of a much larger meadow system, work to reduce the height of fen vegetation here, which had become dominated by reed canary grass, has included the use of Highland cattle as grazers with a conservation mission. Their work has helped to boost numbers of lapwing and snipe and the variety of plants at Aird Meadow.

This is a good place for watching the spring displays of great crested grebes, at one of their Scottish strongholds, and other breeding wildfowl such as mallard, tufted duck, coot and moorhen. Both Aird Meadow and Barr Loch (south-west of the road)

BADGERS

Badgers are clan animals, living where soil conditions and food suit them. Earthworms can form an important part of their diet, so woodland flanked by pasture in areas of fertile soil can be a good location for a badger group's underground home, or 'sett'.

SCOTLAND'S NATURE AND WILDLIFE

HEDGEHOG
(Erinaceus europaeus)

Around dusk by the grassy side of a quiet town street, you might see one, quietly snuffling and trotting on its rounds of local gardens. Plenty of hedgehogs have made their home in Scottish urban areas, where strips of grass under trees and on lawns give some of the feeding opportunities their country cousins enjoy in pasture and along woodland rides.

Worms, beetles and slugs are all to a hedgehog's liking – and much else meaty besides. So if your patch is part of a hedgehog's evening patrol, you could put out a bit of meat-based cat food or dog food to encourage it to stay a while longer. Don't use full strength cow milk, since this can give hedgehogs 'the runs', although much-diluted cow milk or some goat milk is fine.

In October or thereabouts (depending on the weather) hedgehogs begin to hibernate. They live off their fat reserves for about five months, with their bodies cool (but not too cold) and bodily processes on tick-over. Every so often, a hedgehog rouses from hibernation for a short while, and may even leave its winter nest in a mild period. But you usually won't see much hedgehog activity again until late April, when they wake and begin their noisy courtship.

are important for wintering ducks and geese, including greylag geese and whooper swans, wigeon, pochard and goldeneye.

Willow scrub and mixed woodland around the open water gives cover for breeding reed buntings and sedge, grasshopper and willow warblers, while migrant redwings and fieldfares use the trees and bushes in winter. Prominent flowers include meadowsweet, valerian and purple loosestrife at the edge of the marsh, with yellow iris, marsh marigold and marsh cinquefoil in places where the water is slightly deeper, plus bogbean out on the loch.

AYR GORGE WOODLANDS

Much of the broadleaved woodland in west Central Scotland is linked to the main rivers. The woods along the Clyde, described above, are the finest of these. But for an idea of the type of woodlands along a smaller river (that flows down to the Firth of Clyde rather than into the main river), the Ayr Gorge Woodlands (SWT) are excellent. Accessible from a lay-by in Failford, which is a few kilometres west of Mauchline on the A758 to Ayr, these woods have a good network of paths. Sessile oak is the main tree along the wooded ravine, with some birch and a bushier-growth of hazel, holly and rowan. Bluebell, red campion, ramsons, wood sorrel, wood-rush and wood avens all grow here, with heather and blaeberry on more acid ground.

Otters use the river – where dippers, grey wagtails and kingfishers feed – and badgers, red squirrels and roe deer live in the woods. This is also a great place for insects – including many kinds of beetles – and spiders, scores of different species of which have been recorded here.

South-west from where the Clyde makes a dog-leg turn at Cloch Point, across from Dunoon, sit some splendid islands. Long known to people from the metropolis who went 'doon the watter' for some relaxation in the Glasgow Fair fortnight, the names of the main towns on the larger of the islands still have a holiday ring to them for many in the west including, Rothesay (Bute), Millport (Great Cumbrae), Brodick and Whiting Bay (Arran).

CENTRAL LOWLANDS & FIFE

ARRAN

All the Clyde islands, large and small, accessible and not so, are good places for wildlife, blending the interest of sea coasts beside the tide-tugged channels with inland scenes that vary from gentle farmscapes to heathy tops. Queen of all the Clyde's isles is Arran – the largest of the lot and with such contrasts in its scene as to justify visit after visit. Access is by ferry from Ardrossan to Brodick or from Claonaig in Kintyre to Lochranza.

The north of the island is dominated by a huge mass of granite, which looks like a red boil on a geological map. The thin, acidic soils here support an upland flora and fauna which is strongly reminiscent of parts of the Highland mainland. The most well trodden route through Arran's mini-Highlands is the trail up to the summit of Goatfell (NTS) – at 874 metres the highest point on the island. But there is much to recommend walks away from the main drag, to explore other glens within the northern hills, such as along Glen Sannox or Glen Forsa. Red deer roam the hills here as they have done for 1000 years and more – celebrated in a glorious ancient Gaelic poem called *Arran of the Stags*. Golden eagles, ravens and peregrines use the cliffs and crags and glide across ice-carved corries. This is also the southernmost breeding place in Scotland for ptarmigan.

Arctic-alpine plants on higher parts of the hills include alpine buckler ferns and alpine lady's mantle. On Goatfell itself (spectacular for its rock formations) mountain sorrel and mountain saxifrage grow beside streams, and dwarf willow clings to the high tops. One oddity of northern Arran, which has a stronghold on steep granite crags in the Glen Diomhan National Nature Reserve, is the bastard mountain ash – an unfortunate-sounding name for an attractive relative of the rowan. Both it and the Arran whitebeam (another member of the genus *Sorbus*), are found nowhere else in the world except this corner of Arran – but you'll need to fine-tune your tree identification skills to know one when you see it.

Brought to the island in the 1920s by the Duchess of Montrose, the red squirrel now thrives here. A ranger-

KINGFISHER

Adult kingfishers have perhaps the most astonishing colours of any Scottish breeding bird, in a dazzling combination of blues, white and hot orange. Younger kingfishers are duller and more green looking, especially on their head and wings. Lowland rivers suit them best, but a few even nest in the Highlands.

SCOTLAND'S NATURE AND WILDLIFE

COMMON SEAL

Common seals are haul-out experts. As the tide comes in, they can slowly bend their bodies up, like giant bananas, to keep tail and head clear of the water.

guided walk around Brodick Castle (NTS) grounds can often give a better chance of seeing one of these bushy-tailed beauties than many red squirrel searches on the mainland. Across on the opposite coast of the island, looking over to Kintyre, the waters of the Kilbrannan sound are worth scanning for porpoises and dolphins. Here and elsewhere in the Firth of Clyde are also prime areas for the huge basking shark – the second largest fish in the world. But with its numbers at a low ebb, any sighting of these massive plankton feeders is a bonus.

Out from the Ayrshire coast, where the Clyde merges with the North Channel of the Irish Sea, the granite lump of Ailsa Craig holds a large gannet colony. A cruise around the island on a trip from Girvan can give a memorable impression of the scale, noise and smell of a major seabird breeding station. But for those whose sealegs are suspect, the Bass Rock and the nearby Seabird Centre in North Berwick, across on the North Sea coast, are better bets for gannet-watching.

LOCH LOMOND

The first National Park established in Scotland has Britain's largest sheet of inland freshwater as its centrepiece. Morar may be deeper, Ness may hold more water and mysteries, but at 71 square kilometres, Lomond has the biggest surface area. Looking down on it are many hills, including the much-climbed, much-sung-about Ben Lomond. 'Ye'll tak the high road, and I'll tak the low road' runs the old lyric. It's an appropriate pairing for the loch and its surrounds. The southern end of the water is sliced by the Boundary Fault that is the major geological divide between Highland and Lowland Scotland and both water and wildlife have a foot in these camps.

The northern part of Loch Lomond is steep-sided, the waters deep and acidic. In the southern basin, the loch is studded with attractively wooded islands, its spread is wide and the waters richer in food. This variety is one reason why Loch Lomond is home to a great many kinds of fish.

These include salmon and sea trout, which enter via the River Leven, brown and rainbow trout, pike, perch, roach, chub, dace and the powan – an uncommon freshwater herring whose only Scottish waters are here and in Loch Eck. The River Endrick, which meanders into the south-east corner of the loch, has an important population of river lamphey.

Close to the shore at Balmaha – from where it can be reached by boat – the small, hilly island of Inchcailloch within the Loch Lomond National Nature Reserve, straddles the faultline. Contrasting rock types to either side of this divide have different soils and different plants associated with them. These include wavy-hair grass, heather, blaeberry, mosses and ferns typical of acidic peatland close to plants which thrive in richer soils, such as maidenhair spleenwort, woodruff and sanicle. Guelder rose, willow and bog myrtle grow along the shore. A nature trail runs to the summit of the island, through sessile oak and mixed woodland that includes alder and ash in damper areas and Scots pine and larch on higher ground. In summer, the woods here have good numbers of breeding wood, willow and garden warblers, tree pipits, and smaller numbers of redstarts and blackcaps. Great spotted woodpeckers, jays and buzzards also use the island.

Just over 3 kilometres north-west of Balmaha, inland from where Strathcashel point pokes a prominent nose into the loch, is Cashel Farm. This was bought by the Royal Scottish Forestry Society funds, with help from Millennium Forest for Scotland in the late 1990s, with the aim of creating a working Scottish forest of native trees. Within the property, which rises from shore level to 580 metres on Beinn Bhreac, new planting has taken place over hundreds of hectares. Part of the farm has also been fenced to keep deer out in order to protect seedlings and

Red Fox

DID YOU KNOW?

Slugs and snails feed by rasping a tongue-like organ called a radula over food. Covered with thousands of tiny, tooth-like structures, this acts like a sandpaper conveyor belt to strip greenery. Use a hand lens to watch a leaf from below where a slug or snail is in action, and you can get an impression of radula power.

encourage natural tree regeneration.

Woodland walks can be followed along what is planned to be an expanding path network, and a warden is on site for much of the year.

Various butterflies use Cashel, including small heath, ringlet, peacock, orange tip, common blue and red admiral. Birds include both red and black grouse, buzzard, raven, stonechat, whinchat, grasshopper warbler, willow warbler, whitethroat, meadow pipit, tree pipit and reed bunting. As the woodland develops, the wildlife communities at Cashel will change, so who knows what plants, insects, birds and animals may be seen in years to come?

Common Frog

> **DID YOU KNOW?**
> *Adult lacewings are gorgeous insects, with glistening eyes, bright green bodies and finely patterned, see-through flying gear. But they are also voracious predators, able to chew up large numbers of aphids. This makes them an ally to organic gardeners keen to control greenfly without using chemical sprays.*

BEN LOMOND

The walk up Ben Lomond (NTS) itself follows a path from Rowardennan, beside the narrower northern basin of the loch. There is an information centre and ranger centre here. As the southernmost 'Munro' or peak over 3000 feet (914 metres) in Scotland, and as a readily climbed mountain not far from Glasgow, Ben Lomond attracts huge numbers of walkers every year. This reduces the chances of seeing some kinds of wildlife, but the climb up the Ben can still give interesting contrasts in plants and birds.

Curlew, meadow pipit and skylark live on the moorland at lower levels, where bog myrtle grows thickly in wet peaty areas. In stream gullies away from grazing animals, the rich flora includes globeflower, starry and mossy saxifrages and filmy ferns. At higher levels, where ptarmigan, ring ouzel and raven may be seen, Arctic-alpine plants grow on ungrazed ledges.

North again, overlooked beyond the opposite western bank of the loch by the shapely 'Arrochar Alps', the RSPB's reserve at Inversnaid has fine woodland rising up to crags, with open moorland beyond. As with all the areas detailed around the loch, Inversnaid is accessible from the long distance West Highland Way footpath. It also sits at the very end of the B829, 24 kilometres west of Aberfoyle.

A steep nature trail leads through the woodland. Spring flowers include bluebell, wood sorrel, ramsons, wood anemone, lesser celandine, primrose, sanicle and woodruff beneath oak, ash, birch and alders. Mosses and ferns thrive here especially around the waterfalls. Migrant breeding birds include common sandpiper down by the loch, tree pipit, redstart, wood warbler, spotted flycatcher and pied flycatcher (boosted by nestboxes). Buzzards nest on the crags in the wood and black grouse are sometimes seen on the moorland.

QUEEN ELIZABETH FOREST PARK

The huge Queen Elizabeth Forest Park (FC) includes part of the eastern shore of Loch Lomond. But the park's heart is in the Trossachs, in the Loch Ard, Achray and Strathyre Forest, with Aberfoyle as the best starting point for exploration of the huge network of trails. Designated in 1953 to mark the coronation of Queen Elizabeth, the tens of thousands of hectares of ground in the forest park include different types of woodland. Plantations of Sitka spruce, Norway spruce, Douglas fir and larch are a major theme. There are also areas with mixed planted broadleaves and conifers and long established native woodland, such as the Fairy Knowe wood near Aberfoyle, as well as tracts of moorland, loch and mountain.

The Queen Elizabeth Forest Park visitor centre, on the A821 'Duke's Road' above and just to the north of Aberfoyle, is open daily between March and October. Exhibitions and audio-visual displays give information on forest life and the centre is also a starting point for a number of themed trails. These include a waterfall trail, an oak coppice trail, which reveals aspects of traditional forest management, and a Highland Boundary Fault Trail that follows the faultline itself.

The forest is a good place for birds of prey and owls, including short-eared and long-eared owls, peregrine and merlin, found near crags and open hill, hen harrier, sighted over moorland, buzzard and sparrowhawk. Jay, pheasant, woodpigeon and goldcrest use even the denser plantations. Oakwoods in the area have green and great spotted woodpeckers and tree pipits. Larger mammals include roe deer, and there are some red squirrels.

FLANDERS MOSS

Across the flood plain of the infant River Forth, east of the B8222 between Kippen and Thornhill, sits the largest surviving raised bog in Britain. East

Flanders Moss, which includes areas managed as a National Nature Reserve and a Scottish Wildlife Trust reserve, is all that remains of a once vast wetland. Centuries ago, the Forth Valley boglands stretched from Aberfoyle to the west to Stirling in the east – a spread of nearly 30 kilometres.

Thousands of years earlier, between 8500 and 6800 years ago, the low ground here was on the seabed. At that time, raised sea level – a consequence of the melting of the great ice age glaciers – flooded huge areas of land east and

BOG ASPHODEL

The bog asphodel is one of the glories of Scottish boggy areas from mid to late summer, when its golden-yellow flowers open in six-pointed stars over bog moss and heather. In winter, the seed heads can stay on the stems to catch the pale rays of low sunbeams.

SCOTLAND'S NATURE AND WILDLIFE

ADDER

Reptiles, like this adder, are cold-blooded. Basking in sunshine on warm rocks or in open patches on a moor can help them become active. Male adders have contrasting pale grey and black markings. Females are dull brown with fainter zigzag markings.

west in this part of Scotland. A neck of dry land only 8 kilometres wide was all that separated the sea in the Loch Lomond basin from the sea in the Forth Valley. The Highlands (which begin over the line of the Menteith Hills, that look down on the bogland from the north) nearly became an island! With that in mind, it's not so surprising that whale bones were once found in the peat here, a place that is now far inland.

The big push for drainage of Flanders Moss came in the late 1700s. Henry Home – Lord Kames – was a man of many talents and a leading figure in that flowering of Scottish art, science and culture known as the 'Scottish Enlightenment'. When his wife inherited her brother's estate at Blair Drummond, Henry (then 70) set about the business of making agricultural 'improvements'.

Through a system of reservoirs and a giant water wheel, he arranged for water taken from the River Teith to be released in deluging blasts to carry away great chunks of bogland peat down to the Forth. These were cut by people – later given the nickname of 'moss lairds' – who had been given areas of the bog to work on long leases, with the first seven years rent-free.

The effect of this and later peat removal and drainage was immense, converting huge acreages of bog into farmland. In the twentieth century, this was followed by extensive planting of conifers, especially to the west of the area – further drying and changing the moss – and commercial extraction of peat. An original 69,000 hectares shrunk over the centuries to 4000 hectares. It's something of a miracle that a good dollop of wilderness and wet has survived here. Now, work by the Forestry Commission, in partnership with Scottish Natural Heritage, the Scottish Wildlife Trust and others is helping to regenerate some parts of the bog, through damming of drainage ditches and removal of conifer plantations.

One of the best ways to appreciate the sheer expanse of Flanders Moss is to look south from one of the interpretation points along the A873 (at the South Common, Thornhill and the Flanders View tea room lay-by) or across from the many hills that flank the valley.

Many kinds of sphagnum bog mosses – the plants that make up most of the peat and store much of the bog's water – grow in wetter areas, with drier parts dominated by ling, cross-leaved heath and cotton grass. Other plant life is unusually varied for a bog and includes cranberry, bog rosemary (referred to by botanists by its spacey-sounding Latin name 'Andromeda'), and Labrador tea (a plant more usually associated with the barrens of North America).

The many kinds of insects include the four-spotted chaser dragonfly, the brindled beauty moth (whose caterpillars feed on bog myrtle) and the Rannoch sprawler moth. Adders live here, roe deer are common and, unusually for a lowland site, mountain hares breed out on the bog.

LAKE OF MENTEITH

In winter, hen harriers roost on the Moss and thousands of pink-footed geese visit the area, including the nearby Lake of Menteith. This is the only water in Scotland with the name 'lake'. This probably arose from a mix-up with the Scots word laigh, which means 'low ground' from the Gaelic *leachd* translated as 'sloping ground'. Whatever its etymological roots, the Lake is worth checking for other water birds, including goldeneye and whooper swans in winter and heron and goosander in summer.

The Lake is well known for its rainbow trout, and for the beauty of the ruined Augustine Priory on Inchmaholme, the largest of its three islands.

FIFE AND KINROSS

Facing east, the peninsula that holds the lands of Fife and Kinross has a special blend of land and sea. A long coastline meanders around its fringes, from the mudflats of the Tay estuaries' southern edge past massive sand dunes, rocky shores and broad bays to the Forth bridges. Within the Forth itself sits a sprinkling of islands, including two of the finest seabird havens along the entire British mainland.

TENTSMUIR POINT NATIONAL NATURE RESERVE

The sands and forests at the north-east corner of Fife are a major coastal link between the outer Tay and the estuary of the River Eden beside St Andrews. Tentsmuir Forest (FC) covers some 1500

SCOTLAND'S NATURE AND WILDLIFE

> **DID YOU KNOW?**
>
> Small rodents communicate a great deal of information to each other by scent, including the scent of their own urine. An adult male bank vole leaves a urine trail to help him attract females. This contains a chemical whose production depends on male hormones.

hectares and is criss-crossed with paths, giving access to open areas and ponds as well as forest walks among Scots and Corsican pines. Three species of bat roost in the forest, but the main focus for many wildlife enthusiasts in the area lies beyond, where the trees give way to lower vegetation and the land meets the sea.

Tentsmuir Point National Nature Reserve contains one of the fastest-growing lengths of coast in the country. The rate of advance is so rapid here that stones once set on the shore to mark salmon fishers' netting stations now lie well under the conifers, while concrete anti-tank blocks placed near the water in the 1940s are now almost a kilometre from the sea. Accessible from either Tayport village or from the Forestry Commission's Kinshaldy beach car park – signed from a minor road into the forest from the B945 north of Leuchars – this area is excellent for both birds and vegetation.

In winter, the Abertay Sands offshore can hold thousands of waders, including grey plover, sanderling, bar-tailed godwit, dunlin and oystercatcher. Many thousands of pink-footed geese (plus some greylags) roost here, while large flocks of seaduck are a feature from here, westward into the mouth of the Tay and southwards towards St Andrews Bay. Eider ducks are a major part of the sea duck gangs – with the occasional king eider seen around Tayport – together with common scoters and long-tailed duck. Year round, common seals and grey seals use the sandbanks as a haul-out.

The dunes at Tentsmuir, together with the hollows or 'slacks' behind them and the woodland fringe beyond, are home to around 400 species of plants. They also give a classic demonstration of how plants stabilise new sandy ground and gradually change its character with their different communities. Sea rocket and sea sandwort on the foreshore gives way to tall, dune-binding, lyme and marram grasses. Beyond, lichen-rich heath spreads to meet alder, birch and willow scrub. Choice plants such as the beautiful, white-petalled grass-of-Parnassus, purple milk vetch, common storksbill, common and seaside centaury grow on sandy land, providing food for butterflies and other insects.

MINNOW
(Phoxinus phoxinus)

It's the smallest carp in the country. The carp family includes the familiar goldfish and various species sought by anglers, but only a few, such as rudd, are able to cope with the cool conditions in Scotland. Gone are the days when the minnow itself might be caught for food and served up by the gallon at medieval banquets!

Clean, oxygenated water suits minnows, so fairly fast-flowing Scottish streams and rivers are to its liking, as are lochs which have clean, gravelly areas for summer spawning. Minnows are fast breeders, able to mate at the end of their first year, and one female can lay hundreds of eggs over several seasons during her adulthood; spawning, like much else in a minnow's life, is a communal activity, performed in a shoal.

Males in mating finery get flushed with rose-red along their flanks and develop little bumps, called tubercles, on their heads. The tubercles are made of keratin – the protein that forms our fingernails and hair – and are sloughed off after spawning.

CENTRAL LOWLANDS & FIFE

EDEN ESTUARY

Between Guardbridge and the end of the West Sands at St Andrews, the Eden Estuary Local Nature Reserve can hold impressive numbers of waders and wildfowl, including perhaps the largest concentration of black-tailed godwits in Scotland. There is effectively no access along most of the north shore of the estuary beside the Leuchars RAF base, but there are various ways to approach the inner estuary and the southern shore.

A short path from the A919 to Dundee, beside the Guardbridge paper mill, gives an entry point not far from where the River Eden meets the tidal mudflats. A recommended approach is to visit the observation centre built by Fife Council on the south side of the paper mill, which has views over the estuary and river. Nearer St Andrews, the outer estuary can be visited from the Eden Course car park of the Royal and Ancient Golf Club by walking to Balgove Bay.

Summer bird interest on the Eden Estuary includes shelduck and eider duck, but the place comes into its own between autumn and spring, when great numbers of wildfowl and waders pass through on migration or stop there to spend the winter. In addition to the black-tailed godwit interest, the estuary is also a good place for wintering grey plover, together with flocks of oystercatcher, knot, dunlin, bar-tailed godwit, redshank and some pink-footed geese. Scarce birds to watch out for in autumn include little stint and curlew sandpiper.

ISLE OF MAY NNR

Guarding the mouth of the Firth of Forth, and sitting closer to Fife than the southern shore, the Isle of May National Nature Reserve has huge historical and wildlife importance. This was a popular place of pilgrimage in the Middle Ages – a side trip for travellers who had journeyed to St Andrews. It was also the site of the first permanently manned lighthouse in Scotland, built in 1636. The main lighthouse at the crown of the island became fully automated in 1989,

SHELDUCK

The shelduck is a large duck (as big as a small goose) that feeds on mudflats and nests in burrows in dunes. It sifts the ooze at the surface of the mud, using side-to-side head movements to sieve small crustaceans and molluscs, such as spire shells, from the gritty soup.

SCOTLAND'S NATURE AND WILDLIFE

GREY SEALS, ISLE OF MAY

The colony of grey seals on the Isle of May National Nature Reserve, in the Firth of Forth, has increased significantly since the 1980s. Seals from here can range far and wide, such as south to the Farne Islands, or north along the Grampian coast and beyond.

with ownership of the island passing to the Nature Conservancy Council (now SNH). Work by volunteers making short visits to the Isle of May Bird Observatory and ornithologists studying seabirds and other wildlife has given the Isle of May an international reputation for the scientific work carried out there.

Through the summer, boats from both Crail and Anstruther – two of the attractive fishing communities in the 'East Neuk' of Fife – south of St Andrews, give the opportunity to make a day trip to the Isle of May. Rewards for the 8 kilometre crossing, which can take 40 minutes or so, include views of the rugged cliffs that rise along much of the island's western edge, the possibility of seeing grey seals in the water and the chance to experience one of the most accessible, large puffin colonies in Britain and Ireland at close range.

Puffin numbers on 'the May' have increased rapidly in recent decades, swelling from a handful of pairs in the early 1960s to the current level of more than 20,000 pairs. There is no guarantee that a day trip will coincide with one of the times when large numbers of puffins come ashore – this happens every three or four days on average. But you can be sure of seeing large numbers of puffins on and over the water between May and mid-August, mingled with some of the thousands of other auks, guillemots and razorbills, which breed on the cliffs here. Other prominent members of the Isle of May's seabird community include the shags and fulmars, thousands of herring and lesser black-backed gulls, kittiwakes, and a growing number of breeding common and Arctic terns.

A track runs along the spine of the island, past the top lighthouse and links the landing places at the north-west and south-east. From it you can get close views of breeding eider duck and an impression of the lush vegetation. Fertilised by copious amounts of phosphate-rich seabird droppings, but also shaped by salt-spray and North Sea gales, prominent plants include sea campion, sea pink (or 'thrift'), sorrel, scurvy, grass red fescue and different kinds of orache.

In autumn and winter, when the island is largely inaccessible to visitors, the Isle of May is an important east coast breeding rookery for grey seals. Some seals can usually be seen around the island in summer, when the clear water can also reveal thick beds of kelp and other seaweeds inshore and different species of jellyfish riding the currents.

BARNYARDS MARSH

Situated between the village of Kilconquhar and the hamlet of Barnyards, Barnyards Marsh (SWT) is part of a larger wetland area. This is a good place for wetland plants, especially sedges. These include, lesser pond sedge (more common in eastern England than in Scotland), brown sedge, white sedge and bottle sedge.

Orchids found here include northern marsh. Other typical wet ground plants here are ragged robin, meadowsweet and marsh marigold.

Sedge warblers and reed buntings breed and snipe overwinter. Access to a path through the reserve is a short distance from the unclassified Colinsburgh Road, which runs north-west from Kilconquhar Kirk.

LOCH LEVEN NATIONAL NATURE RESERVE

Roughly halfway between Edinburgh and Perth, and snuggling in against Fife where the heights of West Lomond drop to the plain below, the tiny county of Kinross is big on wildlife interest. Key to this is Loch Leven National Nature Reserve and Vane Farm (RSPB), which together comprise a place of huge importance for breeding, feeding and wintering wildfowl and waders.

The loch can be viewed well from several places, including Kirkgate Park just east of Kinross and across from the Castle Island (prison for Mary, Queen of Scots in 1567-68) and at the RSPB's Vane Farm Nature Centre. This is on the south side of the B9097 Glenrothes road, 3.2 kilometres east of Junction 5 on the M90. Behind Vane Farm are two nature trails that climb Vane Hill, from where you can take in an excellent loch panorama.

Loch Leven is the most extensive stretch of lowland freshwater in central Scotland. Formed in a hollow where a giant block of ice sat stranded at the end of the last ice age, the shallow waters of the loch are famous for their brown trout. Both fish and birds benefit from the rich

Wood Sorrel

SCOTLAND'S NATURE AND WILDLIFE

WIGEON

A prominent white wing flash and a creamy yellow forehead are two of a drake wigeon's distinctive features. Females are much more muted in colouration than males, as an aid to camouflaging them on the nest.

soup of invertebrates in the water, including Daphnia water fleas and small crustaceans.

The National Nature Reserve has the largest concentration of breeding ducks found anywhere in the UK. Over 1000 pairs of duck nest here, mostly among tussocks on St Serf's Island. Hundreds of tufted duck, plus mallard, gadwall, wigeon, shoveler and shelduck share the island with thousands of breeding black-headed gulls. Lapwing, curlew, oystercatcher, redshank and snipe, ringed plover and common sandpiper breed on wet grassland at the loch margins. In autumn, waders on passage, including golden plover, dunlin, greenshank, ruff, spotted redshank and black-tailed godwit, can feed on mud exposed when loch levels are lower.

Wet grassland around the loch holds orchids such as lesser butterfly and northern marsh orchids. Yellow flag and amphibious bistort grow in lagoon areas, and the reserve has a number of rare plants, including holy grass.

In late autumn, the loch and its fringes become a major entry point to Scotland for thousands of wildfowl. These include around 200 whooper swans from Russia, together with thousands of geese from Iceland and Greenland. Upwards of 20,000 pink-footed and greylag geese, plus a handful of white-fronted, bean, barnacle, brent and even the occasional snow goose winter on and around the loch.

CENTRAL LOWLANDS & FIFE

LOTHIANS AND BERWICK

There are swathes of greenspace at the heart of Edinburgh, and many other parts of the city beyond. Think of Princes Street Gardens – surely one of the most inspired pieces of undeveloped ground in any British city, flanking the Scottish capital's busiest shopping street and giving a leafy counterpoint to the starkness of the Castle crags above – and you start to get the picture.

You can get up close and personal with grey squirrels here – love them or loathe them. And there's something about the dialect of the local chaffinches around central Edinburgh that's got more than a whiff of tree frog about it.

However, it's the green fringes that can make a city such as Edinburgh really liveable for many of its residents and visitors alike. Edinburgh can offer some fine tastes of nature among the stones and tarmac. Not exactly unchained wilds, but not totally tame or urbanised either.

THE WATER OF LEITH

Central to the capital's green wedges is a real gem – the Water of Leith. This small river starts life up in the Pentland Hills and meanders a few tens of kilometres through farmland before it hits the outer edge of the city at the village of Balerno. For the next 16 kilometres or so, it's Edinburgh's home river, even more than the Forth. Although the estuary is a backdrop to the city, when viewed from a high point, such as around the Royal Mile or up on Calton Hill, the Water of Leith is right there at the core of it, chuckling its way beside the buildings and bustle or easing through calmer stretches. Designated an Urban Wildlife Site by the City of Edinburgh Council, it runs beyond Balerno close to the Lanark Road for a while, through Currie, Juniper Green and Slateford before hitting the fringes of the city centre at Wester Coates, Dean, Stockbridge and Warriston. Eventually, it spills out to meet the salt of the Forth at Leith.

You can follow the urban course of the river for much of its length by using the Water of Leith Walkway, and in places connect with a wider network of paths where parkland comes up to the banks. A visitor centre – the Water of Leith Heritage Centre – in a renovated schoolhouse on Lanark Road, gives a wealth of information about the history, wildlife and conservation work along the water. This is accessible from the walkway stretch between Juniper Green and Slateford.

COLINTON DELL

But you can dip in to the river margins at many places. Just use a large-scale tourist map of the city that shows the watercourse and you won't go far wrong. A good place to sample the water is at Colinton Dell on the south-west outskirts of the city. Here, as at Dean Village close to Princes Street, the river runs through a steep gorge. The Dell can be reached by walking towards Balerno from a car park under the main bridge over the river at Colinton, or by walking upstream from the Dell Inn beside Slateford Bridge.

Colinton Dell has large areas of mature deciduous woodland, with the odd conifer such as cedar of Lebanon, bushy patches and open grassland. In

---

DID YOU KNOW?

The mental 'picture' that a bat can have of its surroundings, based on echo-sounding in darkness, is more detailed than human vision produces in daylight.

SCOTLAND'S NATURE AND WILDLIFE

SEVEN-SPOT LADYBIRD
(Coccinella 7-punctata)

Many different species of ladybird live in Scotland, including 16 which have been recorded in the Highlands. One of the commonest and most widespread of these is the seven-spot. Its abundance is appropriate since it's the seven-spots that put the 'lady' in ladybird in the first place.

The name comes from 'Our Lady' – the Virgin Mary. The red colour of the seven spot's wing cases recalls the colour of cloak that Mary seems to favour in old paintings, while its spots symbolise the seven joys and sorrows of the Virgin.

Ladybird spotting can be a matter of doing just that – counting spots. The other very common ladybird in Scotland is the two spot, which (you've guessed it) usually has a single large spot on each wing case. Some confusing variations occur, however, such as two-spots with dark wing cases and more than the standard issue spot number. Studying these is a fascinating research subject in its own right.

Most impressive Scottish-dwelling species of all, is the eyed ladybird (*Anatis ocellata*) which lives in conifers, especially pines. This grows about 8 millimetres long, making it the biggest ladybird in Britain, and has seven or eight dark spots on each wing case, each spot circled in yellow.

DID YOU KNOW?
Some of the world's most impressive reefs of cold water coral grow on the seabed of Scotland's 'Atlantic Frontier' north and west of the Outer Hebrides.

spring, bluebells grow beneath the trees, and ramsons – with their strong whiff of crushed garlic somehow more Loire than Lothians – cover broad patches of the valley sides. Spring is also a time for willow warbler and chiffchaff song here and, in summer, wood warblers can sometimes show up. More than 80 species of birds have been recorded in the Dell, including great spotted woodpecker and sparrowhawk.

At other places along the river, birdlife includes grey wagtails and dippers on fast-flowing reaches, such as Balerno to Slateford, and Roseburn to Stockbridge, herons, mallard ducks, mute swans and the occasional kingfisher. Eleven species of fish, including brown trout, now live in the channel, where you might also find caddis fly larvae and freshwater leeches, or see mayflies dancing on warm evenings.

DUDDINGSTON LOCH

If the Water of Leith is Edinburgh's wild ribbon, Duddingston Loch and Bawsinch (Scottish Development Department and SWT) is a small oasis. The loch sits below Arthur's Seat within Holyrood Park. Public access is restricted to the northern shore along the road through the park between Hangman's Rock and a church at Old Church Lane. The loch has an interesting history. It was dredged in the eighteenth century to get lime-rich 'marl' for nearby farms. These excavations uncovered antlers of ancient elk and deer, human remains and other artefacts from the Bronze Age.

Greylag geese were brought to Duddingston in 1961 and still breed here, and there are many hybrids resulting from inter-breeding with other species, including canada geese. Other breeding wildfowl include mute swans, great crested grebe, little grebe, moorhen, coot and tufted duck. In winter, the loch attracts good numbers of duck, including tufted duck, pochard, teal, some goldeneye and the occasional goosander. Pochard numbers used to be higher but gatherings of a few dozen are still found.

A band of marshland across from the public area has reedbeds, sometimes used by breeding herons, with woodland behind. Sedge warblers also breed in the reeds and the woods shelter blackcap, chiffchaff and green woodpecker. In autumn, pied wagtails roost in the eastern reedbed, which can be watched from the adjacent road.

ABERLADY BAY

Aberlady Bay (East Lothian Council), which fans its mudflats out against the Forth where the Peffer Burn meets the sea beside Aberlady village, is the oldest local nature reserve in Britain. Administered by the Local Authority since 1952, the Bay and its surrounding coastland are big on bird, plant and geological interest. Access is from a car park 0.8 kilometres beyond the village beside the A198 Edinburgh to North Berwick road. From here a track goes over a footbridge across the Peffer Burn and on northwards to Gullane Point with a left branch that goes on to the coast.

The mudflats are so extensive at low-tide as to make the Bay seem vast and even the swirling flocks of hundreds of waders seem small. Aberlady has salt marsh, freshwater marsh, pools, dunes, woodland and sea buckthorn scrub. Each of these has its own possibilities for different wildlife. And in an eastern coastal location such as this, those possibilities include seasonal ringing of the changes as migrant birds drop in to estuary or shore in autumn and spring, then move on to who knows where.

Aberlady has been blessed with a sprinkling of rare wader visitors, including caspian plover, sharp-tailed sandpiper, white-rumped sandpiper and Baird's sandpiper – all long-haul travellers from as far afield as the Canadian Arctic. But this is also a place where less exotic, but never-the-less tricky to spot waders in other places, such as curlew sandpiper and little stint turn up most autumns.

Wader flocks here can repay a visit on even a grey autumn or winter's day. Oystercatcher, ringed plover, golden plover and grey plover, knot, sanderling, snipe, bar-tailed godwit, curlew and redshank can be here in strength, challenging identification skills for even the most seasoned watcher – for who knows what scarcer species might be there among the knot of knots?

Roe Deer

REGIONAL HIGHLIGHT: ABERLADY BAY

DESIGNATION:
Local Nature Reserve.

LANDSCAPE:
Coastline with mudflats, salt and freshwater marsh, dunes and pools.

HIGHLIGHTS:
Unusual vagrants such as white-rumped sandpiper and Caspian plover are among the rarities that have visited the bay. Common wading birds and wildfowl, including mallard, wigeon and pink-footed geese, are more usual, plus a host of other birds. Orchids, burnet rose, moonwort and bog pimpernel can be found on and around the dunes.

BEST TIME:
Autumn and winter for waders, including the more rare species, and various wildfowl.

FACILITIES:
Car park; reserve open all year round.

ADMISSION:
Free.

DIRECTIONS:
Access from the car park by Aberlady, off A198.

SCOTLAND'S NATURE AND WILDLIFE

Rookery

Wintering wildfowl include hundreds of mallard and wigeon out on the mud, flocks of sea-duck, with eiders, common scoters and long-tailed duck, plus red-necked and slavonian grebes on the sea beyond (best scanned from Gullane Point). Thousands of pink-footed geese use the bay as a winter roost.

Eider, ringed plover and shelduck are among the summer breeders. Marl Loch, opposite an area of salt marsh, has breeding water rail and lesser whitethroat, with abundant sedge warblers in the marsh and bogbean, amphibian bistort and intermediate bladderwort in the water. Notable vegetation elsewhere includes the moss and lichen cover on the fixed dunes, with autumn gentian, grass-of-Parnassus, burnet rose and moonwort in some areas. Wetter areas between dunes have bog pimpernel, early marsh and other orchids, and many species of sedges.

A small chain of islands, each distinctively shaped, pocks the water just a short distance out from the coast near North Berwick. Eyebroughty, Fidra, the Lamb, Craigleith, the Bass Rock – all are important for breeding seabirds, the Bass in the major league as possibly the largest single rock colony of North Atlantic gannets in the world.

THE SCOTTISH SEABIRD CENTRE

Thanks to the Scottish Seabird Centre at North Berwick, visitors can now enjoy live TV relays of some of the seabird action on the nearby islands. While still ashore, visitors can find out about seabird ecology and conservation and ogle the offshore through high-power telescopes. Built on a rocky promontory at North Berwick harbour, the centre has full disabled access, a shop, catering facilities and a pleasant view out over the Forth.

A visit to the Seabird Centre should whet the appetites of many, and with the Bass Rock just a gannet glide away, North Berwick is a great departure point for a trip out on a boat (check at the harbour for times) to see a major seabird colony at close range. Gannet numbers on the Bass have swelled from 6000 to 8000 occupied nest sites in 1962 to possibly 40,000 or more now. The spectacle of these big birds – even at a distance from a boat – is tremendous. Long winged, noisy, yet graceful in both flight and in postures used ashore, the gannet's real jaw-dropper is the way it can fold its wings back and plunge, like a feathered missile, to grab fish from just beneath the sea surface.

Aside from gannets, the Bass is also home to guillemots, razorbills, puffins, fulmars, shags, kittiwakes, herring gulls, lesser black-backs and some great black-backs, with a smattering of rock pipits and regularly breeding pied wagtails, starling, dunnock and feral pigeon. One interesting plant which grows on the Bass is tree mallow – perhaps brought here for its medicinal properties.

JOHN MUIR COUNTRY PARK

Just a few kilometres south-east of North Berwick and the Bass, broadly speaking, from here to Northumberland, is the John Muir Country Park (East Lothian

---

DID YOU KNOW?

The sea level in central Scotland was once so high (beyond the end of the last ice age) that whales swam in what is now the upper valley of the Forth, to the west of Stirling.

CENTRAL LOWLANDS & FIFE

Council). Named after the Dunbar born naturalist, inventor and writer who moved to the United States as a boy and later became a founding father of the National Parks system, the country park includes a huge area around the broad expanse of Tyninghame Bay.

This is where the River Tyne meets the sea. A headland with the intriguing name of St Baldred's Cradle curves across the northern end, and two long sand spits – Sandy Hirst and Spike Island – shelter the inner estuary. These spits are used by breeding ringed plover, their sea buckthorn can shelter migrant birds and the salt marsh on the west side of the Sandy Hirst can give a vantage over roosting curlews and bar-tailed godwits.

Other wintering waders include oystercatcher, dunlin, knot, redshank, grey plover and turnstone. Scores of mute and whooper swans winter here, while wigeon (up to 1000), mallard and teal feed around the marshland and pink-footed and greylag geese roost on the estuary.

Summer plant interest includes wild thyme, ling, cross-leaved heath and lichens in parts of the dunes, meadow saxifrage, cowslip and primrose on the steep cliffs at Dunbar, and sea campion and common scurvy grass, with buckthorn plantain and bloody cranesbill around Whitberry Point. A nature trail, with information boards along the coastal grassland and clifftop route, starts from car parks at the north end of Dunbar High Street or from the shore at Belhaven, east of Dunbar.

GANNETS, BASS ROCK

The gannetry on the Bass Rock, close to the town of North Berwick, is probably the first seabird colony to be described in world literature. It is mentioned in The Seafarer, *a poem that still survives in a manuscript from around 1000 AD, but which was probably written in the late 600s by an Anglo-Saxon who visited East Lothian.*

SCOTLAND'S NATURE AND WILDLIFE

Eastern Lowlands

The eastern fringes of Scotland, from the Moray Firth down to the Tay, have long been occupied and used by farmers. Neolithic settlers left many a mark around these coastlands, in cairns raised 4000 years ago or more, and in standing stones and shards of pottery.

Fast forward to the present (leapfrogging so much, including the times of the Picts, for whom these Eastern Lowlands were a hub), and agriculture still figures strongly in the look and the life of the area. So it makes sense in watching wildlife here not to focus exclusively on reserves and other choice wildlife sites (mainly dotted around the coast), but to try and get an idea what some of the farmlands hold in store.

A walk along a minor Black Isle road, for example, beside small family farms still practising a mixed husbandry of cattle, sheep, root and cereal crops, can be rewarded with views of finch flocks in winter, gulls and sheep on stubbles, and signs of fox, such as hairs on wire fences. In Aberdeenshire the farmland scene would often feature large groups of rooks and could perhaps reward searches for signs of badgers near fields and otters along rivers.

Planted woods of many kinds are also a fundamental part of the look of these lowlands. Conifer woods along the southern and inner coasts of the Moray Firth include a major amount of Scots pine. The benefit of this is that some wildlife more often associated with native woodlands could be encountered on a walk through a planted forest. This includes red squirrels and pine martens, and pinewood plants such as creeping lady's tresses orchid.

Elsewhere, clumps of trees within farmland often merit a closer look as providing small oases of unkempt greenery for wildlife. Their shrubby fringes can be used by breeding warblers and rabbits, while their interior hold evidence of roe deer.

The long coast of the Eastern Lowlands has huge stretches of soft shore, in the mudflats of estuary systems and bays, and in the shifting expanses of sandy dunes. Wading birds and wildfowl home in on the muds, such as those close to the industrial complexes at Nigg, skirting the town of Montrose, and in the more tranquil setting of the Ythan estuary.

The sands, at first sight, look less promising for wildlife. But go in summer to places like Forvie, and the colours of flowers among the dunes, their nectar feeding a range of butterflies and other insects, can seem all the more impressive for springing from such desert-like conditions.

Hard shores are also here in abundance, including some with cliffs that hold large numbers of breeding seabirds. These birds look to the North Sea for their summer livelihood, and their colonies are far less numerous than in the seabird havens of the North Isles. But they bring an element of surprise to the eastern fringes through their occasional bursts of noise, smell and bustle. Puffins near the neep fields, guillemots just beyond the furrows – that's part of what can make this area special.

Greenshank

SCOTLAND'S NATURE AND WILDLIFE

INNER MORAY FIRTH

BOTTLENOSE DOLPHIN
Bottlenose dolphins are adept at leaping clear of the water, sometimes in unison with other dolphins in their group. This may form part of their social communication. Underwater, dolphins use clicks, whistles and other sounds, both to keep in touch with each other and to locate and stun prey.

INVERNESS

Capital of the Highlands and one of the fastest-growing urban areas in Britain, Inverness still holds some excellent wildlife-watching areas within and around its city limits. The heart of town is perhaps the most surprising of these.

Where the River Ness flows past Inverness Castle and on under several bridges, sections of gravel near the banks are favourite loafing and washing areas for a variety of gulls, some of which may be off duty rooftop nesters during the summer. Sit quietly on the riverside grass along here and you might see a dipper or a grey wagtail feeding, or red-breasted mergansers in mid-channel. Further upstream, the Ness Islands give wooded shelter for migrant and resident songbirds as well as further opportunities to look out for birds using the river, including the occasional kingfisher.

Immediately to the west of the Kessock Bridge, which links Inverness and the Black Isle, there are prime dolphin-watching vantages at both North Kessock and South Kessock. The narrows here are a feeding area for some of the Moray Firth's resident bottlenose dolphin population. You can also get excellent views of them at many times of the year at the narrows between Chanonry Point near Fortrose, Fort George and around Cromarty.

BEAULY FIRTH

Westward again from the Kessock Channel, the shallows and mudflats of the Beauly Firth are a major British stronghold for goosanders, more than 600 of which can gather here in winter. From May onwards this is also a moulting area for Canada geese. These geese began their summer gathering on the Beauly Firth during the 1950s. Subsequent studies have revealed – amazingly – that they come here from as far away as Yorkshire. It's a striking example of an introduced species, first brought to Britain in the seventeenth century, developing a new migration

EASTERN LOWLANDS

route within a colonised county.

CROMARTY FIRTH

Flanking the Black Isle's northern shores, the Cromarty Firth is an important place for wildfowl, waders and common seals, also known as harbour seals. Best seal-watching is from lay-bys both on the Cromarty Firth Bridge, beside the A9 north-east of the bridge, and at the Clanland Centre at Ferryton. Dozens of common seals can haul-out on sandbanks at low tide around here. At higher tides, it's not unusual to see seals balanced on their bellies on sea-washed rocks, bodies arched up in banana curves as they try to keep dry.

NIGG AND UDALE

Towards the seaward end of the estuary, the big bays of Nigg and Udale face each other across a deep water boat channel and oil rig anchorage. These bays teem with mud-dwelling molluscs, other invertebrates and plants which feed large numbers of wildfowl and waders. Nigg, best viewed from the shore beside Barbaraville and Milton, holds half the total intertidal area of the Cromarty Firth. The Udale RSPB reserve has an excellent hide at a parking area beside the B9163 just west of Jemimaville.

Large beds of eelgrass in both bays give grazing for thousands of wigeon in autumn and spring, during movements to and from Icelandic breeding grounds. Oystercatcher and curlew numbers can be high at any time of year, joined by big flocks of knot, redshank and dunlin in autumn and winter, and a sprinkling of greenshank, ruff and black-tailed godwits. Beds of glasswort are an interesting feature on the upper part of Udale, forming a fringe below the salt marsh.

CULBIN, ROSEISLE AND LOSSIE

Think 'conifer plantation' and you might well conjure up an image of a stand of Sitka spruce, stereotypically dark, difficult to walk through and devoid of much obvious interest among the needle carpet. The coastal plantations in Nairn and Moray are different. Between Nairn and Forres, the Forestry Commission managed forests of Culbin, Roseisle and Lossie are big on pines, a mix of Scots and Corsican. The upshot is that some choice native flora and fauna has been able to survive and even thrive in these

---

COMMON SEAL
(Phoca vitulina)

The smaller of the two seals that breed in Scotland, this puppy-faced character is outnumbered many times over by the larger, Roman-nosed grey seal. If in doubt about which of the two species you're watching, check the nostrils as well as the head shape. Common seal nostrils slant down in a 'v' shape to almost touch, while grey seal nostrils are nearly parallel slits, set in a flatter-topped, longer head. But identification can still be tricky if you're looking at animals in the water. More than nine out of ten common seals in Britain are Scottish dwelling. Females give birth to a single pup in midsummer, which can swim as soon as the tide washes in over the sandbank or hard rock maternity area. Mating takes place at sea in July. At that time, males display by roaring underwater and by making short stylised dives.

Studies in Orkney and the Moray Firth have shown that calls vary from place to place, perhaps as a result of differences in local marine conditions. So it's quite possible that male common seals in widely separated locations have different accents.

DID YOU KNOW?

Domestic pigeons, including the ones that flock in city squares and streets, are descendants of rock doves. Some parts of the northern Scottish coast and islands still hold populations of wild rock doves, which like to breed on cave ledges (hence the town pigeons' liking for old buildings).

SCOTLAND'S NATURE AND WILDLIFE

> **DID YOU KNOW?**
>
> A whole community of insects can live on a single thistle head. This can include moth caterpillars, weevil larvae, aphids, thrips, beetles, gall-forming flies and a variety of parasitic insects that lay eggs on and in the young of other species.

woods. Their many tracks are well worth exploring to get an idea of plants and creatures you might normally associate with ancient pinewood remnants elsewhere.

Pine cone seeds give food for both crossbills and red squirrels here, and there is a healthy breeding population of crested tits. These cresties are usually much more widely spaced than their relatives in the older Highland pinewoods, but their trilling calls help to locate them at a distance. Plantation-dwelling pine martens will normally be elusive, but you might see signs of them through droppings along trails.

Culbin Forest, accessible from a car park at Wellhill, grows on one of the largest sand dune systems in Britain, with some of the tree-stabilised sandhills topping 30 metres. This was once fertile farmland, but in the autumn of 1686 (so the story goes) a tempest blew vast quantities of sand over the area, ruining the harvest. Over many years, continuing sand blows covered farmhouses and fields alike. Two centuries later, an Elgin writer commented how 'to make one's way across the flood of sand, even for a little distance, was no easy task'.

Experimental tree planting began here in 1888, but the main push started in the 1920s, when sand dunes were first covered with a thatch of branches before seedlings were planted amongst them. By the late 1960s, the trees finally stilled the swirling of the sand. Now, in addition to the animals and birds you might encounter here, including widespread coal tits, goldcrests, siskins and chaffinches, the plant life can give some surprises in the shape of some of the best expanses of lichen heath (rich in *Cladonia* species) anywhere in the north.

CULBIN BAR

Beyond the woods, the 7 kilometre stretch of Culbin Bar, accessible only with care at low tides, but impressive enough as a seascape feature in the distance, is part of a massive shingle system. This is linked by shared coastal processes with the shingles at the mouth of the Spey, to the east. The RSPB's Culbin Sands reserve includes a mix of salt marsh, dunes, pinewoods and bushy scrub. It holds ringed plover and terns in summer, snow buntings along the beach and dunes in winter, bar-tailed godwit, oystercatcher and knot roosts, and winter flocks of sea duck offshore.

FINDHORN BAY

East of Culbin, the Findhorn Bay Local Nature Reserve has a variety of trails through different kinds of vegetated shingles and dunes flanking Findhorn village, and along the shore of both estuary and firth. These include a route along the 'Ee' – a hooked spit of sand and shingle that curves across the mouth of the bay, channelling the Findhorn River over a sand bar between the village peninsula and the pines of Culbin.

The heart of the Ee is rich in flowers, including wild thyme, Scots lovage and biting stonecrop. The spit also gives a vantage to look out over the bay – the shore is used by osprey and redshank, and the waters used by both common and grey seals. Day flying burnet moths are common in the sand dunes to the east, where dune crests also give panoramic views across a huge sweep of

EASTERN LOWLANDS

the Moray Firth. In winter, thousands of greylag and pinkfeet geese use the bay.

SPEY BAY

The channel of the River Spey where it flows down to meet the sea is a braided, shifting mosaic of rushing water, bare gravel and wooded islands thick with alder. It's a wild place, which holds nesting areas for common and Arctic terns, redshank and duck and good fishing shallows for ospreys.

The mouth of the river and the huge banks of vegetated shingle to the west lie within the Scottish Wildlife Trust's Spey Bay reserve. Best approached on foot along tracks leading out from Kingston, this has a mixture of heathland, woodland, damp dune hollows and freshwater marsh. The burnet rose is prominent among the stones here at any time of the year, whether blooming in summer or with its small red haws in winter.

Other notable plants include coralroot orchid, and common and intermediate wintergreens. Kidney vetch provides food for the caterpillars of colonies of small blue butterflies here. East of the river mouth, the Moray Firth Wildlife Centre, housed in an old salmon fishing station, gives good interpretation and wildlife viewing facilities.

Jutting east in a rounded wedge, the fertile farmlands of Buchan, big on the straight lines of modern field boundaries over fairly flat plains, are bounded by a

ARCTIC TERN

From some angles, the arctic tern can seem more wing than bird. Its outer wing feathers (the primaries) are translucent – one of the ways you can tell it apart in good light from the common tern. The other is that the arctic tern's bill is all red, while the common tern's has a black spot at the end.

SCOTLAND'S NATURE AND WILDLIFE

PURPLE SANDPIPER
Purple sandpipers breed from northern Europe up to the high arctic. Large numbers spend the winter in Scotland.

> **DID YOU KNOW?**
> More grey seals breed in Scotland than anywhere else in the world, but individaul greys can travel between several countries, such as to the Faroe Islands and Ireland, in the course of a single year.

wilder coast. Beaches, coves and cliffs edge the northern shore along the outer Moray Firth. A softer fringe, punctuated by some spectacular cliffy outcrops, flanks the North Sea.

TROUP TO CRUDEN

The area near Gardenstown and Pennan gives a flavour of this salty rim, often given the cold shoulder by wildlife seekers from beyond the region, but worth some exploration. A series of moist, narrow ravines shelters great examples of herb-rich grassland, flushes and scrub here. As along most of the length of this shore of the Firth, it's also worth looking out to sea in case any bottlenose dolphins are passing; although the main outer Firth hot spots are further east, in Cullen Bay, Findochty and Portknockie.

TROUP HEAD

The major seabird breeding area in this part of the north-east is around Troup Head, where cliffs more than 100 metres high extend for several kilometres between Crovie and Aberdour Bay. Troup Head can be approached by a stiff walk from the fishing village of Crovie. Closer access is only feasible with permission from local farms. Lion's Head, west of Pennan (famous for the red phonebox which featured in the film Local Hero) can be approached from a car park off the B9031 at Cullikhan. A faint path follows the clifftops in the area and promontories give good views of nesting seabirds. But the cliffs are steep and need great caution to enjoy safely.

Troup – the only gannet colony on the Scottish mainland – is also Scotland's newest. These big, dazzling white seabirds catch the eye here, both ashore at their nests and offshore as they flap and glide in search of fish. Other breeding seabirds include many thousands of pairs of kittiwake and guillemot, smaller numbers of razorbill and fulmar, herring gulls and a handful of puffins. The rocky shoreline between Rosehearty and Fraserburgh is a good place for waders in winter, including redshank, oystercatcher, turnstone and purple sandpiper. Fraserburgh Harbour, a major fish market, is popular with

EASTERN LOWLANDS

gulls, and worth checking in winter for pale-plumaged glaucous and Iceland gulls.

LOCH OF STRATHBEG

Far out to the north-east between Peterhead and Fraserburgh, the RSPB's Loch of Strathbeg reserve includes marsh, dune, farmland and woodland around the largest dune pool in Britain. The loch was once a coastal bay, connected by a narrow channel to the sea. But in 1720, a severe easterly gale blew a bar of sand and shingle into the channel, blocking the inlet and forming a shallow, brackish loch. Surrounding land flooded, fen and marsh formed and castle of Rattray, which once lay on the loch's southern shore, was abandoned. Human loss was wildlife's gain. Despite repeated attempts at drainage in the past, the loch remains a site of prime importance for wildfowl, with an interesting variety of plants in its lime-rich soils. Strathbeg is one of the best sites in Britain for wintering pink-footed geese – over 30,000 in an average season and with a record count of nearly twice that number.

Lapwing

Smaller numbers of Icelandic-breeding greylag geese, plus some barnacle geese from the Spitzbergen population (stopping over in October on their way to the Solway Firth wintering grounds) also occur. Numbers of grey geese usually build up during September, with the birds roosting on the loch and feeding on surrounding farms.

Come November, several hundred

REGIONAL HIGHLIGHT: LOCH OF STRATHBEG

DESIGNATION:
RSPB reserve.

LANDSCAPE:
Loch, marsh, dune and woodland.

HIGHLIGHTS:
A popular spot for pink-footed geese, along with greylag and barnacle geese in smaller numbers. Mute and whooper swans, water rails, reed buntings, teal and goldeneye can also be seen around the loch. Other wildlife includes otters, roe deer, foxes and butterflies, while plants of interest include creeping spearwort, Baltic rush and early marsh orchid.

BEST TIME:
Pink-footed geese between autumn and spring. Other geese, ducks and whooper swans in winter, along with lapwings, golden plovers and curlews. Great-crested glebes and sandwich terns in summer.

FACILITIES:
A visitor centre and observation room with toilets and car park; (centre not fully accessible to disabled visitors). Open all year round.

ADMISSION:
Free - Donation

DIRECTIONS:
Near Crimond on the A90, S of Fraserburgh.

CONTACT:
RSPB Loch of Strathbeg Reserve, Starnafin, Crimond, Fraserburgh AB43 8QN

Tel: 01346 532017

www.rspb.org.uk

BOTTLENOSE DOLPHIN
(Tursiops truncatus)

The last resident population of bottlenose dolphin in the North Sea lives in the waters from the Moray Firth, south along the coast to St Andrews Bay. There are also very small groups which regularly use parts of the Western Isles, around Tiree, Coll and Barra.

The big fin on a dolphin's back – the dorsal fin – can vary a bit from animal to animal. Different sizes, shapes, differences in skin tone and wear and tear, including teeth marks from other dolphins, can all add up to a fin being unique to a particular individual.

Using thousands of photographs of dorsal fins, scientists based at Cromarty on the Black Isle and in St Andrews have been able to discover that there are around 130 animals in the north-east population. This is few enough to make people concerned about the animals' future numbers, and has lead to plans for special conservation measures to help dolphins in the Moray Firth.

Distinctive dorsal fins are also a good way for people who just like to watch dolphins to keep track of favourite individuals. One called 'Runny Paint' – with several white marks like brush strokes on the fin – was first photographed and named in 1989, for example. Since then, Runny has been seen at St Andrews, Dundee and Aberdeen as well as back in the Moray Firth.

DID YOU KNOW?

Male ducks typically have little or nothing to do with the incubation of eggs or rearing young. So while the female ducks tend to be well camouflaged, the males are feathered dandies, big on colour and attitude.

---

whooper swans and flocks of moulting mute swans also use the loch, together with wintering wigeon, mallard, tufted duck, teal, goldeneye, red-breasted merganser and goosander. Curlew and golden plover feed in the fields. Summer breeders include hundreds of sandwich terns, common terns, and a range of ducks, while water rails use the marshland, and sedge warbler and reed buntings nest in the reedbeds.

Increasing enrichment of the loch's waters has reduced the variety and number of larger plants in it, but there is a fine range of flowering plants elsewhere, including grass-of-Parnassus, field gentian, Baltic rush and Scots lovage on the dunes, and angelica, early marsh orchid and greater butterfly orchid in the marsh. One of the most intriguing plants here is creeping spearwort. This rarity is thought to originate from material eaten by geese in Iceland and airlifted to Britain – mostly to goose roosts.

Otters are regularly seen on the reserve, roe deer are common and feed out to the waters edge, and foxes benefit from the rabbit warrens in the dunes. Butterflies include grayling and dark green fritillary. The reserve can be approached from a visitor centre at Starnafin, near Crimond, and hides give fine views of the pools.

LONGHAVEN CLIFFS

The granite cliffs to the south of Buchan Ness are a beautiful sea-sculpted and shattered succession of small inlets, stacks, caves and arches. At Longhaven Cliffs SWT reserve, thousands of seabirds breed, including numerous kittiwakes and guillemots and smaller numbers of fulmars, razorbills, puffins, shag and herring gulls.

Clifftop vegetation has an unusual type of maritime heath, with bell heather, devil's-bit scabious, crowberry and grass-of–Parnassus. Roseroot, thrift and sea campion cover the cliffs, while more sheltered bays and inlets have a woodland-like mix of primrose, bluebell, red campion, marsh marigold and lesser celandine. Access is off the A920 down a track to a quarry inland from Yoags Haven.

Just south of Longhaven is the small settlement of Bullers of Buchan named after the collapsed cave in the nearby sea cliff. The sea rushes through

EASTERN LOWLANDS

a natural archway here into a cavern with a 30-metre-high opening, called the Pot. When James Boswell and Samuel Johnson came here in 1773, Boswell described this feature as a 'monstrous cauldron'. Puffins burrow in the clifftop vegetation close to the Bullers, above a good mix of other seabirds, including gulls, razorbills, guillemot, shags and cormorants.

YTHAN TO DEE

The winding course of the River Ythan is like a journey in snatches of song and story, so close is it twined with places and names that loom large in ballads and history. 'There's mony a bonny lass in the Howe O' Auchterless, there's mony a bonny jean in the Garioch – oh, there's mony a bonny quine in the streets o' Aberdeen, but the floo'er o' them aw bides in Fyvie-oh.'

She must have been quite a stunner, that lass from Ythan-side whose beauty still sings down the ages. Then there was 'Mad Jack Byron' – another kettle of passions entirely – father of the poet Byron, who squandered the lands of Gight. Even without its famous, bird-thronged entrance to the sea, the Ythan is fascinating water. But the estuary has its own claim to fame. Thanks to work done by generations of scientists from the University of Aberdeen, many using the field station of Culterty as a base, this is now perhaps the most studied estuary in the world.

GREYLAG GOOSE

A native population of a few thousand greylag geese is thinly scattered over Caithness, Sutherland, western Ross-shire and the Hebrides north of Mull. In autumn, Scottish greylag ranks are swelled by the arrival of tens of thousands of birds from the Icelandic population.

SCOTLAND'S NATURE AND WILDLIFE

EIDER DUCK

The eider duck is widespread around most Scottish coasts, but the largest colonies are on the east coast, with the area from the Ythan estuary, south to near Dundee and out to the Isle of May having the biggest concentrations.

In winter, the mouth of the Tay off Tentsmuir NNR has huge flocks.

Modest in size it may be – about 8 kilometres long, 300 metres wide on average and only 600 metres at its widest – but you could fill a library with the data that has been gathered here and the resulting publications on everything from mud to eiders. The size matters, for the narrowness of the river's final run has made it easier to study many different aspects of the place – from single species to whole systems of energy flow – that would be hard in a larger area.

That's some of the Ythan's global significance. But for wildlife watchers, especially those with an eye for birds, the intimate scale of things here brings the boon of good, close views of many different species at a place not far (19 kilometres) from Aberdeen.

There are various access points – near the golf course close to the Ythan Hotel, off the A92 at Newburgh, at the Waterside Bridge over the river north of Newburgh and down a track to a hide, built by the local council, overlooking the inner estuary. Birdwatchers benefit from the way the road follows the estuary edge for much of its length. Many of the birds here, including eider, shelduck and waders, are accustomed to people and their vehicles and so are fairly tame.

One of the best places to watch eiders is when thousands gather off Newburgh beach to feed on submerged mussel beds. The river mouth (which sits between the Ythan and Sands of Forvie National Nature Reserves) is also popular with other ducks, including

EASTERN LOWLANDS

scaup and long-tailed duck in winter, and red-breasted mergansers.

Good wader watching is further upriver, near where the Tarty Burn enters the river amid the mudflat of the Sleek. Curlews, ringed plover, bar-tailed godwit, knot, golden and grey plover, greenshank, redshank and snipe are all possibilities here at different seasons. As a guide, curlew numbers tend to peak here in July, redshank and oystercatcher in August, golden plover and knot in September, lapwing in November and dunlin in January.

Winter is when flocks of greylag and pink-footed geese use the river and surrounding fields. The hide at Waulkmill may give a chance of watching these without disturbing them, and of appreciating the mute swans which favour this part of the river. Among the other wildfowl, locally burrow-nesting shelduck – always dapper with their coloured plumage panels set against striking white – add vibrancy to even the greyest of North Sea coastal days.

> ### RED KITE
> #### (Milvus milvus)
>
> Persecuted to extinction in Scotland in the 1800s, the red kite is now making a comeback. The Black Isle, at the heart of the Inner Moray Firth, was the launchpad for reintroduction.
>
> Between 1989 and 1993, the RSPB and the Nature Conservancy Council (forerunner of Scottish Natural Heritage) imported 93 young kites from Sweden. After release, the young pioneers were given food-handouts at secret locations, but were free to go their own way.
>
> First breeding was in 1992, when a pair reared a single chick. Since then, the Scottish population has steadily climbed, despite setbacks from a small level of continuing illegal persecution. By 2000, more than 70 chicks were hatched by several dozen pairs.
>
> The Inner Moray Firth is still an excellent place to watch for kites. Their long wings are noticeable in the air, but a red kite's most striking feature is its deeply forked tail. The bird bends and flexes this to adjust its airtrim, seeming to react to the slightest shifts of breeze.
>
> Commuters on the A9 trunk road between Inverness and the Cromarty Firth Bridge often get a view of a red kite above the highway. But for safer kite watching, the North Kessock tourist information centre, off the northbound carriageway just beyond the Kessock Bridge, is a better bet in spring and summer. Information panels and other printed material give the background to the bird's resurgence, and in recent years, a video link to an occupied nest has given great views of a kite family at home.

SANDS OF FORVIE

The Sands of Forvie National Nature Reserve (SNH) lies immediately to the north of the Ythan, between the river and Collieston. A track on the right off the B9003 to Collieston leads to the Forvie Centre, where there is information about the reserve. Tracks go from here into moorland areas and into the sandy heart of the reserve.

This is one of the finest dune systems in Britain, with an array of different types of vegetation on the lime-poor sands. There are mobile 'yellow' dunes, gripped by marram grass but shifting in the winds, wet hollows, 'grey' dunes plastered in lichens, rabbit-grazed grassland and swathes of maritime heath rich in heather, crowberry and matgrass.

The upshot of this habitat variety in a fairly harsh environment is a great mix of plants. Around 350 species of flowering plants have been recorded here – some striking, like various kinds of orchids; some subtle, like the rare colony of curved sedge and the many species of mosses and liverworts (some with strong links to Scandinavia).

SCOTLAND'S NATURE AND WILDLIFE

COMMON SUNDEW
Small but deadly (if you're as wee as a midge or some other tiny insect), the common sundew supplements its diet in food-poor, boggy places with some fresh prey. Sticky droplets on tentacle-like prongs trap the victims, which the plant then slowly digests.

Butterflies at Forvie include the small pearl-bordered fritillary and dark green fritillary. Green-veined white and small heath are the commonest butterflies here, and around 250 species of moth have been recorded, including moorland-users such as eggar and fox moths and the large, day-flying emperor moth.

Forvie holds the largest breeding concentration of eider in Britain among its dunes and moorland. At its southern end there is a large tern colony. Sandwich terns are the most numerous (this is the biggest Scottish colony), together with common and Arctic terns and a small number of little terns. Shelduck nest in abandoned rabbit burrows in the dunes. This spectacular concentration of breeding birds makes it crucial for visitors to keep to the tracks between April and August, and to avoid entering the ternery. In winter, parties of snow buntings feed among the dunes.

ABERDEEN AND SCOTSTOUN MOOR

Aberdeen is a city blessed with some good wildlife areas, including several local nature reserves. Set between housing areas north of the River Don, Scotstoun Moor was described in 1893 as a 'garden of delights to every nature lover'. Reduced from its former spread, this LNR still holds a good blend of rough grassland, wetland scrub and woodland. Access is from the B977, on a bus route about 6.5 kilometres north of the city centre.

The northern part of Scotstoun Moor is a mix of gorse scrub and plantation woodland – good for yellowhammer, blue tit and chaffinch. The southern part is a heathy peat bog, home to the scarce black bog-rush and sundews. A network of paths through the reserve provides an easy way to watch meadow pipits here, and to look out for short-eared owls, foxes and roe deer.

ARNHALL MOSS

At Westhill, Arnhall Moss LNR – accessible by various buses and with a car park beside the local bowling green and tennis courts – has one of the last raised bogs in Aberdeenshire.

Here, you can see bog cotton, blaeberry and different kinds of sphagnum bog mosses. There's a path network which leads across the moss and into drier, wooded areas in the northern section. Downy birch, rowan and willows grow here – the latter giving food for the caterpillars of swallow prominent moths.

DONMOUTH & HARBOUR

Where the River Don meets the sea, beside the A92 a few kilometres north of the city centre, the estuary in the Donmouth LNR gives excellent scope for seeing waders, terns and seabirds. Sandwich, common and Arctic terns fish here in summer, with little and black tern also recorded. Skuas can come by in late summer, which is also a good time to watch out for little stint and other passage waders. Seals use the sand spit near the mouth of the river.

The salt marshes and sand dunes hold a variety of insects and flowers in what is the first area of natural coastline north of Aberdeen Harbour. The harbour itself, and to the south of it the lighthouse and Girdleness area, are popular places to watch for migrant birds passing through in spring and autumn. Just off the harbour, the sea is worth scanning for wigeon, eider and other ducks. This is also a good area to watch for bottlenose dolphins from the Moray Firth population early in the year. Groups of dolphins sometimes use the area and the harbour entrance and beyond, even bow-riding large boats.

> **GREY GEESE**
> *(Anser spp.)*
>
> Four species of geese with large amounts of grey in their plumage – pink-footed, greylag, white-fronted and bean – winter in Scotland. Greylag and pinkfeet are by far the commonest of these, with greylag also the most widespread.
>
> Scotland has a modest population of breeding greylag, thinly scattered over Caithness, Sutherland and the Hebrides. But the bulk of the winter population is geese that breed in lowland areas of Iceland. The greylag's winter range in Britain contracted northwards between the early 1900s and the 1960s. As it did so, north-east Scotland became a more important greylag wintering area than before.
>
> As with greylags, Scotland is home to the great majority of pink-footed geese that winter in Britain. These arrive in autumn from breeding areas in central Iceland and the east coast of Greenland. Strongholds are in the lowland eastern areas and (in late winter) the Solway.
>
> Islay is the main Scottish wintering place for the Greenland white-fronted goose. Here, thousands scatter themselves widely in small flocks to feed in stubble, grassland, pasture and bogs.
>
> Amazingly, more than a century ago, the bean goose was the most abundant of the grey geese visiting Scotland. Now you'd be lucky to see any. Traditional areas once favoured by bean geese are around the Solway, Loch Lomond and in the Carron Valley.

> *DID YOU KNOW?*
>
> *The full patterning on some flowers only shows up in ultra-violet light. This is because pollinating insects can see wavelengths that are beyond the range of human eyesight.*

HOWE OF THE MEARNS TO ARBROATH

From Stonehaven to the River North Esk and inland to the foothills of the Grampian Mountains lies a country of fertile farmland, fringed by cliffs, sandy and stony beaches. This is the Howe of the Mearns, evoked in Lewis Grassic Gibbon's classic novel of the early twentieth-century *Sunset Song*.

There are many meandering routes through the core of this red-earth land, and an awesome viewpoint over the whole scene from the road which runs from Clatterin' Brig past Cairn O' Mount. But for wildlife-watching, the prime sites are coastal.

> **DID YOU KNOW?**
>
> A centipede has one pair of legs on each body segment, a millipede two pairs on most of their segments.

FOWLSHEUGH

Fowlsheugh RSPB reserve, reached via a minor road off the A922 south of Stonehaven, is one of the most accessible major seabird colonies in Britain. Cliffs, formed about 400 million years ago by boulders and pebbles from a large river, rise to 65 metres here. They give nesting space to as many as 130,000 seabirds within the reserve, which runs northwards from Crawton.

Guillemots comprise about half the total number of seabirds here, in the second largest colony in Britain and Ireland (beaten only by Handa in north-west Sutherland). The next most numerous seabird is the kittiwake, most seafaring of the British gulls, some 60,000 of which plaster their guano and weed constructed nests to the crags.

When the blizzards of kittiwakes are in full cry (calling their name 'kitt-ee-waak') and the serried crowds of guillemots are growling, the sound of this place can be as impressive as the sight. Add a strong blast of sun-warmed guano, and it's a multi-sensuous delight (or challenge).

REGIONAL HIGHLIGHT: ST CYRUS

DESIGNATION:
National Nature Reserve.

LANDSCAPE:
Sand dunes, salt marsh and cliffs.

HIGHLIGHTS:
The reserve's fertile soil provides optimum conditions for a variety of plants and insects, including butterflies and over 200 species of moth. Breeding birds include little terns, Arctic terns, stonechats, whinchats, whitethroats and warblers.

BEST TIME:
Spring/summer for plants and breeding birds, winter for wading birds.

FACILITIES:
Visitor Centre (open Apr–Oct), with car park, toilets and an exhibition.

ADMISSION:
Free.

DIRECTIONS:
On A92, six miles N of Montrose.

CONTACT:
SNH, The Old Lifeboat Station, Nether Warburton, St Cyrus, Montrose DD10 0DG

Tel: 01674 830736

www.snh.org.uk

www.nnr-scotland.org.uk

Several thousand razorbills nest in crevices and cracks among the cliffs, with a small number of puffin burrows near the top, also the preferred area for herring gulls and fulmars. A few pairs of shag prefer caves at the base of the cliff, with small numbers of eiders offshore. One of the benefits of Fowlsheugh (purchased in the mid-1970s using funds raised by the Young Ornithologists Club) is that deep clefts in the cliffs make it relatively easy to get close views of birds nesting nearby across the chasms.

ST CYRUS

An ancient line of cliffs, once wave-washed, now landlocked in the wake of past changes of sea level, also gives nesting room for fulmars and herring gulls at St Cyrus National Nature Reserve (SNH). Little terns breed together with Arctic terns and waders at the south end of the reserve, and other breeding birds include whinchat, stonechat, grasshopper warbler, and whitethroat.

But the real glory of this place, just 5 kilometres north of Montrose, is in the number and variety of flowers and insects that thrive in the mix of habitats here. Included in these are foreshore, salt marsh, sand dunes, dune pasture, scree and cliffs, each with its own distinctive flora and fauna. Several plants, including the clustered bellflower, are at their northern British limit here. The cliffs, which are dry, sheltered and south-east facing, hold over 200 of the 350 higher plant species which have been recorded on the reserve. Some of these, found on or just below the cliffs, are national rarities, such as Nottingham catchfly,

knotted clover, rough clover and maiden pink. Late spring is a wonderful time on the lower cliffs, when yellow spikes of great mullein blend with the reds of marjoram and paler tones of maiden pinks.

There are maiden pinks on the grassy dune pastures, as well as meadow saxifrage, purple milk vetch and bloody cranesbill. More open parts of the dunes to seaward hold spring vetch and sea rocket among the tough dune grasses. The blend of flowers at St Cyrus, including campion and bluebell, can give vibrant swathes of colour from late

SHAG

Much commoner than the cormorant in Scotland, the shag – like its white-cheeked relative – is a precision sea-going fish finder and catcher, often in water just offshore. So if you watch from a high lookout, you might be lucky enough to see one in action under the clear water far below.

SCOTLAND'S NATURE AND WILDLIFE

DID YOU KNOW?

Polecats have now disappeared from Scotland, although you can find polecat ferrets in places, as escaped ferrets revert to type. Because of their pungent smell, polecats used to be known as 'fou-marts' (foul martens), in contrast to the less nostril-challenging pine marten, which was the 'sweet mart'.

spring into summer.

Thanks to the warmth and shelter here, St Cyrus is also a haven for insects. These include all five Scottish-dwelling species of grasshopper and cricket, as well as many kinds of butterflies and moths. Over 200 moths have been recorded, including the cinnabar (near its northern limit in Britain), fox moth, Mother Shipton, bordered grey and six-spot burnet. The 13 species of butterflies include small copper, small blue and grayling.

MONTROSE BASIN

Where the River South Esk flows down to meet the North Sea, its estuary – the Montrose Basin local nature reserve – presses its mudflats to the rim of the town from which it takes its name. Relatively unpolluted and untamed by industrial development, this enclosed basin is a major feeding, breeding and wintering place for thousands of wildfowl and waders.

The major landowner here is the Scottish Wildlife Trust, which administers the reserve with a consortium of other partners, including the National Trust for Scotland and the local council. The SWT has a wildlife centre with good viewing and interpretive facilities off the A92 at the south side of the Basin. This is a recommended first stop for orientation and for directions to other vantages and access points at widely scattered places around the estuary. For anyone arriving by train, the station railway bridge gives an excellent look-out over the northern basin.

The Montrose Basin holds a bustle of birds at any season, but winter is prime time for sheer weight of numbers. This is when knot from Iceland, bar-tailed godwit from Finland and wigeon from other parts of the sub-Arctic join flocks of less far-travelled curlew, oystercatcher and lapwing on the estuary.

Stars of the winter show are the grey geese, including up to 30,000 pinkfeet and several thousand greylags. When the big skeins muster to go down to roost at evening, or swirl up into the early morning sky, the sight and sound of them is part of the seasonal atmosphere of the town itself – a wild presence above the streets and buildings. October and November are peak months for the goose spectacle, although several thousand usually stay here throughout the winter.

The Basin is an internationally important moulting and wintering area for mute swans with up to 300 arriving in July and August. It is also used by large numbers of eider, mallard and shelduck, smaller numbers of teal and red-breasted merganser, and the only regular flock of pintails in this part of Scotland. Passage of waders can also be impressive, especially in May, July and August. With so much bird interest at Montrose, it can be hard to focus on other wildlife, but the mussel beds along the South Esk are impressive, and the river hold eels, salmon and sea trout.

SEATON CLIFFS

Northwards from Arbroath, a ribbon of soft red cliffs winds between farmland and sea. A coastal trail runs through the

Chequered Skipper

SWT's Seaton Cliffs reserve here. Easiest access is from Arbroath promenade, where a footpath leads up a brae at the end of a car park. Waves have worked on lines of weakness on the sandstone rocks to form coves, arches, pinnacles and caves. These provide nest sites for various birds, including herring gulls and fulmars. Descendants of Arbroath town pigeons, now indistinguishable from their wild rock dove ancestors, breed in the caves. House martins have also rediscovered their roots here, building mud nests under overhangs, a traditional habit long since abandoned in favour of nesting on buildings by most other Scottish martins.

Spring and summer flowers, including primroses and violets grow by the path. Thrift and sea campion are widespread, with kidney vetch nearer the cliffs and some purple milk vetch. Damper lime-rich areas support a large population of banded snails among lime-loving plants such as the clustered bellflower and carline thistle. Six-spot burnet moths and butterflies such as the common blue, visit the trailside flowers and solitary mining bees burrow in the sandy path-side banks. Gentler slopes covered with luxuriant vegetation break the line of cliffs, with the thick woodland of Seaton Den contrasting with the exposed clifftop.

BAR-TAILED GODWIT

Bar-tailed godwits prefer to feed on sandy estuaries. So most of the places where it concentrates, in winter or on passage to and from other estuaries or breeding grounds, are on the east coast. The inner Moray Firth, from the Dornoch Firth south to Nairn, is one of the good areas for them. They can wade belly-deep in water and immerse their heads to search the mud for food.

SCOTLAND'S NATURE AND WILDLIFE

Central Highlands

Many features combine to make the Central Highlands a magnet for wildlife enthusiasts. Part of the allure is in the concentration of species and habitats that are scarce or widely scattered in other places. Mountain ground rich in Arctic-alpine plants in the Breadalbane Hills and on the heights overlooking the Angus glens; the largest remnants of Caledonian forest in the country, in places from Rannoch, through to Strathspey and over to Deeside; major swathes of ling-purpled grouse moor; a clutch of large rivers, including the Tay – the mightiest, in terms of flow, in all Britain; the broadest expanses of high-level ground on the plateaux of the Cairngorms; more than one quarter of all the species listed as meriting special action to conserve biodiversity – these are some of the features that make the Central Highlands a wildlife treasure trove.

But beyond the natural 'top 20' charts of best this, broadest that, rarest whatever (appealing though the subjects of those listings are) is a blend of scenes where the more commonplace, as well as the exceptional, holds huge attraction. Along the course of the River Spey, for example, it's not only the glimpses of pine-rich old forest that catch the eye, but the many birchwoods, large and small, that cloak slopes away from the river. Breeding waders and other waterbirds, including red-breasted mergansers, common sandpipers, wagtails and dippers are not uncommon nationally, but their abundance along the streams and rivers of the Central Highlands is a vital part of the look and sound of these places for anyone who enjoys wildlife.

Visit one of the habitats elevated to celebrity status in the national rankings, and you're well-nigh guaranteed some wildlife pleasure. Quite simply, the distinctive appearance of a place like an old pinewood, a stretch of high altitude fell-field or a moor that purples a whole hillside can almost be reward enough for the effort spent getting there.

The species you could encounter are the icing on the cake. But in the Central Highlands, some of those species could have the cachet of rarity, whether the dotterel on the hill, the unusual ants and boreal forest flowers in the woods, the bird of prey over the moor, or the lamprey in the river. Another bonus of the area is the scope it gives for going from low ground to high through a sequence of fairly natural wildlife zones. From river level in a strath, through native woodland, past moorland on middle slopes and up to a summit ridge is a journey you could make in many places in the Central Highlands, encountering the distinctive communities of species linked to each major part of the habitat sequence.

Scottish Crossbill

Like other regions described in this book, the Central Highlands is a huge and complex area. So appreciating the variety of scenes and wildlife it holds means not expecting to 'do it all' in a few visits. Decades could seem insufficient to do justice to what this mix of strath and wood, farm and moor, hill and glen has in store. But in another way, each day spent sampling the Central Highland scene is likely to be a day well spent.

SCOTLAND'S NATURE AND WILDLIFE

TAY COUNTRY – THE WILD WEST

The country drained by the River Tay is at the very heart of mainland Scotland. At 193 kilometres from source to sea, and more than 20 kilometres ahead of the Spey or Clyde, the Tay is the nation's longest river. The catchment is vast, with headwaters of the main river and its tributaries rising in both the West Highlands and the southern fringes of the Cairngorms over an area of some 6475 square kilometres.

Loch Tummel, Loch Rannoch, Loch Ericht, the Garry, the Lyon, plus the Almond and the Isla – all these waters and many more play their part. Swelled by this combined force of burns, lochs and rivers, the Tay disgorges more water to the sea than any other river in the United Kingdom. On the journey to that destination, it cuts across the Highland Boundary Fault – the divide between Highland and Lowland Scotland.

LOCH TAY AND BEN LAWERS

At the core of the great Tay watershed is Loch Tay, a beautiful water set within hills to match. With Loch Tay at the centre of the river system, Ben Lawers is the crowning glory, and a fitting place for what is one of the top areas in Britain for mountain plants. Purchased by the National Trust for Scotland in 1950, and managed as a National Nature Reserve in partnership with Scottish Natural Heritage, the reserve includes the south side of mountains in the Lawers range, rising from above the north side of Loch Tay for some 13 kilometres to close by Killin.

An information point, car park, and nature trails – where guided walks can be arranged – can be reached off the A827 to Killin by turning up the minor road to Glen

---

REGIONAL HIGHLIGHT: BEN LAWERS

DESIGNATION:
National Nature Reserve (NTS, SNH).

LANDSCAPE:
Mountainous.

HIGHLIGHTS:
Rich in arctic-alpines including moss campion, sheep's fescue, mountain pansy and rock speedwell, along with tall herbs, montane scrub and woodland plants such as yellow saxifrage and oak fern. Moths and butterflies common to the area include the fox and emperor moths, small tortoiseshell, small heath and the rare small mountain-ringlet butterfly.

BEST TIME:
July for the small mountain-ringlet butterfly. Summer for arctic-alpines.

FACILITIES:
Car park, nature trail.

ADMISSION:
Free.

DIRECTIONS:
Six miles NE of Killin, off A827.

CONTACT:
Ben Lawers NNR office,
Lynedoch,
Main Street,
Killin FK21 8UW

Tel: 01567 820988

www.nts.org.uk

www.nnr-scotland.org.uk

CENTRAL HIGHLANDS

Lyon at Edramucky. At 1214 metres, this is Perthshire's highest mountain, and one of the top ten in Scotland, with views on a clear day stretching from the Atlantic to the North Sea.

The rocks at high altitudes have a great influence on the wealth of plant life in the mountain. From the summit nearly down to the car park area, these are largely sediments, laid down some 600 million years ago and changed around 510 million years ago by enormous heat and pressure during major earth upheavals to crumbly mica-schists. These still have a high lime content (an excellent plant booster) and break down in flakes to form good water-retaining soil.

Unusually, the folding of the Earth's surface that generated the heat to transform the old sediments also shoved them up and over younger rocks. So the plant-friendly old rocks sit high in the hills, where a host of Arctic-alpine species make use of them.

The crumbly, silver-flecked mica-schists are part of the secret of the high level plant richness in Breadalbane and a little bit beyond. Exploration of the area by a local minister, the Rev. John Stuart of Killin, gave the first inkling of this special flora. He helped another botanising cleric, the Rev. John Lightfoot, whose ground-breaking book *Flora Scotica*, published in 1778, first drew attention to the Breadalbane range.

Ironically, just at the time that Ben Lawers and its neighbours were being recognised as floral treasure troves, big changes were happening to the vegetation of the hills and glens. Numerous sheep had arrived on the scene, so much so that a mere 21 years after Lightfoot's book was published, another writer commented that 'since the introduction of sheep on a large scale, the verdure (green grass) is ascending to the very summit'. This was enough to gladden the hearts of local shepherds and lairds, but a problem for many of the plants, including some which have probably never regained the strength they had in Stuart and Lightfoot's day.

For the NTS, an important part of the work at Ben Lawers in recent years had been to reverse some of these changes and restore original flora and other plants. This includes work to boost 'montane scrub' – a low growth of bushes at and beyond the upper-fringe of mountainside

PURPLE SAXIFRAGE

The purple saxifrage can be a good indicator of where more lime-rich pockets outcrop on otherwise acid and food-poor mountains. It is incredibly hardy, has a circumpolar spread in the northern hemisphere, and has been seen as close to the North Pole as the north coast of Greenland.

SCOTLAND'S NATURE AND WILDLIFE

RED DEER
In places where food can run short at times, the number of female red deer can have an impact on the number of males. If hinds become particularly numerous, stag numbers can fall. This is one of many discoveries from long-term studies of red deer in Scotland.

woodland.

This type of vegetation is particularly sparse in Scotland, in comparison with places such as Norway, and there is now a major push to better understand it and expand its extent. Ben Lawers has some of the best remaining patches of montane scrub in the country, including the largest known population of mountain willow in Britain. Significantly, this has developed on steep, rocky slopes that are difficult for grazing animals to reach. The same applies to some other specialist mountain willows that grow on crags and rocky ledges here, including downy, dark-leaved and net-leaved willow, together with scattered plants of woolly willow.

The alpine grasslands at Ben Lawers are rich in the tussock-forming moss campion, growing among alpine lady's mantle and sheep's fescue. Moss campion also grows on crags in the company of that classic flower of lime-rich, exposed places, mountain avens.

Many other Arctic-alpines grow here such as cyphel, sibbaldia, mountain pansy, alpine forget-me-not, alpine fleabane, alpine gentian, mountain sandwort, rock speedwell and various mountain grasses and saxifrages. Tall herb communities on damp mica schist ledges are a beautiful feature, with a mixture that characteristically includes plants such as roseroot, water avens, wild angelica, wood cranesbill, melancholy thistle and globeflower, with a sprinkling of rarities such as rock whitlowgrass and alpine cinquefoil.

Woodland plants, such as oak fern, wood anemone and moschatel grow in shady places among the rocks. There is an interesting mix of sedges and rushes in high-level wet areas, with yellow saxifrage and common yellow sedge growing together in wet gravelly areas.

The variety of lichens at Ben Lawers is enormous and there is also a rich insect fauna. Moths include northern eggar, fox moth, emperor moth and yellow underwing. Several species of butterfly are common on the high ground, including green-veined white, small tortoiseshell, small pear-bordered fritillary and small heath. But the star turn among these regularly seen butterflies are the small mountain-ringlet, the core of whose Scottish population is in the Breadalbane

CENTRAL HIGHLANDS

hills. July is a good time to look out for this species.

Birds in the area include raven, ring ouzel, red grouse, ptarmigan, dipper and curlew, plus widespread meadow pipits and wheatears.

BLACK WOOD OF RANNOCH

About 15 kilometres to the north-west of Ben Lawers' summit, up and over Glen Lyon is the Tay Forest Park beside Loch Rannoch. Within it is the Black Wood of Rannoch (FC), where a Caledonian Forest reserve holds the largest remaining native pinewood in Perthshire.

Access is off the minor road along the south side of Loch Rannoch at Caie, a few kilometres to the west of Kinloch Rannoch. There are picnic sites and trails within the forest park. The Black Wood's survival is something of a miracle. Hundreds of thousands of trees were offered for sale by the local laird in 1798 and a network of canals and sluices was dug to float timber by way of the Tummel and the Tay to Dundee. It is said that some of the big Rannoch trunks didn't stop there, but floated on as far as Holland and Denmark! The scheme was later abandoned, but further pressure on the wood came from fenced in deer, fellings in the Second World War and the planting of commercially forested conifers.

Work to remove non-native trees at the Black Wood's edge and to reduce grazing pressure from roe and red deer is helping the ancient pinewood to expand from its core area of 300 hectares. This, in turn, should boost a great range of wildlife, such as the pine martens which have been increasing in number here.

> ### RED SQUIRREL
> *(Sciurus vulgaris)*
>
> With its tufted ears, bushy tail and perky expression, the red squirrel is high on the list of Scotland's most popular mammals. It's been in decline in many areas, but still has some excellent strongholds, including in the plantation forests of Dumfries and Galloway and the native and estate policy woodlands of the Central Highlands.
>
> Scots pinewoods in Strathspey are a classic location for seeing red squirrels. But they also thrive in mixed woodlands in Perthshire, alongside North-American-origin grey squirrels.
>
> This suggests that Nutkin's recent woes can't all be laid at the door of the greys. Helping reds to reclaim lost ground will be a big challenge for wildlife workers in years to come.

Red squirrels also live in the wood along with birds such as Scottish crossbill, capercaillie, redstart and treecreeper.

Scots pine is the principal tree in the Black Wood, with goat willow and bird cherry. Other vegetation includes common wintergreen and lesser twayblade and the rarer serrated wintergreen and coralroot orchid, together with a special old pinewood community of lichens and fungi. The Black Wood and its fringing birchwoods are particularly noted for insects, and the area has been a focus of attention for entomologists since the mid-nineteenth century. Scottish wood ants live among the pines, with the occasional timberman beetle, the males of which have antennae longer than their bodies. Moths in the vicinity include the splendidly named, but elusive Rannoch sprawler, which lays its eggs on old birch trees and is patterned to be camouflaged against a background of gnarled birch bark. Another moth which takes its name from the area is the Rannoch looper.

> *DID YOU KNOW?*
> 'Fairy rings' of fungus form when an underground net of fungal tissue called a mycelium (that can be very, very long-lived) spreads out in a circle from the point where a fungal spore became established. At least, that's what the botanists say...

133

SCOTLAND'S NATURE AND WILDLIFE

RANNOCH MOOR

Beyond Loch Eighheach, to the west of Loch Rannoch, the B846 ends at Rannoch station. For many kilometres to the west and south-west of here, the lochs, bogs and heaths of Rannoch Moor – one of the wildest stretches of country in Scotland – stretch away. Part of this rugged, soggy land drains eastward within the Tay catchment. The rest is across the other side of Scotland's watershed, and drains to the west. Access to the moor is easiest from its western edge, beside the historic Kings House Hotel off the A82 to Glencoe.

Rannoch Moor sits in a granite-lined cauldron, scooped out by glacial action in the last ice age. It rides high at about 300 metres above sea level, so can be cold, bleak and windswept. The blanket bog is broken up by rocky knolls and small valleys with water in the deeper troughs and holes. The largest loch, Loch Laidon, also sits along a major fault line. If you're equipped for changes in the weather, and even relish a dash of the elemental in your enjoyment of wildlife and landscape, then sampling a taste of Rannoch Bog could be just the ticket. Sphagnum bog mosses of many kinds are here of you've and eye for the details of colour that can separate the species, and reveal something of the conditions beneath – such as intense green in wet hollows and paler green to claret on flatter surfaces.

It has been soggy here for a long time, yet in places where the peat has dried and eroded, old stumps, trunks and roots of pine trees are sometimes revealed, some of which are thousands of years old.

Bog bean does well in open water, and there are three species of bladderwort – carnivorous plants that supplement their diet with aquatic insects. Some lochans are fringed with bottle sedge, with white and yellow lilies in the open water.

Star of the Rannoch plants is the delicate, hard to spot Rannoch rush. This grows sparsely in wet hollows among the bog mosses and has a whiff of the fugitive about it, as seems fitting for a denizen of the furthest Rannoch wilds. Widespread in the bogs of Central and northern Europe, remains of Rannoch rush have also been found in peat in many parts of Britain. The living plant was first recorded in Yorkshire in 1787 and was also known in Shropshire, Cheshire, Inverness-shire and Argyll. Peat cutting, drainage and tree planting led to the plants extinction at these places, so that Rannoch Moor is now the last British location for the rush that bears its name. A final twist is that the plant is not a true rush, but is most closely related to arrowgrasses.

Birds on the moor include curlew and red grouse in heathery areas and red-breasted mergansers on the lochs. Both red and roe deer use the area.

SCHIEHALLION

Sitting not far from the eastern end of Loch Rannoch and overlooking Dunalastair Water, the pointed quartz-rich cone of Schiehallion (John Muir Trust) is one of the most prominent mountain landmarks in this

Salmon

DID YOU KNOW?

The Shetland mouse-ear is a tuft-forming, white flowered plant that grows nowhere else in the world but the Shetland island of Unst.

CENTRAL HIGHLANDS

part of the Highlands. Famous for its relevance to science, as the place where the Astronomer Royal, Maskelyne, made measurements to try and calculate the density of the Earth, Schiehallion is also with its pointed shape, the classic fairy hill in Scotland.

Whether you set any store by the wee folk or not, there's no doubt that some of the vegetation to be found in places around the mountains skirts has a touch of the unusual for a Scottish site. The reason is the Dalradian limestone which crops up in places off this road between Kinloch Rannoch and the B846 beside Loch Kinardochy as limestone pavement.

This is weird-looking stuff, with smooth surfaces cuts through clefts (called 'grykes'), which can shelter a good range of plants. These include species more usually linked with woodland, such as dog's mercury, herb bennett, wood sorrel and wood anemone. Grasses on the limestone include quaking grass, with other plants such as rockrose and globeflower in places.

TAY COUNTRY – WOOD & WATER

ABERFELDY

Aberfeldy is a place with music at its core. The village sits by the Tay, straddling both banks of the Urlar Burn where it flows down from the hills to meet the main river. 'Urlar' is a word with huge

HEATH SPOTTED ORCHID

Heath spotted orchids are the commonest orchids in Scotland. The intensity and tone of petal colour can vary a great deal, and some individual plants that have white flowers can look very striking. The leaves are dappled with purplish blotches.

associations for lovers of Highland bagpipe music.

In pibroch – the complex variations from an initial theme which thrill many bagpipe buffs and leave others baffled – the melody, or 'ground' on which the structure of sound is built is the 'urlar'.

But that's not the only musical link in the water that runs through Aberfeldy. Better known is a song written by Robert Burns, *The Birks of Aberfeldie*, which marks his visit to the Falls of Moness – a little way up the burn from the village – in late August 1787.

True to his form in many lyrics, the poet is keen to get a 'bonnie lassie' to join him here on a country walk, where the 'little birdies blithely sing, while o'er their heads the hazels hing, Or lightly flit on wanton wing, In the Birks (birches) of Aberfeldie'. And as with some of his other well known songs, he uses an old tune and reshapes some elements of another song to suit his purpose. In this case it's the *Birks of Abergeldie* – a place with plenty of birch trees not far from Balmoral in Deeside – which provided the building blocks. That's why Dorothy Wordsworth says she couldn't find any birches in the burn gorge by Aberfeldy when she came here with her brother in 1803, and why birch is not a very prominent part of the local trees today.

The blessing of Burns's work, despite its using poetic licence with this part of the Perthshire scene, is that it has helped to give enthusiasm for maintaining a woodland walk up the Den of Moness for more then 200 years. Visit today, and you can be rewarded with a tranquil blend of woodland, water and wildlife. Access to a nature trail, following a path with seats and viewpoints alongside the burn (also known as the Moness Burn), is from car parks off the A826 at the southern edge of Aberfeldy.

Woodland on the lower slopes of the den is a mix of ash, wych elm and some hazel plus introduced beech trees and with willows in wetter parts. Flowers under the broadleaved trees include ramsons, red campion, wood cranesbill, sweet woodruff, common wintergreen and wood vetch. The damp, shady parts of the Den are rich in ferns and mosses, such as the beautifully named, and beautiful looking tamarisk-leaved feather moss. On the upper slopes the woodland changes from ash and elm to oak and (yes, they're here after all) birch. Cow-wheat, chickweed wintergreen, harebells and bitter vetch grow here.

Birds in the wooded den include grey and pied wagtails and dipper along the burn. Both green and great spotted woodpecker live in the woods, plus redstart, wood and willow warblers, spotted and pied flycatchers, various thrush and tit species, woodcock and sparrowhawk.

SCOTTISH CROSSBILL
(*Loxia scotica*)

This species, exclusive to Scotland, lives all year round in the centre and east of the Highlands, in the Scots pine woods of the old Caledonian forest.

Like the more widespread common crossbill, the Scottish species has an odd beak. The upper mandible curves across and droops over the lower one. This allows a crossbill to prise open cones and then use its tongue to extract pine seeds, the Scottish crossbill's staple diet.

Telling the Scots and commoners apart is tricky, but those in the know reckon that the native species has a deeper voice and looks a bit bulkier. Whatever the precise identification, these are fascinating birds and a living link to the wildlife of the great 'boreal' forests of the northern world.

CENTRAL HIGHLANDS

KILLIECRANKIE

A blend of oak-rich woodland, pasture and birchwood on steep western slopes above the River Garry makes the Killiecrankie area a treat for the eye at any season. Within areas owned by the RSPB and NTS, a range of trails gives visitors a chance to sample the woodland scene and learn something of the area's history. Most famously this includes the Battle of Killiecrankie in 1689, when Jacobites led by 'Bonnie Dundee' defeated a government force. One redcoat managed to escape capture by the rebels by jumping across the Garry at 'Soldiers Leap'.

The RSPB reserve runs from the gorge of the Garry to the heathland several hundred metes above. Access to waymarked trails is from a car park at Balrobbie Farm, on an unclassified road off the B8079 at Killiecrankie. Oakwoods on the lower slopes have green and great spotted woodpecker, pied flycatcher, redstart and wood warbler, with tree pipits, siskins and redpolls in the birches above. Plants include a good variety of ferns and mosses, wood vetch, yellow saxifrage and shining cranesbill. Butterflies include Scotch argus and pearl-bordered fritillary.

Deeper into the gorge, where some of the same bird species as in the RSPB reserve can be seen, the NTS ground at the Pass of Killiecrankie has steep, rough paths leading through woodland to the River Garry and Soldier's Leap. A visitor centre here features information

ATLANTIC SALMON

A salmon leaping to return to its spawning beds upstream is a potent symbol, not only of a healthy river, but of spirit and tenacity. The Celts thought of salmon as symbolic of wisdom, as described in tales of salmon that ate of the nuts of knowledge that fell into a magical pool.

SCOTLAND'S NATURE AND WILDLIFE

DID YOU KNOW?

The fulmar has distinctive breathing holes like flared nostrils at the top of its beak. Like the Manx shearwater, storm petrel and Leach's petrel, which also breed in Scotland, the fulmar is a 'tubenose' and a close relative of albatrosses (none of which breed in the northern hemisphere).

about natural history, and there is a ranger service.

Trails from here link to Pitlochry, through mixed woodland further downstream on the Garry, and by the north bank of the River Tummel, including the waterfall at the Linn of Tummel. There are also Forestry Commission walks in the mixed woods near the shores of Loch Faskally, to the north of the town.

Grey wagtail and dipper can be seen at the loch fringe at many times of the year, plus common sandpiper in summer and kingfisher in autumn. Winter wildfowl include little grebe, greylag goose, wigeon, teal, mallard, pochard, tufted duck and goldeneye.

PITLOCHRY DAM

At the town end of the reservoir, the Pitlochry Dam and power station (last part of a massive hydro-electric scheme driven by the channelled waters of the Tummel-Garry system) has a built-in fish ladder. This is accessible by a short walk from car parks at the south side of Pitlochry. Viewing panels allow close observation of the wild salmon which use the fish pass to move up and over the 86.5-metre-high dam to get to the loch and river beyond.

Golden Plover

TUMMEL SHINGLE ISLANDS

Just upstream from where the Tummel meets the Tay, the SWT's Tummel Shingle Islands reserve has an interesting mixture of woodland, pools, river and bare gravel. Formed by the natural shunting and shifting of river gravels, and so prone to drastic reshaping in big spates, the islands have a great range of flowering plants in their different habitats. Over 350 species have been noted here, including some, such as sea campion, more commonly found on the coast. Goldilocks buttercup grows in the woodland (a blend of birch and Scots pine with some juniper and alder); thyme, meadow rue, globeflower, cowslip and yellow rattle in the grassy areas; and mountain sorrel and sea campion on the open shingles. Birds using the reserve include common tern and various waders such as common sandpiper, redshank oystercatcher and lapwing.

This is a good place for insects, including many kinds of craneflies. Scotch argus and common blue are among the butterflies that use the grassland areas. Access is by a marked path along the west bank, above the river, starting off the A827 just over the bridge from Ballinluig. Take care not to block the steel barrier or entrance to the nearby joiner's workshop if parking off the road.

LOCH OF THE LOWES

A little over 3 kilometres to the north-east of Dunkeld, off a minor road which runs south-east from the A923, a car park gives access to the SWT's Loch of the Lowes reserve. The loch is one of three that sit in the low ground of the Luna Burn between Dunkeld and Butterstone.

Once the location of a significant

fishery for eels, the Loch of the Lowes has now become more associated with ospreys than with any of the other wildlife that lives here. Ospreys have been visiting the loch since 1969 and have bred successfully particularly in recent years. The Lowes gives one of the best chances within medium distance of most major Scottish cities to see these magnificent fish catchers at home. The regular eyrie is viewable from a hide beyond the SWT visitor centre where there are also video, audio and fixed displays and a number of TV monitors screening pictures from wildlife hot spots around the loch and beyond. The reserve and visitor centre is open from April until the end of September.

Aside from the ospreys, the bird interest at the Lowes includes great crested grebes. This was the first place in Scotland where great crested grebes were breeding (in 1870). Now a few pairs usually share the water and reedbeds with little grebes and other breeding wildfowl, including mallard, teal, tufted duck and Canada geese. Greylag geese use the loch as a winter roost.

Woodland around the Lowes holds many kinds of trees and shrubs, including several species of willow. Migrant breeders here include tree pipit, redstart, spotted flycatcher and garden warbler, plus sedge warbler and resident reed bunting in the reeds. Other woodland dwellers are woodcock, green and great spotted woodpeckers and winter groups of siskins and redpolls.

Within the loch, some plants, such as quillwort, shoreweed, water lobelia and bogbean are typical of food-poor upland lochs. These grow close to others more adapted to nutrient-rich silts (once dredged here for use as fertilizer), such as yellow water-lily and amphibious bistort. Beneath the water, a population of the rare slender naiad thrives alongside commoner species such as water milfoil.

TAY ESTUARY

The large Tay estuary begins to the south-east of Perth. This is a major area for wildfowl and waders and holds the largest single reedbed in Britain, an important breeding place for sedge warblers and water rail, and a roost for

LAPWING

The lapwing, green plover, peesie, teuchit or curracag (and many other names besides) is a bird that likes to nest in fairly short vegetation in pastures. An old cow pat can even serve, on occasion, as a cup for the four eggs. Males have slightly longer crests and blacker chest bands than the females.

swallows and martins. Reeds are still commercially harvested here to supply thatching materials. From the point of view of wildlife watching, the reeds are a mixed blessing since they can block visibility of large chunks of the estuary. Some of the better vantage points for scanning the north shore of the estuary are at Invergowrie Bay, to the west of Dundee.

The River Dee issues from the heart of the Cairngorms on the Braeriach plateau and drops more than a kilometre in its

UPPER DEESIDE

140 kilometre run from source in the mountains to sea at Aberdeen. Along much of this course it flows cool and clean through ground greened by many woods, including those of so-called 'Royal Deeside' where it flows through the Balmoral Estate.

Close to the higher reaches, major areas of native pinewood survive at Mar in Glen Quoich, Glen Derry and Glen Luibeg. These hold a blend of pinewood birds and mammals, including Scottish crossbill, crested tit and red squirrel. The minor road which loops nearby past the Linn of Dee and Inverey can also be particularly good for seeing red deer.

MORRONE BIRKWOOD

A few kilometres downstream, at the edge of Braemar, the Morrone Birkwood National Nature Reserve (SNH) is intriguing, since it shares some characteristics with birchwoods in parts of Norway. Downy birch is the main tree here, with abundant juniper scrub beneath, the most luxuriant and extensive on this type of soil anywhere in Scotland. Isolated outcrops of lime-rich rock enrich the grassland and marshy areas within the reserve, boosting the variety of plants that grow here.

Some 250 species of flowering plants and ferns have been recorded at Morrone, compared with less than half that number in woods of similar size on more acid soil. These include rare plants usually associated with Scots pinewoods, such as twinflower, and the more common but no less beautiful chickweed wintergreen, with its matt olive-green leaves and pointed circle of pure white flower. Early marsh and fragrant orchids grow in the open areas, together with yellow mountain saxifrage, alpine rush, Scottish asphodel and hair sedge in wetter

WOOD ANTS
(*Formica spp.*)

There are several species of ants that build large mound nests of twigs and leaf litter (especially conifer needles) in Scottish woods. One of these is the Scottish wood ant (*Formica aquilonia*), which is confined to the Highlands.

Its huge nests can be up to 1 metre high and measure 3 metres around the base. Each nest holds several queen ants and 100,000 or more workers. Small tracks run from the nests to nearby trees, where workers tend aphids to 'milk' them for sugar-rich honeydew (in return for giving the aphids some protection) and hunt for prey such as caterpillars.

A related species (*Formica lugubris*) can share some birch and pinewood areas in north-east Scotland with the Scottish wood ant. Rarest of all the mound builders is the narrow-headed ant (*Formica exsecta*), whose stronghold for the whole of Britain is in the native pine and birchwoods of Strathspey, including the Glenmore Forest Park. Its nests are modest (only about one-third of a metre across and fairly low), with 1000 or so workers.

areas. Under the trees there are globeflower, alpine bistort, spignel, wood cranesbill and lesser twayblade, with serrated wintergreen, small white orchid and holly fern on the crags.

The shape of the trees and shrubs at Morrone, and the extent of the wood, has been greatly influenced by browsing red deer. But Morrone is an amazing survivor. Study of pollen grains trapped in different layers of its soil shows that the mix of trees and plants here has not changed much over several thousand years. This makes Morrone a living link to a kind of birchwood that may once have been much more widespread on glen sides with richer soils.

Among the varied insect fauna is a bug known only by its scientific name of *Dikaneura contraria*, which was unknown outside the Pyrenees until it was discovered at Morrone in 1970. Another reminder of the mountain links which Morrone provides comes in the form of the ring ouzels which sometimes use the crags. Access is restricted to the gravel tracks within the reserve, which start at a car park beside a small loch at the top of Chapel Brae in Braemar.

Not far downriver from Braemar is the castle of Balmoral and its surrounding estate. First visited by Queen Victoria in the late 1840s, then purchased by Albert, the Prince Consort, in 1852, the scenery here, from river to the highest tops, was an abiding passion for Victoria over the following half-century. She would spend as much as a third of the year here, in spring and through the autumn. Her personal assistant on the estate was John Brown, a blunt-spoken man who was a fiercely loyal and devoted servant to the monarch.

GLEN MUICK AND LOCHNAGAR

Nowadays, Victoria's descendants are able to spend much less of the year here. Other visitors focus their outdoor interest within the estate on Glen Muick and Lochnagar. If you can cope with sharing the wilds with large numbers of others (some 180,000 people can come here in some years) a trip up the glen offers some magnificent scenery, and the chance of seeing some mountain plants, birds and animals.

A low-level track leads from a visitor centre at Spittal up to Loch Muick.

BLACK GROUSE
The black grouse lives in the wooded fringes of moors. Like the capercaillie, its chicks can benefit from good growths of blaeberry among heath and heather plants, where they find insect prey. Blackcocks 'lek' in spring and summer to attract females ('greyhens'), who come to eye-up the talent at communal display areas where the males strut, posture and compete to be top cock in the lek.

SCOTLAND'S NATURE AND WILDLIFE

> **DID YOU KNOW?**
>
> Young's helleborine is a very rare orchid known only from old coal bings (the spoil heaps from mine workings) in central Scotland and northern England.

The name Spittal is more appealing than it sounds. The surrounding hills have several high-level routes, once used by cattle drovers to move beasts on long journeys to distant markets. The Highland cattle moved in this way through much of the droving era would have been black, rather than the redheads later favoured by Queen Victoria. Drovers using the track over the Capel Mount to Glen Clova would pause to rest at the 'spittal' or 'hospice' beside where the visitor centre now stands in Glen Muick.

The glen is a good place to see red deer at close range. A mix of shrubs grows near the loch shore, including crowberry, blaeberry, bearberry and cowberry among the heather, with sundew and butterwort in damper patches. Snipe, redshank and common sandpipers use the loch margins and northern eggar moths and emperor moths live on the moorland.

Above the loch tower the crags and buttresses of Lochnagar, set against an ice-rounded sweep of corrie and cleft with gullies that funnel shattered rocks to the screes below. This was the scene that inspired Lord Byron to pen his song in praise of the 'steep frowning glories of dark Lochnagar' in the nineteenth century (still belted out by climbers in some far-flung hostelries in the twenty-first century). Then the Prince of Wales drew inspiration here for the popular children's story, *The Old Man of Lochnagar*.

These works of literature suggest one good way of appreciating the beauty of Lochnagar – from a distance. The route up the hill here is steep and exposed, and could benefit from a few more feet staying in the glen than tramping to its heights. People that do venture some of the way up may see golden plover, dunlin,

---

REGIONAL HIGHLIGHT: **GLENMORE FOREST PARK**

DESIGNATION:
Forest Park (FC) including a Caledonian Forest Reserve.

LANDSCAPE:
Woodland.

HIGHLIGHTS:
Wood-dwelling ants are a feature of the forest floor, while birds include Scottish crossbills, redstart, crested tit, goldcrest and willow warblers. Look out too for plants such as juniper, crowberry, heather and common wintergreens. Through the Cairngorm Reindeer Centre, visitors can join a herder on the hillside and see reindeer at close proximity.

BEST TIME:
Late spring through autumn for birds, plants and insects.

FACILITIES:
Visitor centre (open all year round) with café, shop, audio-visual presentation and exhibition, along with a car park and picnic area.

ADMISSION:
Free - Parking charges

DIRECTIONS:
Seven miles from Aviemore on the ski road.

CONTACT:
Glenmore Forest Park Visitor Centre
Tel: 01479 861220
www.scotland.forestry.gov.uk

Cairngorm Reindeer
Tel: 01479 861228
www.cairngormreindeer.co.uk

red grouse and ptarmigan, with mountain hares on the moorland. Preferable for many is to look skywards in hope of a golden eagle seen from the glen floor, or an exploration of the network of footpaths in the lower woods of the area, now being promoted by the Upper Deeside Access Trust.

GLEN TANAR NNR

Most accessible of the surviving Caledonian pinewoods in Deeside is at Glen Tanar Estate, near Aboyne, where the Water of Tanar flows to join the main river at its right bank. As in Strathspey, logs cut from here were once floated down the Dee in times of spate (these were used as ship timber in Aberdeen). From the 1940s onwards, regeneration of the old woods, through fencing to protect seedlings from deer and active planting, helped to secure and expand what is now the third-largest native pinewood in Britain. More than 4000 hectares of this are within the Glen Tanar National Nature Reserve.

Access is from the south Deeside road just short of 5 kilometres south-west of Aboyne. The Braeloine visitor centre, down the estate road, has various kinds of interpretation including innovative special needs versions of a trail guide in audio, large print and symbols, giving information about forest history and ecology. There is a network of waymarked walks, mostly on estate tracks, with some rough footpaths, ranging from less than two kilometres to longer routes.

Glen Tanar has an unusually wide range of ages of Scots pines, from grannies now in their third century of life, to small trees newly sprouting beyond the big cone bearers. One of the great pleasures of this place is to see the sheer extent of this natural spread of the forest. Under the trees, where heather, blaeberry, cowberry, grass and mosses cover the ground, creeping lady's tresses orchid and chickweed wintergreen are widespread, with some lesser twayblade, twinflower, common wintergreen and intermediated wintergreen.

Among the birds, the populations of capercaillie and black grouse (often struggling to survive in other areas) are still strong here. This is probably the most important place in Britain for Scottish crossbill, so it's worth looking out for cones prised apart and dropped from

GOLDEN EAGLE

Golden eagles are most often seen in flight, when the wings look broad, long and with finger-like ends to the outermost feathers. If you are lucky enough to see an adult eagle perched, the paleness of the plumes at the back of the head (which give the bird its name) can be striking. Young golden eagles, by contrast, are a rich chocolate brown.

SCOTLAND'S NATURE AND WILDLIFE

BIRCH TREE

Birch trees can be fast growing, able to transform open heathland to woodland within a very few decades. This has happened at Muir of Dinnet. Some can be long lived, particularly in upland areas where they grow more slowly and can survive, in some cases, for more than 200 years.

above by the birds, as well as cones nibbled by the local red squirrels.

MUIR OF DINNET NNR

Muir of Dinnet National Nature Reserve, between Ballater and Aboyne, has an intriguing mix of heathland, birchwoods, open water and burn. A visitor centre with a car park at the Burn o' Vat, beside the A97 road to Huntly, offers displays, a leaflet about the reserve and access to walks.

Only a few decades ago, the writer, Cuthbert Graham, commented how 'to the regret of many, the heather-carpeted moor' at Dinnet was 'with increasing rapidity turning into a jungle of birchen scrub'. That process, begun when muir burning stopped here, has continued, but what may have been a cause of regret for some in the past is now a source of pleasure for many in the present. Swathes of fine birchwood with trees of many shapes and sizes now spread across many hectares here, the colour and textures contrasting with the darker, more intense tones of the moorland.

Within young growth of birches and pine here, work by the British Trust for Ornithology indicates that the bird communities are big on willow warblers, chaffinch, meadow pipit and tree pipit. Older scrub, with dead wood to provide more opportunities for hole-nesting, has great tits, treecreepers and redstarts.

The reserve has many features formed during and after the last ice age. The Burn o' Vat flows in one of the deep meltwater channels in the area, and the massive rock-walled chamber from which the burn takes its name (some 16 metres deep and 22 metres across) may also have been formed by the action of water-swirled rocks after the ice age. Its granite walls hold a good variety of ferns and mosses.

The two lochs at Dinnet formed as 'kettleholes' when chunks of slowly melting ice sat there, long after the surrounding glacier had gone. Together, the Dinnet lochs are a wetland of international importance for wildfowl. Numbers of ducks slowly increased here from the late 1970s, and a greylag goose roost became established, now the largest roost in Britain for birds from the Icelandic greylag goose population. In November 1995, a staggering 36,000 of these birds were counted here. Quite some number, but just think of the noise!

CENTRAL HIGHLANDS

Perhaps that's what puts the 'din' in modern Dinnet.

This area experiences some of the coldest winter conditions for a lowland British location. In severe winters, the lochs can be frozen for up to three months, during which time the wildfowl move elsewhere. At other times in winter, wigeon, mallard, tufted duck, goldeneye, goosander and coot visit the lochs in large numbers.

In summer, these reed-fringed waters (well used throughout the year by otters) have both yellow and white water lilies. Hundreds of moth species have been recorded here, including Kentish glory, while butterflies include pearl-bordered fritillary and northern brown argus.

Just north-east of Kingussie and downstream to Kincraig, the Spey shows what other rivers could do if they were

CAIRNGORMS – SPEY WETLANDS

less tamed and artificially channelled. The scenic meanders of the river course here are full of the piping of common sandpipers, low-flying sand martins and dancing flies in summer. But it's the soggy luxuriance out from the right bank (assuming you're headed downstream), which is a natural marvel.

INSH MARSHES

Now extensively owned and run as an RSPB reserve, the Insh Marshes is one of the few areas in the whole of Britain where you can experience a partly natural flood plain of a major river. It's a place of great importance for birds, insects and other fauna, which has survived against the odds in the past.

Attempts at drainage from at least the eighteenth century onwards failed to dry-out the flood plain, not least because the torrents from the Spey in spate washed away embankments. In 1973, the RSPB bought a small area of land here. Since then, the reserve has grown through further purchases and agreements, and now covers some 1000 hectares. Water is a key to the whole place – swelling in winter floods, dwindling in summer – and it feeds a mix of different kinds of vegetation. Grassland, fen with sedges, open water, heath, bushy scrub and

INSH MARSHES
The Insh Marshes, on the floodplain of the River Spey near Kingussie, is one of the finest wetlands in Scotland. A huge variety of insects uses the area (including the Kincraig blackfly). Birds include water rails and spotted crakes in summer and whooper swans and hen harriers in winter.

TWINFLOWER
Twinflower is one of the characteristic plants of the conifer-dominated boreal forest that girdles the northern world. Within Scotland, the Caledonian forests of pine and birch are a western outlier of the boreal and are home to some of this special vegetation.

woodland are all here, each giving fresh possibilities for wildlife.

A car park with information centre lies beside the B970, past the historic Ruthven Barracks, scene of a final Jacobite attempt after the defeat at Culloden. From here, there is access to a couple of marked trails and to two wooden hides that overlook several pools. This is a great site for birdwatching at any time of year. The number of breeding waders here is tremendous with between 700 and 1000 breeding pairs such as lapwing, redshank, curlew and snipe. Ten species of wildfowl nest, including teal, mallard, wigeon, tufted duck and the largest population of breeding goldeneyes in Britain. The goldeneyes have benefited from a long-running scheme to provide them with tree-mounted nestboxes at various places along the strath.

This is also one of the best sites in Britain for the rare spotted crake. Its common relative, the water rail, nests here too, but both birds are very elusive, preferring to stalk among the rushes rather than reveal themselves much in the open. A remedy for this, from a human standpoint, is to visit the outskirts of the reserve on a still summer's evening. Listen closely, and among the sounds of skirling lapwing and thrumming snipe you could be lucky enough to hear the weird squeals and grunts of the local water rails in full cry.

Ospreys also breed, and other rarities which have nested at the Insh Marshes in the past include bluethroat, wryneck, redwing, wood sandpiper, whooper swan and marsh harrier. When the marshes flood in water, fresh flocks of wildfowl move in, the most notable of which is the Icelandic whooper swan, for which the site is internationally important.

The swan flock is also unique in the UK, since it feeds on nothing else but natural vegetation – grazing sedges, rushes and wetland grasses on the marsh rather than feeding on farmland pastures and stubbles. It's a fine example of how a fairly natural system, given room to follow its own seasonal patterns, can support a creature in a way that reduces conflict with other land users. There is also a substantial roost of hen harriers in denser, tussocky areas during the winter.

The reserve has a rich insect fauna, including some 250 recorded moths (Rannoch sprawler and Kentish glory among them), 19 butterflies (including

Scotch argus) and more than 130 species of beetle. Plant variety is fascinating, with an amazing 24 species of sedges, including the rare string sedge. The vast area of sedge-covered fen is particularly unusual for a Scottish location. Least yellow water lily, awlwort and pillwort are among the aquatic plants.

RIVER SPEY

The River Spey itself is a tremendous resource for wildlife. The second-longest river in Scotland, and one of the least polluted, the whole river has been given European Union recognition for its conservation importance.

Some of this is linked to creatures which are hard to see, including the freshwater pearl mussel, which can live for more than a century, helps to clean water and is linked to the lives of salmon and trout. Another scarce, endangered, but elusive river dweller is the sea lamprey, which uses a sucker-like mouth to clamp onto fish before drinking their blood.

Easier to see than the creatures themselves are the signs of fish – from schools of minnows in the shallows, to the rings in the water made by salmon and trout. The Spey has one of the most important salmon fisheries in Scotland, so there are often good chances to watch the art and craft of fly-fishing from along the banksides. Not surprisingly, the Spey is also one of the best freshwater places in Scotland for otters.

Farmland in Strathspey is also the top mainland agricultural area in Britain and Ireland for breeding waders. Numbers of lapwing, redshank, curlew and snipe are all unusually high here, with the biggest concentrations linked to farmland traditionally grazed by livestock, especially cattle.

CAIRNGORMS WEST – FOREST & WOODS

From a distance, many people think of the Cairngorms area in terms of mountains. This is not surprising, given the sheer extent of high ground here, the concentration of downhill ski centres and knowledge of some of the mountain birds and alpine plants that live here.

But once you're in the area itself, either as a visitor or as a resident, there's often a shift in what seems to be the key elements of the landscape. The mountains are ever present, but the backdrop is more accessible, and what fills most of the view. That scene filler is mainly native woodland threaded through with burns and the major rivers that drain the huge catchments in the hills.

The low ground along the straths (river valleys) below the mountains and the mid-ground of the glen sides holds more woodland of native origin than anywhere else in Scotland. It's a splendid concentration, and it's growing, not just in the sense of individual trees seeing out their natural lifespan (which in the case of Scots pines can be many centuries), but also through massive expansion of the area occupied by native trees.

In the Cairngorms, the old forests are on the march, boosted by major schemes to create a 'Forest of Spey' on the north-western skirts of the mountain core and an expanded Deeside Forest to the east. Many kinds of trees thrive in these areas, and as restoration schemes

> **DID YOU KNOW?**
> *Each branch of egg wrack (or knotted wrack – a seaweed that can be common along western sea lochs) usually forms one air-filled bladder each year. So by counting bladders, you can get an idea of the age of a branch.*

SCOTLAND'S NATURE AND WILDLIFE

SALMON
(Salmo salar)

Revered by the Celts as a symbol of knowledge, the Atlantic salmon is a remarkable fish. It begins its life as an egg and youngster in freshwater, then migrates to sea (as a 'smolt') for the main feeding and growth stage.

Once at sea, the salmon can spend between one and four years away from the river where it hatched. Its life at sea is fraught with dangers posed by commercial fisheries, its return home to spawn complicated by chemical pollutants in lochs and rivers and by sea lice (that attach to fish gills) from fish farms along the west coast.

Clean water, well bubbled with air and with fine gravel as its bed is part of the river requirements of breeding salmon. An association with the now rare freshwater pearl mussel may also play a part in salmon success.

DID YOU KNOW?

The red grouse makes more use of heather than any other bird in the world, relying on it for food (either from heather shoots or from insects that live on the plants) and shelter throughout the year.

progress, the variety within parts of the forest is likely to increase.

The tree to the fore of Cairngorms forests is the Scots pine. On lower slopes and along glens on the northern and north-western flanks of the mountains, the forests of Abernethy, Glenmore, Rothiemurchus, Inshriach/Invereshie and Glen Feshie make up the biggest area of fairly continuous semi-natural woodland in the whole of Britain.

There are thousands of hectares of this pine-rich cover in the main Spey group of forests, with a few hundred hectares more in the nearby valley of the River Dulnain. To the east, other important pinewoods grow at Mar (in the woods of Glen Quoich, Glen Derry and Glen Luibeg), at Ballochbuie and at the largest eastern pinewood areas – Glen Tanar (see Upper Deeside). These ancient woods have been greatly changed over many centuries by fire, grazing and felling, but they still hold a beauty, atmosphere and distinctive wildlife that sets them apart from other British woodlands.

Many people gain as strong a sense of wild nature in these green places as on the vast mountain barrens. A good way to experience some of that nature, and to appreciate the variety of scenes within contrasting areas of the Caledonian forest, is to explore some of the areas close to the Spey between Kingussie and Boat of Garten.

CRAIGELLACHIE

The town of Aviemore, at the heart of this area, is the commercial and holiday hub of Strathspey. Immediately across the A9 from the town is the Craigellachie National Nature Reserve, accessible by underpass from a car park beside the artificial ski slope. Silver and downy birches are the principle trees here, rising up a hillside which has outcrops of sheer cliffs.

A walk in the reserve up the path under Craigellachie Rock is worthwhile at any time of the year, since it gives an excellent way of looking out over the broad plain between here and the highest tops of the Cairngorms which lie more than 10 kilometres away over the forests of Rothiemurchus and Glenmore. It gives a sense of scale and perspective, emphasising the great size of the natural features in the Cairngorms, without having to go up one of the mountains at the core.

Wildlife to watch out for in Craigellachie includes resident great spotted woodpecker and a variety of tits, breeding redstarts, wood warblers, tree pipits and spotted flycatchers, and peregrine falcon overhead. Wildcats also

CENTRAL HIGHLANDS

use parts of the area.

The ground is covered in grasses and mosses, including Sphagnum bog mosses in wetter areas. Common rock-rose and alpine bistort grow in a few places, with shining cranesbill, alternate-leaved golden saxifrage and serrated wintergreen on rocks. The rich insect fauna includes the Rannoch sprawler and Kentish glory moths.

ROTHIEMURCHUS ESTATE

Flanking the town to the east is Rothiemurchus Estate, home of the Grants of Rothiemurchus for more than 400 years and a good place for low-level pinewood strolls. Orientation and information is provided at a visitor centre beside the A951 ski road between Aviemore and Coylumbridge.

A few hundred metres closer to Aviemore is the estate trout fishery, well worth visiting in summer. Locally bred ospreys use it as a fast-food takeaway, making it one of the best places in Scotland to see an osprey fishing at close range. Viewing is from a bird hide, and there is a small charge for entry to the fishery.

Another popular part of Rothiemurchus is Loch an Eilein. This is a scenic stretch of water at any time of the year, and particularly gorgeous on a sunny summer's day, when the birches are in fresh leaf, their cascades of pale green contrasting with the bottle green of pines and grey browns of the mountains.

CAPERCAILLIE

During the breeding season, a cock capercaillie puts a huge amount of time and energy into display. He fans his tail, puffs out body and throat feathers and makes a strange, popping call. Caper numbers have fallen in Scotland (in part due to changing climate) and the best advice for would-be watchers is to leave the birds well alone.

SCOTLAND'S NATURE AND WILDLIFE

REINDEER

Reindeer were part of Scotland's fauna when tundra conditions returned after the end of the last Ice Age. These natives died out. But since the 1950s, a herd of reindeer, now owned by the Glenmore Reindeer Company, has grazed the flanks of the Cairngorms. Both males and females have antlers.

information and a point of entry to the trails here. Paths from the car park lead around the loch (just under 5 kilometres), with a small extension possible around the tiny Loch Gamhna.

Breeding birds in the forest here include the small perching birds for which the Caledonian pinewoods are famous – Scottish crossbill and crested tit. Redstarts, wood and willow warblers and great spotted woodpeckers are among the others. Red-throated divers, teal, goldeneye, wigeon and the occasional fishing osprey use the loch itself.

A ruined castle on an islet in the loch is thought to be at least 600-years-old. It was the scene of a fierce skirmish between Jacobite attackers and Grant defenders after the Battle of Cromdale in 1690. In the 1800s, it also held one of the last remaining osprey eyries in Scotland, infamously plundered after a swim across the waters by the Victorian hunting-shooting-naturalist, Charles St John.

Another visitor centre and official car park (small charge payable), accessible from an unclassified road off the B970 from Inverdruie to Kincraig, gives

GLENMORE FOREST PARK

Coming down from the mountain edge to meet part of the Rothiemurchus boundary is the Glenmore Forest Park (FC). The Forest Park visitor centre sits within the hamlet of Glenmore, just short of 10 kilometres along the A951 from Aviemore. This has various facilities, including an audio-visual presentation and displays about native pinewoods and the work being carried out to restore them.

Once a fairly heavy-duty plantation forest for the production of timber from exotic conifers, Glenmore has seen mammoth changes from the 1990s onwards. Large areas of Sitka spruce and other introduced trees have been felled to make room for expansion of natural-style woodland. A major network of trails, including colour-coded routes, runs through different parts of Glenmore, ranging from short routes for all abilities (including one in a damp piece of woodland not far from the visitor centre) to longer paths over both low and medium altitude ground.

Glenmore is a very good place to see wood-dwelling ants, which include both a widespread species – wood ant – and a rare one, the narrow-headed ant. The ants make large nests constructed from pine needles, rising as high as a metre or so from above the ground, often near the sides of forest trails.

Close to the Glenmore Forest Centre is the Cairngorms Reindeer Centre. From here, you can arrange to accompany guides to see some of the Cairngorm Reindeer Herd – the only free-ranging group of introduced reindeer in Britain, several dozen of which spend the year further up the mountain.

of redstart and tree pipit, and a mix of others, including coal tit, crested tit and goldcrest. The floor of the valley, which was once flooded from time to time to provide a rush of water to float timber down to the Spey, is thick with heather, blaeberry and crowberry. Shrub cover includes some fine stands of juniper in both its low-growing and upright forms.

Many species of plants have been recorded here, but look out for common wintergreens alongside the path to the south of the Green Lochan. This lochan, whose waters are a striking shade of bluey green throughout the year, is one of several green-coloured lochans around the Cairngorms.

DID YOU KNOW?

Some pods of orcas (also known as killer whales) live in Scottish waters. The grey seal is one of the creatures they can hunt. They sometimes set a trap, where a group divides and one part panics a seal towards the others who are waiting in ambush.

PASS OF RYVOAN

To see some of the restoration work at Glenmore and to appreciate the structure of the old woodland here travel through the Pass of Ryvoan, accessible along a track running from the forest visitor centre, past Glenmore Lodge and into the Pass itself.

Ryvoan is an important through route in this part of the mountains, linking Abernethy and Glenmore. As the expansion of tree cover continues, it will be a vital corridor for wildlife moving between different large blocks of forest. A lovely aspect of Ryvoan is the way that the woodland cloaks large swathes of its steep sides, revealing the mix of trees more easily than on level ground and giving the opportunity to see and hear birds some distance away. The 'chup' flight call of crossbills is one to listen out for here.

The breeding bird community in the Pass majors on wren, willow warblers and chaffinch, with smaller numbers

ABERNETHY FOREST RESERVE

Beyond the Green Lochan, the path forks, one route leading into the hills, the westernmost going on to Abernethy Forest Reserve (RSPB). This is part of a mega-reserve, formed when the RSPB purchased land to link the Loch Garten and Abernethy reserves into one vast holding. From Boat of Garten, at 235 metres above sea level, to the summit of Ben MacDui at 1100 metres, this is now the largest nature reserve in Britain. Within it are large expanses of mountain and moorland, in addition to the Caledonian forest at its core. Much of the forest, purchased with money raised through an appeal to RSPB members, benefits from a lack of disturbance from people – a boon to the local breeding capercaillie and black grouse for example.

Yellow Iris

SCOTLAND'S NATURE AND WILDLIFE

OSPREY

Although ospreys have now spread to many areas, the scene of their re-colonisation of Scotland, close to Loch Garten, is still world famous and a popular spot for visitors who come to use the special viewing facilities there. After catching a fish (which it does with a precision grab while flying) an osprey typically gives itself a shake in the air.

LOCH GARTEN OSPREY CENTRE

The best way to get an impression of the wildlife here, without putting it at risk, is to go to the RSPB's Loch Garten Osprey Centre. This can be reached by following the B970 east of Boat of Garten, just off the A95 north of Aviemore, in the direction of Nethy Bridge. The reserve is signposted from this road. A good time to visit is in the summer, when the observation post and shop are open from mid-April to August. In winter, goldeneye, goosander and greylag geese use the loch.

This is home to some of the most watched ospreys. Generations of these dapper fish-catchers have reared broods here under scrutiny from nearby hides. Ospreys have been nesting here since 1959, and visitors can now get a closer view of the eyrie action than ever, thanks to closed-circuit TV beaming live pictures to the osprey centre. But nothing beats the sight of the bird off-screen, such as an adult perched on a branch beside the nest tree, or one flying in with a fish clutched in its talons.

Elsewhere in this part of the reserve, there are Scottish crossbills, crested tits, siskin, redstart, sparrowhawk and the occasional capercaillie in the woods, with black grouse at the forest edges and out on the moorland. Breeding wildfowl on Loch Garten include teal, wigeon and little grebe, and goldeneye breed in nearby tree mounted boxes.

CAIRNGORMS EAST – CAENLOCHAN

The hills and the glens at this eastern edge of the Cairngorms are certainly picturesque. More lime-rich rock occurs here in the soft schists than in the acidic granites of the massif's core. The blessing of this comes in variety of mountain flora, making the Caenlochan National Nature Reserve and its surrounds one of the top places for wild Arctic-alpine plants in Britain.

A blend of steep moorland, hill, pasture, plateau and cliffs, Caenlochan rises in a sweep of mountain ground above Glen Isla, Glen Doll, and Glen Shee. The main car parks on the A93 Cairnwell road give a good approach to the western side. The ancient routes of Jock's Road and the Monega Pass link Caenlochan to the glens, while a public footpath passes through the Forestry Commission plantation at the head of Glen Doll and gives entry from the east. The size of the reserve has been reduced in recent years, but the area still allows visitors to see some of the distinctive wildlife of the high Cairngorms without

OSPREY
(Pandion haliaetus)

The return of the osprey to Scotland as an expanding part of the country's bird fauna is one of the major conservation success stories of the past half century. After the extinction of the osprey as a British breeder in 1916, it wasn't until 1954 that a pair bred again, at a secret location in Strathspey.

Then there was a gap (marred by the theft of a clutch of eggs in 1958) before the first chicks were hatched in 1959 at the now world-famous site at Loch Garten, in the RSPB's Abernethy reserve, near the 'osprey village' of Boat of Garten. The millionth visitor was welcomed to Loch Garten several years ago. Many tens of thousands of other people have also enjoyed watching ospreys at the SWT's Loch of the Lowes reserve near Dunkeld.

CENTRAL HIGHLANDS

penetrating the mountain's central wilds. A combination of high altitude, a fairly continental climate (with sharp contrasts between winter and summer) and a wide variety of rock and soil types has led to Caenlochan's importance for mountain plants and other wildlife, including mountain birds.

To walk in these hills you need to be well prepared. Snow can fall in any month, the winds bite, and whatever the weather, each 100 metres of climb up the hill usually means a one degree Celsius drop in temperature.

Some of the best places for Arctic-alpine plants here are small and inaccessible ledges, which look like hanging gardens of colour and greenery. But you can still enjoy them from across a gully or by looking along a slope through binoculars. This applies to the rare alpine sow-thistles in Caenlochan Glen that grow on a ledge out of reach of most sheep and deer.

A broad ledge near Glen Doll also has the best surviving relic of montane willow scrub in the country, consisting of a mixture of woolly willow and downy willow. In other northern countries such as Norway, this type of vegetation typically grows between the normal treeline and the highest plateau and tops, but is very scarce in Scotland.

The mountain flora here is diverse, with a mix of widespread species, such as roseroot, red campion, water avens, globeflower and wood cranesbill. Other plants among the many botanical highlights at Caenlochan include alpine milk-vetch, yellow oxytropis, alpine sowthistle, alpine fleabane and snow gentian, as well as rare sedges and grasses such as alpine timothy. Where serpentine outcrops at Meikle Kilrannoch beyond Glen Clova, the largest of the two British colonies of alpine catchfly grows among the rock debris.

Like some other specialist Arctic-alpines, it occurs on both sides of the Atlantic, in Scandinavia, Britain and on serpentine barrens in North America. Alpine catchfly was first discovered here by George Don of Forfar in 1795. It was Don, a nurseryman by trade, who first drew the wider world's attention to the plant riches of the area. His achievements were enormous. He found a sedge and a hawkweed completely new to science here, and three others – including the

ORANGE TIP

Among the several kinds of white butterfly in Scotland, the male orange tip is perhaps the most striking.

Much of his black-tipped forewings is a tangerine colour. Perhaps that's why the French call this butterfly 'the dawn' (although they must have some particularly fruity sunrises to match the orange tip's brightness).

There's no orange on the end of the female's wings, but her hind wings share the same greyish freckling as the males on top, with a more prominent greenish-brown blotching underneath. This is a butterfly on the move in Scotland, and its fortunes have ebbed and flowed over the last 200 years.

Once widespread, from the Borders to Glasgow in the west and up to the Moray Firth in the east, it dwindled and died out in many places. But in the mid 1950s, it started to regain old ground, appearing at Aviemore in 1954 and becoming more common, especially in the north-east. Now it is also widespread across central Scotland and is continuing to push beyond its old strongholds in other places.

Life for orange tip caterpillars is tough. They are cannibalistic, so only one usually survives on a larval foodplant. This is usually lady's smock, although orange tips also use other cabbage family wild plants in Scotland, including garlic mustard, hedge mustard and charlock.

alpine catchfly – never before recorded in Britain.

In Don's own words, in the preface to his *Herbarium Britannicum*, he 'repeatedly ranged over the great mountains of Angus-shire which surround the great district of Clova, where no one on a similar pursuit... ever preceded him'. But Don, greatest of the pioneering Scottish botanists, was later followed by collectors such as the Victorian fern fanatics who dented the numbers of the rare oblong and alpine woodsia in the areas. Now these plants and other montane wildlife could also be under pressure from changing climate in an era of global warming.

Breeding birds around the Caenlochan tops and plateau include dotterel, which enjoy better breeding success on the schist-based rocks than among the granites further west golden plover and the dunlin. This is also an excellent area for golden eagles.

Other mountain birds include ring ouzel, ptarmigan and a scatter of snow buntings. One of the most striking mammals on the slopes and flats is the mountain hare, and there are substantial herds of red deer in the area. Butterflies include the small mountain ringlet.

The glens that lead away from the hills and down into the fertile lowlands of Angus are worth visiting for their own, softer beauty. Buzzards thrive here, and a variety of other upland birds can be seen from the roads that link high ground and low ground.

CREAG MEAGAIDH

This is a place which marks a divide, in more ways than one. The great whale-backed massif of Creag Meagaidh – the name of both the highest top here and the collective term for the massif which flanks the northern side of the Spean Bridge to Laggan road – straddles 'Druim Alban', the watershed of Scotland.

From the huge summit plateau here you can look west over Loch Moy, where

CRESTED TIT

Crested tits do best in the long-established native pinewoods of the Highlands. Smaller numbers also live in more recent plantations of both Scots pines and other pine species, such as Culbin on the Moray coast. The first clue to a crestie's presence can be a trilling call from among the trees.

the River Roy runs down in the direction of the Atlantic. Just to the east, beyond the falls of Pattach, the infant River Spey begins its journey to the North Sea.

But Creag Meagaidh also marks a divide in thinking – a bold move away from types of land use which depleted the natural store of the Highlands in the past, to ways which are restoring abundant wildlife. When Creag Meagaidh was bought for the nation by the predecessor of Scottish Natural Heritage in 1985 it had been grazed for centuries by cattle, sheep, goats and deer. In times past much of this grazing would have been vital to the communities of people living in surrounding straths and glens.

By the late-twentieth century, however, patterns of settlement and work had changed, with many of the old smallholding areas abandoned and people concentrated in villages many kilometres away from Creag Meagaidh. But high numbers of red deer and sheep continued to restrict the possibilities for growth of native trees and shrubs. A bold decision was made to drastically reduce the red deer population, and many were captured and sold to deer farms. Sheep grazing was also stopped. The pay-off for this policy (opposed by some at the time) now comes in a thousand shades of green and many colours besides. Native trees are spreading across the Creag Meagaidh heaths and grasslands to places they haven't been able to thrive in for generations. Tender plants can grow among them and birds and animals move back to reclaim lost ground.

It's a place of restoration and inspiration, where wildlife will continue to change and grow for decades, even centuries to come. All this has been achieved by simply reducing grazing pressure, and without the use of fences.

With this background to the recent story of the National Nature Reserve, the spectacular setting comes as real icing on the cake. Long before this place was known for nature, it was famous for its scenery and its history. Early Scots kings are said to be buried on the other side of Loch Laggan and are associated with the Isle of Kings in the loch itself. The fugitive Prince Charles Edward Stuart moved from the headwaters of the Roy over the Creag Meagaidh ridge a few months after the Jacobite defeat at Culloden. In 1847, Queen Victoria commented during a visit to nearby Ardverikie, how she was 'delighted' with the scenery, 'which is singularly beautiful, wild and romantic!'

BIRCHES
(Betula spp)

Birches were some of the first large trees to re-colonise Scotland after the end of the last ice age. They still play a pioneering role, seeding into clearings after felling and grasping opportunities for growth on recently bared ground.

Some of the finest birch-rich woods are in the Highlands, but birch is also a very prominent tree in many lowland areas, thanks to its colonising ability. On rich soils, those lowland trees can grow faster than their upland kin, but the down side is that they have shorter lives. A lowland birch is old at 100 years, when a slower-growing uplander of that age could have more than double that span still left to go.

Several kinds of birch grow in Scotland. The silver birch (*Betula pendula*) has a pale trunk, marked with black diamond shapes, and may droop its branches in a weeping form. The downy birch (*Betula pubescens*), which favours wetter parts of the country, has duller bark and fine white hairs on its twigs. The aptly named dwarf birch (*Betula nana*), which lives in some mountain areas and exposed coastal sites, doesn't grow above a metre high and often sprawls as a low shrub close to ground level.

CENTRAL HIGHLANDS

That scenery on the skirts of the mountains is changing, as birchwood expands in the bowl of Coire Ardair, the heart of the reserve. A car park off the A86 Fort William to Inverness road beside Loch Laggan provides a starting point for sampling Creag Meagaidh's varied views and vegetation. Just beyond, at Aberarder Farm, a path runs all the way up Coire Ardair to Lochan a' Choire, under the spectacular cliffs, gullies and buttresses of the corrie wall. These cliffs are highly rated by ice climbers in cold winters, and owe their shape and form to glacial sculpting in the last ice age.

Among the birches (some silver, most downy birch) close to the path, heath-spotted orchids, common cow wheat, primrose and globeflower grow. Beyond the trees, heather is more widespread and there are broad areas rich in blaeberry and crowberry. Some of these show where snow patches lie late in spring. In places where snow stays later still, the blaeberry and crowberry give way to mat grass, lichens, mosses and alpines including alpine lady's mantle. The crags of Coire Ardair and Coire Choille-rais are the richest areas for alpine plants. Here, the plants have survived out of reach of most large grazing animals. Rarities such as alpine speedwell and Highland cudweed grow here, along with downy willow, alpine saxifrage and alpine hawkweeds.

Mountain hares live on the mountain slopes, and Creag Meagaidh is still a good place to look out for red deer; although numbers have been reduced, the intention was always to keep deer as part of the natural system. Pine martens and wildcats use the area, but as usual you are more likely to see droppings than to encounter the creatures themselves.

Ptarmigan and dotterel are both in the higher parts of the reserve, where alpine heaths of woolly hair moss and three-leaved rush soften the ground.

Impressive though the high tops and plateau of Creag Meagaidh are, a visit here can be well worthwhile within part of Coire Ardair alone. Who knows, it might even change the way you think about other areas after you see the possibilities.

NEAR LOCH NESS – WOODS & WATER

The cleft of the Great Glen running from south-west to north-east for around 100 kilometres is one of the most striking landscape features in Scotland. A chain of long, narrow lochs sits in the glacier-worked trench along a major faultline in the Earth's crust.

At the heart of the glen lies the most famous of these waters, Loch Ness. Known more for what fabulous wildlife may not live in it than for its actual fauna, the lure of the unknown draws many to its shores each year. The real wildlife in and around the loch tends to get overlooked in this

SNOW BUNTING

A sprinkling of snow buntings breeds at high altitude in the Scottish mountains. Others come in from the continent in autumn and spend the next few months foraging for seeds among coastal sand dunes. Here, their flurries of flight in small flocks justify their other name of 'snowflake'.

DID YOU KNOW?

The dog whelk is a barnacle-eating shore snail. It can drill a hole through a barnacle's hard casing, send digestive juices in then suck up the resulting liquid like soup through a straw. Refreshing seaside drink, anyone?

mania for monsters. And there's no doubt that Loch Ness is an awesome place.

So what's the reality? It's the largest body of fresh water in the British Isles, holding more than all the lakes and reservoirs in England and Wales put together. It's also deep – very deep. Its maximum depth of 230 metres falls short of the 310 metres plumbed at Loch Morar, but Loch Ness has the greatest average depth of 132 metres.

The underwater profile is amazingly smooth, with steep sides sloping in and down to a fairly flat bottom – the legacy of ice age sculpting. Black sediment coats the floor of this deep basin, and within the murky, peat-clouded waters, life is sparse. Plants root to a depth of around 6 metres around the shores (trifling in comparison to the abyss beyond), and microscopic plankton are thinly spread. Brown trout, char, pike and some minnows spend their whole lives here, and fish stocks are seasonally boosted by migratory salmon and sea trout returning from the sea via the River Ness before spawning.

URQUHART BAY WOODS

It's at the rim of the waters where observable wildlife begins for most people. Fortunately for visitors the bay beside Urquhart Castle (outside Drumnadrochit and the most heavily used look-out for would-be Nessie watchers) has an interesting mix of birds, trees and plants. Where the Rivers Coiltie and Endrick meet at the lochside, a fine alder swamp has formed. Owned by the Woodland Trust Scotland, these Urquhart Bay Woods are thick with alders on the wetter ground, with a mix of ash, rowan, wych elm and bird cherry elsewhere. Tree holes here are used by nesting tits and even goosanders. Other breeding birds include great spotted woodpecker, treecreeper, blackcap, wood and willow warblers.

Dippers, goosanders and grey herons feed beside the Endrick, where grey wagtails, oystercatchers and common sandpipers nest among riverbank stones and overhangs. Butterflies include the orange tip. Access is signed from beside Old Kilmore graveyard, beyond the Benleva Hotel (wellies are advisable footwear for the soggy ground here at many times of the year).

Across the A82 from the natural tree cover of the Urquhart Bay Woods is a different kind of woodland scene, worth visiting for the size of some of its planted trees and for the fine views from the top.

BALMACAAN WOODS

Balmacaan Woods, the first Scottish purchase by the Woodland Trust, adjoins the Craigmonie Woodland to the north. The word 'balmacaan' means a loose, full overcoat with raglan sleeves – the kind that are slanted up to the neckline. Appropriately, the cloak of trees here includes some shapely conifers in its centre. Planted in the nineteenth century, some of these are among the largest of their kind in the country, including a Douglas fir that is nearly 52 metres high.

The rocky outcrop of Craig Mony, once the site of a local gibbet, gives wide views over Loch Ness. A small plantation of Scots pine here is used by red squirrels and crossbills as well as red polls and goldcrests. Elsewhere in the woods, standing dead timber gives nest space for great spotted woodpecker, redstart, great

---

DID YOU KNOW?

Both the wild hyacinth (the plant whose flowers can add a pastel blue haze to lowland woods in late spring) and the harebell (which flowers in mid to late summer) are called 'bluebell' in Scotland. But it's harebell which gets the full accolade as 'Scottish bluebell'. It likes dry grassland, sandy places, machair and rock ledges and has many different common names. How about 'gowks thummles' (cuckoo's thimbles) and *curac-cuthaige* (cuckoo's cap) for starters?

tit and blue tit, while blackcap, chiffchaff and willow warbler use the dense undergrowth. The mix of broadleaves and conifers also supports a range of small mammals, which help to feed local birds of prey and owls, including tawny owl, buzzard and kestrel.

Access is up Balmacaan Road, beyond the supermarket at the southern end of Drumnadrochit, from where a farm track on the right leads to the Woodland Trust area. A network of paths administered by various groups involved in the woods can be followed from there.

Between Drumnadrochit and Inverness, another part of what was once the Balmacaan Estate is having a new lease of life in an exciting community-linked woodland project around Abriachan, nestled just inland from Loch Ness. On and beyond steep-sided slopes, reshaping of conifer plantations, restructuring of native woodland and creation of a path network has produced new possibilities for conservation and enjoyment of local wildlife.

ABRIACHAN FOREST

The impetus for this renaissance has come through the sheer enthusiasm of Abriachan people, young and old, for their home above the Great Glen. In the late 1990s, the community-led Abriachan Forest Trust (AFT) bought 1000 acres of ground – mainly under conifer plantation – from the Forestry Commission. Helped by Woodland Grant Scheme awards, the AFT then began to harvest some of the poorer areas of conifers (largely Sitka spruce and lodgepole pine), and to replant or allow natural re-growth of native species such as birch. Other areas were left to be managed as conifer woodland.

A network of paths leads through many parts of the Abriachan Forest ground, both among the trees and out over the heath and grassland on the open hill. A good place to explore some of the area is from a car park down a track immediately west of Loch Laide. One of the intriguing features close to here is a boardwalk through a conifer plantation. It's hard to explain, but somehow the ability to have straightforward, slightly elevated access through the trees transforms an otherwise

DOTTEREL

The dotterel is a dapper wader that breeds in small numbers among the high-level snowfields of a few Scottish mountains. Females are more brightly coloured than males. In winter, Scottish dotterel live in North Africa.

SCOTLAND'S NATURE AND WILDLIFE

SCOTTISH CROSSBILL

The Scottish crossbill is the only species of bird found in Scotland and nowhere else in the world. Its stronghold is in the pinewoods of the Highlands. It uses its crossed mandibles to prise seeds from pine cones. Common crossbills (which have a slightly higher-pitched call) also breed, and both species provide links to the fauna of the boreal forest in other countries.

standard-issue conifer stand into something much more interesting.

From the boardwalk you can see various fungi, appreciate bark textures, look and listen for goldcrests and siskins, then wend down to a hide overlooking the small loch. The hide can give good views of herons and ducks, and the chance of seeing a slavonian grebe. Nearby pools at the forest fringe (some also beside the boardwalk) support a variety of dragonflies and damselflies, including golden-ringed dragonfly, above peaty water used by frogs.

A reconstructed Bronze Age dwelling made by youth club members with help from a thatcher is worth seeing, along with a shieling – the type of building once used in summer by young people while they herded cattle on the high pastures, made cheese and got closely acquainted with each other.

ABRIACHAN WOODLANDS

Overlooking Loch Ness, and with paths that interlink with Abriachan Forest, the Abriachan Woodlands (WT) cover two areas of mainly native woodland to either side off the Allt Killianan gorge that plunges down from Abriachan. The northernmost of these is difficult to access and relatively little visited. But the second area, on the lochside between the Abriachan Nursery Garden and the Clansman Hotel, has a good system of trails. These can be found close to the car parking areas beside both gardens and hotel. A steep path which runs diagonally through the wood was once used as a

CENTRAL HIGHLANDS

'funeral road' to carry coffins between Abriachan and the burial ground at Kilmore.

The woodland here is mainly birch, with areas of oak and alder and substantial amounts of hazel. Much of this hazel is multi-stemmed, a legacy of former coppicing for hurdles and implements, and the old stems are thick with lichens, including lungwort. Rowan, ash, aspen, wych elm, juniper and holly also grow here. Large areas of bracken cover parts of the woodland floor, but before it burgeons in summer, there's a good show of spring flowers under the broadleaves, including primroses, violets and wood anemones. Dog's mercury, enchanter's nightshade and sanicle are among the later flowers. On sunny days, slow-worms may bask in warm spots beside the paths. It's also worth looking for signs of the red squirrels, pine martens and wildcats which live in the area. Roe and red deer are abundant, plus the occasional sika.

Butterflies in the area include speckled wood and Scotch argus, and local birds include several kinds of tits, warblers and woodcock. Many of the trails within the wood are fairly steep, but the reward comes both from the shapes and forms of the trees and from the views along and across Loch Ness which you can enjoy on a fine day.

LOCH RUTHVEN

Inland from the north-eastern shore of Loch Ness sit several scenic lochs. One of the largest, Loch Duntelchaig, provides water for the City of Inverness – just a few kilometres further on along the Great Glen faultline. Close by is Loch Ruthven, a beautiful stretch of water, fringed by sedge beds and with birchwood, moorland and crags nearby. The eastern end forms part of an RSPB reserve, accessible off the B851 at Croachy (27 kilometres from the A9 at Daviot).

This is the best site in the whole of Britain for summer viewing of the rare and gorgeous slavonian grebe. The Loch Ness area was the launch-pad for the slavonian grebe's occupation of Scotland. The first pair nested here in 1908, part of a natural expansion in the bird's range in northern Europe. Numbers increased slowly until the 1990s, but they never numbered more than a few score of pairs, the majority of which have always been

RED SQUIRREL

The Highland Region is the only part of Scotland where red squirrels live but grey squirrels (descendants of stock introduced from North America) are absent. Parts of the Highlands are also likely to have retained small numbers of red squirrels through the 19th century, when they died out elsewhere. Squirrels have short front legs and long hind legs – an aid for leaping.

SCOTLAND'S NATURE AND WILDLIFE

> ### HEN HARRIER
> (*Circus cyaneus*)
>
> He's an ace performer in the moorland air. The appearance is cool, with a colour scheme of blue-grey wings and wing-tips dipped in black ink that emphasise sleekness and style.
>
> Watch a male dance in the sky to impress a partner – one of several females he'll mate with, given the chance – and his dives and stalls can amaze. When the larger, brown-plumaged female is on eggs or tending the brood in the heather, he'll come in with food drops, passing a vole to her in mid-air. She catches it with a dexterity that could be the envy of many.
>
> Harrier fortunes have been depressed by persecution from people. There should be hundreds more of these fine fliers over many more moors. But with wisdom applied to care of the heathlands, their numbers could rise once again.

hen harrier add feathered spice to the moor and wood.

WEST OF LOCH NESS – WOODED GLENS

Between Invermoriston, close to the south-western end of Loch Ness, and Achnasheen, nearly 50 kilometres away to the north-west, lies a major area of hill country almost free of roads. Seven glens cut through the mountains from Glen Moriston northwards, all with the roughly east-west alignment that is a major theme for many of their kind in the west.

At the core of this area is the village of Cannich. Within a few kilometres of it, the glens of the rivers Affric, Cannich and Farrar hold some of the finest scenery and wildlife in this huge area. They flow into the River Glass, which then feeds the River Beauly, draining a vast area that stretches far across towards the west coast. All three can be reached by road from the east, and have rights of way running through them.

GLEN STRATHFARRAR

Following the A862 south of Beauly, a turn to the right just before the bridge over the River Beauly leads along the A831. This is a scenic route, where the road squeezes between river gorges and steep wooded slopes along to Crask of Aigas before levelling along the alder-rich flood plain in Strathglass. Glen Strathfarrar (NNR) is the first of the glens along this road, accessed by a minor road to the right just before the small village

within 65 kilometres of Inverness.

You can see slavonians in their dowdier black and white winter plumage on the Moray Firth and other places around the Scottish coast. But the slavonians true glory comes in spring and summer, when the birds occupy their breeding lochs from April until late August. Then, the sight of golden eartufts against the black russet and chocolate of other plumage makes them one of the country's finest-looking waterbirds.

From the Loch Ruthven car park, a short trail leads to a hide overlooking a sedge bed used by the grebes. By using this hide and not walking around the shore, birdwatchers can be sure of not disturbing these vulnerable birds, and also be well placed for good views of other species.

Ospreys are regular visitors here, as are red-throated divers, goosanders and other ducks. Away from the loch, whinchat, redpoll, wheatear, and the occasional ring ouzel, short-eared owl and of Struy.

Access on foot or bicycle is unrestricted, but car drivers should note that entry to the glen (run as a National Nature Reserve in partnership between a local estate and Scottish Natural Heritage) is by permit obtainable from the gatekeeper's house near the Struy end of the glen. The reserve is closed to vehicles on Tuesdays and Sunday mornings, with a locked gate ensuring people keep to the rules.

There is also a tight limit on the number of vehicles that can be in the glen at one time, allocated on a first come, first served basis, so if you drive up on a sunny weekend afternoon you might be disappointed. Such restriction, although unusual in Scotland, is slight in comparison to measures at protected areas in some other countries, where you might even need to apply months in advance for permits to some places. It helps to keep the glen very peaceful, both for wildlife and for walkers. The surfaced road runs for some 19 kilometres to Loch Monar dam at the western end of the glen.

One of the beauties of Glen Strathfarrar is the way the native pines and birches spread back from the river up the slopes of the fairly broad strath floor, giving a great sense of depth of view. Both this and the neighbouring glens are important places for native woodland, holding healthy remnants of what was once much more widespread tree cover.

Large areas at the glenside, fenced to reduce deer access, have vigorous, self-sown regrowth of birch, pine, rowan, aspen and other species, demonstrating the huge potential of these uplands to recover from grazing given the chance. In the heart of the native pinewood on the reserve is Coille Garbh or 'Rough Wood', with north-facing wooded crags and terraces rising in steps to the treeline. Old stands of juniper grow beneath the large pines on flatter ground by the river. Timber was once commercially harvested from Glen Strathfarrar's woods, beginning in the 1780s, when logs were floated downriver to sawmills at Aigas. Some of the old Scots pines growing here today would have already been growing as young trees in those earliest days of the logging.

The mix of Caledonian forest birds

SLAVONIAN GREBE

The beautiful head plumes of the Slavonian grebe earn it the title of 'horned grebe' in North America. The Scottish population of this globally widespread bird is tiny and concentrated in a handful of small lochs around Loch Ness and near the Moray Firth coast.

DID YOU KNOW?

Small fish, including young whiting, can take shelter among the tentacles of jellyfish, gaining protection from predators as they drift behind the stinging veil.

SCOTLAND'S NATURE AND WILDLIFE

DID YOU KNOW?

Work by an ornithologist at Aberdeen University has shown that the 'V' formations of flying geese don't just look good – they save energy for flock members. By adopting this in-flight pattern, formation flyers can get extra lift from air disturbed by birds ahead. Tough on the leader, but they do change positions as they travel.

here includes the classic Scottish crossbill and crested tit. Creeping lady's tresses orchid and one-flowered wintergreen grow in places beneath the pines, while richer soil under the birches has lesser celandine, wood anemone, wood sorrel and chickweed wintergreen. Pine martens, red squirrels and roe deer use the woods, with red deer on the moors beyond and otters along the river. This is also golden eagle country.

GLEN CANNICH

The village of Cannich, a few kilometres south of Struy on the A831, gives an entry point to both Glen Cannich and Glen Affric from small roads which fork apart just beyond the settlement. Glen Cannich is the less visited. Here, a road rises to Loch Mullardoch under wooded slopes beside the River Cannich then out onto moorland. The mix of birds here includes buzzard, raven, crested tit, dipper and grey heron and there are many red deer in the area.

GLEN AFFRIC

The Glen Affric National Nature Reserve (FC), reached by single-track road beyond the Fasnakyle power station, holds the largest surviving Caledonian forest remnants outside the Cairngorms, and some of the most extensive native woodland restoration projects. Once heavily planted with introduced conifers for commercial forestry, more recent work by the Forestry Commission has cleared large areas of these exotics, making room for native pine, birch and other trees to expand.

At the same time, volunteers working for 'Trees for Life' – the native woodland charity based at the Findhorn Foundation in Moray – have planted huge numbers of native tree seedlings to begin the re-afforestation of parts of the glen made treeless by past grazing. This massive effort is in close co-operation with the Forestry Commission and other landowners. Together with the Forestry Commission's own work, it is showing that restoration of a network of native woodlands linking east and west coasts in this part of the Highlands could one day be possible.

A good starting place for exploration of the Affric woodlands is the FC car park at Dog Falls. Colour-coded trails can be walked from here, providing circular routes of a couple of hours or so that include excellent viewpoints through the trees and along this lovely glen. It is also possible to follow the road to two car parks further up the glen, beside the north shore of Loch Beinn a' Mheadhoin and close to Loch Affric. The River Affric car park (16 kilometres into the glen) is at the end of the public road.

The blend of wildlife among the pines and birches includes a near full house of Caledonian forest birds, with crested tit, Scottish crossbill, capercaillie and black grouse all resident, and tree pipit and redstart as visiting breeders. Sparrowhawk, buzzard, golden eagle and kestrel all use the area, plus occasional osprey and merlin.

Out on the lochs, both red and black-throated divers can be watched for, plus commoner red-breasted mergansers, goosanders and mallards. Along water margins of both lochs and river, grey wagtails and dippers feed and breed. Larger mammals include pine marten,

CENTRAL HIGHLANDS

wildcat, roe deer and red deer.

An impressive variety of lichens grows on and under the trees. Some 177 different species have been recorded in West Affric, including 24 species of Cladonia lichens. Creeping lady's tresses orchid and twinflower are among the pinewood plants. At the Coire Loch – accessible from Dog Falls car park – 14 species of dragonfly and damselfly have been seen.

BUZZARD

Buzzards are much commoner and more widespread than golden eagles, with a more rounded wing shape and shorter neck. Rabbits can be a staple food for them, as can carrion, supplemented in some places by worms picked from ploughed fields and pastures.

SCOTLAND'S NATURE AND WILDLIFE

West Highlands & Argyll

Nowhere in Scotland is particularly far, by the standards of most other countries, from the sea. But in the West Highlands, the interweaving of sea and land is intimate; the influence of the ocean pervasive. Atlantic driven rains, sweeping in from the south-west, are part of that marriage of water and earth.

The areas of highest rainfall in Scotland are here, with mountains receiving more than the glens below. So gear that can shrug-off the worst the sky can throw at you should be part of West Highland kit in all but the most settled of conditions. Gains from the rains are many, including a lushness and variety of lower plants that gives the western Scottish woodlands fair claim to the title of temperate rainforests.

Oakwoods are the classic West Highland forest type, and within them, mosses, liverworts and lichens cling to every branch and trunk, smooth every boulder and stump. Even if you can't name the many species – and let's face it, only a handful of experts can – there's a pleasure in seeing the sheer diversity of forms they take, and in appreciating their many shades of green. The bird community in the woods has a distinctive oakwood tang, with a blend that can include wood warbler, tree pipit and redstart in its mix, perhaps with the occasional pied flycatcher if you're lucky.

The sea makes its presence felt in the mildness of the climate too – a blessing from the North Atlantic Drift. This massive marine flow – with distant connections to the Gulf Stream, which does not, contrary to popular belief, come anywhere near Scotland – acts as a heat pump. It brings warmth from middle latitudes up to these coasts, which might otherwise be much, much colder.

Otter

In contrast to present-day mildness, a major amount of the sculpting that brings sea and land together here was done at times of extreme cold, when the scene was set for the entry of the sea lochs. There are more than 80 sea lochs along the west coast – there are so many and the majority are so deeply pushed among flanking uplands as to be one of the defining elements of the whole area.

Sea lochs are Scottish fjords, trenched and moulded by the power of ice. Each has a unique shape, although typically with a narrower, shallower entrance and a wider, deeper basin beyond. This happened because the ice mass was greater near land, and as it melted seaward, glacier-transported rock was dumped to form the sills at sea loch entrances.

The beauty of the sea lochs is that they make marine life accessible along much of the west, including in places well screened from the main force of the storm-driven sea. Eider ducks, seals, neatly zoned brown seaweeds in sheltered bays, salt marsh and its flowers where the shallows meet land at the head of the loch – those are some of the species and habitats to seek. Better still, catch a glimpse as you walk a western wood, as you listen to birdsong, or hear gull calls from far below as you stand on the ridge of a coastal hill.

SCOTLAND'S NATURE AND WILDLIFE

FERAL GOAT

The feral goats that live in some coastal and upland areas are descendants of domestic animals. Goats were once common as livestock. Free living goats have an enormous range of coat colours. Mating is in October and November, when billies clash by rearing-up and butting heads. Kids (sometimes twins) are born in January.

The coastline of Scotland's Atlantic rim, from the Mull of Kintyre northwards, is huge. Inlets large and small, from the merest dimple of a few tens of metres to a sea loch biting deep into the mountain fringe, combine with headlands and other features to produce a wrinkled edge of thousands of kilometres.

Getting to know this western frontier would take a lifetime at shore level. Add the high ground set close behind, where the hills can rise sharply and burns and rivers cut short courses to the sea, and the west mainland seems like a whole country in itself. Few, if any parts of this domain should disappoint a walker with an eye for wildlife and for the play of light and water on rock and sand. But some places stand out as giving excellent samples of parts of the wider west, and an inkling of what else might be in store if you choose to venture further.

TORRIDON

Torridon – west of the A896 between Sheildaig and Kinlochewe – is one such area. There's no ignoring the mountains here. They set the scene, hold the eye, shape the mood and mould the wildlife communities. Angular and ancient, the cliffs can soar skywards to spectacular buttresses and narrow summit ridges, some so strewn with shattered quartzite that they glisten white under grey skies or blue.

The Torridonian sandstone that makes up the main bulk of these ranges was laid down as sediment some 800 million years ago. At that time, this part of Scotland was linked to what is now south-east Greenland. Huge rivers dumped their sands and gravels to pile over what is now the West Highlands, heaping them almost unbelievably high. Over an enormous sweep of time, the sediments rose to a depth of more than 7 kilometres, later to be eroded down by the action of rain, flood and frost.

So what remains here, impressive though it is, is little more than the stump of something much, much larger. And to cap it all, literally, is quartz laid down in quiet seas much later than the sandstones – less than 600 million years ago. Shoved over the older rocks when continents collided, the quartz now sparkles below and up to the highest tops.

Two major mountain systems dominate Torridon. Liathach, also known as 'the grey one' (NTS), is the southernmost of these. Its scale is awesome – a mass of sandstone topped by an 8 kilometre ridge links eight separate tops. Two of these are more than 1000 metres above the salty waters of upper Loch Torridon, just an eagle's glide below. Tackling the highest ground here is not for the faint-hearted or the ill-prepared. But you can get an impression of some of the mountain grandeur, and the associated wildlife, by exploring old stalkers' paths at low level from near the NTS countryside centre. Open between May and September, the centre is situated by the A896 at Torridon, and has information on local geology and wildlife.

This area is well known for its herds of red deer and for its golden eagles. At ground level, interesting plants include dwarf willow – a tiny tree well adapted to harsh environments, which thrives better in Torridon than just about anywhere else in mainland Scotland. The willow grows close to another couple of tough mountain survivors – stiff sedge and fir clubmoss.

BEINN EIGHE NATIONAL NATURE RESERVE

Linking with the Torridon estate and covering another great chunk of ground from north beyond Liathach to the shores of Loch Maree, the Beinn Eighe National Nature Reserve (SNH) has a superb range of West Highland wildlife. Best access from the point of view of seeing a mixture of vegetation, birds and other fauna is from the A832, just over 3 kilometres north-west of Kinlochewe.

A visitor centre is open here between Easter and September, with access to woodland and mountain close by.

This was the first National Nature Reserve in Britain, designated in 1951 as much for the value of its ancient pinewood as for the mountain ground beyond. The largest remaining area of Scots pinewood is Coille na Glas Leitir (Wood of the Grey Slope), which cloaks

DID YOU KNOW?

The pitch of a male toad's croak is related to his body size. So if a male is trying to mate with a female and is challenged by other males, he may decide to shout it out. If he's a large toad, this can be enough to deter the competition. If he's not, then let battle commence.

REGIONAL HIGHLIGHT: BEINN EIGHE NATIONAL NATURE RESERVE

DESIGNATION:
National Nature Reserve (SNH).

LANDSCAPE:
Pinewood and mountain terrain.

HIGHLIGHTS:
A huge range of wildlife including pine martens, deer, mountain hares and various species of dragonfly. Mosses, heather and liverworts thrive, as do ferns and arctic-alpines. Birds include Scottish crossbills, siskins, redpolls and ptarmigan.

BEST TIME:
Summer for dragonflies and pinewood birds; autumn for deer rut; winter for moss and liverwort colours.

FACILITIES:
Visitor centre (open Easter–Oct) with exhibition and audio-visual presentation; shop, picnic area, toilet plus nature trails.

ADMISSION:
Free.

DIRECTIONS:
Of A832, two miles NW of Kinlochewe.

CONTACT:
SNH, Anancaun, Kinlochewe,
Ross-shire IV22 2PD
Tel: 01445 760254
www.snh.org.uk
www.nnr-scotland.org.uk

SCOTLAND'S NATURE AND WILDLIFE

HIGHLAND MIDGE
(Culicoides impunctatus)

To many it's the bane of the west, the biter that takes the edge off the wider scene. On summer evenings when the air is still, midge swarms can make quiet contemplation by a Highland loch impossible, unless you're kitted-out like an invading alien to resist the wee blighters' attacks.

One species of biting midge is behind most of the summer midge onslaughts on people. It's only the females that do it, often soon after lift-off from the land surface where she lived as a non-flying youngster.

After going through four different larval stages in the water film over damp soil or bog, the female midge takes flight. She's ready to mate within a day of her emergence. That done, she seeks a blood meal to give a protein source for her eggs – though she could lay a first batch without one.

July and August are the months when Highland midge populations peak. Female midges seem to be attracted more to some people than others, perhaps due to differences in body odour and sweat. They may also use airborne chemical message carriers – pheromones to help locate each other to form swarms and mate.

long-established at Beinn Eighe, both in terms of the individual trees – some of which are more than 350 years old – and because it is likely that pine woodland has grown here for more than 8000 years. Ancestors of some of Beinn Eighe's pines may have survived the ice age in a refuge far to the south-east. So perhaps that's why the trees are different (in terms of chemicals associated with resin and turpentines in their wood) from pines in the woods farther east.

More obvious contrasts with the eastern pinewoods are that there is very little juniper here among the trees; although prostrate juniper does well at higher altitudes on the ridges of the mountain massif. There are also no red squirrels, crested tits or capercaillie, and twinflower and some other special pinewood plants are absent – perhaps a reflection of high rainfall.

But never mind the absentees, check the residents. This area is well known for its pine martens, for example, which live in the woods and range beyond them – even visiting gardens of some householders who welcome them. As usual with martens, you'll be more likely to see their droppings on the trail than to spot the animals themselves. Scottish crossbills breed here, sharing the woodland with redpolls, siskins, redstarts and tree pipits. The flora beneath the pines includes creeping lady's tresses, lesser twayblade and chickweed wintergreen. Where the pines are closely spaced, crowberry and mosses thrive.

In more open areas, tall bushy heather thrives, sprouting with blaeberry over a spongy carpet of bog mosses. In rocky places up the hillside – away from the reach of grazing roe and red deer –

the hillside above the south shore of Loch Maree, not far from the SNH visitor centre. A nature trail of about 1.5 kilometres runs through the wood, with access from a culvert under the main road. Visitors can enjoy a circular walk up, around and down the slope and back near the lochside to the starting place at a parking area. There is also a mountain trail that begins beside the same car park and culvert. It covers 6.5 kilometres and climbs to 550 metres before looping back downhill to the start. The walk is a prospect for those well-prepared and fit enough for a four hour hike in the hills.

The Scots pines are

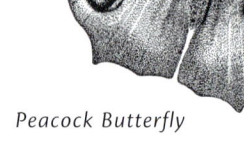

Peacock Butterfly

WEST HIGHLANDS & ARGYLL

there is globeflower, with its butterballs of yellow flower, water avens, common wintergreen and melancholy thistle. Thanks to the damp conditions here, the range of mosses and liverworts, both on and around the trees, is excellent. This is also a great place for a range of insect life, including an impressive tally of 13 species of dragonflies, such as the rare azure hawker and the more widespread (and because of its large size, visible) gold-ringed dragonfly.

At the halfway stage of the woodland trail is a log-built shelter and viewpoint known as the 'conservation cabin', which is constructed from wind-blown pines. Close to it is a rock plinth with layers showing various natural formations in the area. This includes a specimen of 'pipe rock'. Familiar to those who tramp the high levels of the Torridon mountains, pipe rock contains tubes of paler-coloured material that are the fossilised burrows of marine worms. These creatures were active several hundred million years ago and are among the earliest recognisable many-celled creatures in the world.

Above the treeline at Beinn Eighe, especially from about 450 metres upwards, there are some good expanses of dwarf shrub heath, with dwarf juniper, alpine bearberry, trailing azalea and dwarf cornel. Mountain hares (good prey for eagles) graze the middle slopes, which are also hunted by peregrine and buzzards. Ptarmigan live among the shattered rocks right up to the high tops, where the summit heaths hold plants such as

GOLDEN-RINGED DRAGONFLY

The golden-ringed dragonfly is the largest of this ancient group of insects in Scotland. Unlike most dragonflies and damselflies, which use still water as a nursery for their young, the larvae of golden-ringed dragonflies live in flowing waters of burns. They emerge after several years for a few weeks of life as free-flying adults.

SCOTLAND'S NATURE AND WILDLIFE

PTARMIGAN

Ptarmigan can be beautifully camouflaged among the rocks of the mountains where they live all year. Moulting at different times of the year allows them to shift from snowy-white winter plumage to finely barred buff, white and grey to suit the season.

mossy saxifrage and thrift. The screes are great places for ferns – such as parsley fern, beech fern and lemon-scented fern – mosses and liverworts, all of which like the moist, shady conditions among the rocks on steep slopes.

Loch Maree is a bonny stretch of water that runs north-west from the outskirts of Beinn Eighe's main pinewood, along to within a few kilometres of the sea near Poolewe. It has a fine cluster of islands with their own capping of old pines and some oaks. Also designated as a reserve, the islands and the surrounding water – reflecting the magnificent shapes of Beinn Airidh Charn, Beinn Lair and Slioch to the north-east – are best appreciated from the shore that flanks the Slattadale Forest (FC). There are good stopping places and picnic areas beside the A832, from where you can get to the water's edge. From here, you can look for red- and black-throated divers and common sandpipers in summer, and dipper and grey wagtail throughout the year.

INVEREWE GARDENS

Just north of Poolewe on the A832, Inverewe Garden (NTS) is a real green oasis. Set on a craggy promontory overlooking the salt marsh and seaweedy shallows of inner Loch Ewe, with wider views out seaward over open water, Inverewe has a lot to recommend it for visitors who want a good prospect of the sea from sheltered surroundings, or an earful of spring birdsong.

BEN NEVIS

Glen Nevis (part JMT) is an impressive place. Above looms the 1344 metre mass of Ben Nevis, the highest mountain in Britain and Ireland. So you'd have to travel a very, very long way before you could experience the kind of vertical range of landscape – from glen bottom near sea level up to the high, cold shoulders of the Ben – that exists here. A very well-trodden path up the Ben (for those fit, well-shod and prepared for several hours of hiking) begins from above the north bank of the River Nevis. The glen beneath is a softer and very pleasant option.

Some reckon that this is one of the most beautiful of all Scottish glens. A gentle section downstream, where alders sprout along the riverbank and native woods with birch and pine hug the hillside, gives way to the steeper-sided middle section, which is reminiscent of the Alps. In the upper part where the water of the Nevis flows through a gorge, the dramatic waterfall of An Steall slips, glides and crashes down to meet it from the lower cliffs of Sgurr a' Mhaim. Native trees in this part of the glen include old pines, birch, rowan and holly.

Many people tramp the big Ben and its fringes, so the wildlife viewing possibilities here are a bit different from some less popular areas. But the mix of the dramatic mountains of the Mamores with the gentler riverside scene still makes this well worth sampling – lucky walkers may even see a golden eagle overhead from time to time.

ARIUNDLE NATIONAL NATURE RESERVE

The edges of the West Highlands and Argyll are blessed with many excellent woodlands, often with a great deal of sessile oak in their mix of native trees. The Ariundle National Nature Reserve in the glen of the Strontian River (accessible from a car park off a minor road beside Scotstoun, just north of the A867 at

> **DID YOU KNOW?**
> Some water voles do not live close to flowing water. This could be a lifeline for some of Scotland's mountain-dwelling water voles, at a time when their lowland kin are being wiped out by introduced mink.

REGIONAL HIGHLIGHT: ARIUNDLE NATIONAL NATURE RESERVE

DESIGNATION:
National Nature Reserve (SNH).

LANDSCAPE:
Pinewood and mountain terrain.

HIGHLIGHTS:
An abundance of mosses, liverworts and lichens grow here, along with wood sorrel, lesser celandine, bugle and bluebells. Birds include tree pipits, redstarts and warblers.

BEST TIME:
Spring and summer for flowers and birds.

FACILITIES:
Car park (open all year round) and nature trails.

ADMISSION:
Free.

DIRECTIONS:
Off A884/A861, N of Strontian.

CONTACT:
www.snh.org.uk

www.nnr-scotland.co.uk

CHEQUERED SKIPPER
(Carterocephalus palaemon)

This small butterfly of open woodland used to occur in central England, especially the East Midlands. It is thought to have gone extinct in England by 1976. Now western Scotland is the only part of Britain where it lives, spread fairly widely around north Argyll and Lochaber.

It was discovered in Scotland in 1939 and, before 1974, had only been recorded in a couple of places. This patchy record doesn't mean the species wasn't already present, but reflects the shortage of clued in butterfly-watchers seeking them in the right places. That principle still holds true for a great many kinds of insects today – showing the need for more people to take a keen interest in them.

Part of the difficulty of finding signs of chequered skippers is that their caterpillars live in a tube formed from a single blade of whichever grass its egg was laid on. The caterpillar binds the edges with silken threads and eats above and below its tube – a good field sign if you know what to look for, but otherwise great camouflage. Purple moor grass is its favourite Scottish home and nibble, also serving as a winter leaf-blade tent when the caterpillar hibernates.

Adult chequered skippers can be on the wing in places like clearings, rides and edges of western oakwoods between early May and early June. In fine weather, they bask with wings wide open and use purple-flowered plants, especially bugle (if available), as a major source of nectar.

---

bloom while the resident tits, chaffinches, robins and wrens are in full song and willow warblers are fresh-in from Africa. By the time bluebells and bugle are adding other colours to the woodland floor, redstarts, tree pipits and wood warblers will be adding their songs to the Ariundle soundscape.

You can hear, see and smell echoes of this oakwood at other places to the south, with some particularly fine opportunities in Knapdale. Set at the top of the Kintyre Peninsula – that finger of Scotland that reaches down as if stretching out for Northern Ireland – Knapdale is suffused with a sense of water. Sea salt, river ozone and bog reek are part of it, from the long bites of Loch Sween and Loch Caolisport, the meanderings of the River Add, the moss humps of the Moine Mor and the clean cut of the Crinan Canal.

CRINAN WOOD

This last waterway – a fine piece of civil engineering that links Lochgilphead to the Sound of Jura across a few kilometres of land – presses against the edge of Crinan Wood (WT) in its final stages. A footpath runs through the wood. Accessible both from Crinan (take the B841 from Lochgilphead) and from the canal towpath beside a swing bridge, the footpath is punctuated by some interesting sculptures and has great views out over the bogland to the east, coast to the north and islands to the west. Trees here have been shaped by the prevailing westerly winds and the salt-laden sea air. Lichen growth is tremendous, and many kinds of mosses soften boulders and branches.

In addition to the classic community

Strontian) is one of the finest of these. Ariundle is a real 'Atlantic' oakwood, one of several in the Loch Sunart area, where wet, humid conditions help a wealth of lower plants and ferns to thrive. So if you want to get an idea of some of the many shapes that small, moisture-loving plants, such as mosses and liverworts can take, Ariundle is a good place to visit.

Around 250 different species of mosses, liverworts and lichens grow here. But it is also a good place for spring flowers. Lesser celandine, wood sorrel and wood anemone are among those that of oakwood birds including redstarts, wood warblers and tree pipits, you're quite likely to hear sounds of gulls and mallard ducks from the nearby canal, river and sea beyond as you make your way among Crinan's trees. Celandines, wood anemones, bluebells and wood sorrel grow here, and over more acidic soil there is plenty of blaeberry.

TAYNISH NATIONAL NATURE RESERVE

The Taynish National Nature Reserve is only a few kilometres beyond Crinan, down the B8025 beside Loch Sween at the small fishing village of Tayvallich. From the reserve car park, 1.5 kilometres south of the village, waymarked routes lead through the woodland. Here, the cover of oaks opens in places to marshy and grassy areas. This combination of woodland and plant-rich open ground may be one reason why Taynish is such a great place for butterflies.

These include a good population of the marsh fritillary – a beautifully patterned butterfly which has vanished from many of its former breeding places. The marsh fritillaries at Taynish are, not surprisingly, the Scottish form – completely isolated from populations in England and Wales. Twenty-one other butterfly species have been recorded at Taynish. Among these are other fritillaries, including the small pearl-bordered and dark green, plus Scotch argus, green hairstreak, purple hairstreak and speckled wood, and various other more common and widespread species. The butterflies here benefit from some of the more than 300 species of plants.

As you would expect from an Atlantic oakwood, the mosses, liverworts and lichens are superb. Among the flowering plants, the narrow-leaved helleborine, found in less acidic soils is an orchid highlight. Beyond the wood, otters hunt the sheltered shallows of Loch Sween, looking for some of the fish and crabs that live among the seaweeds.

WOOD SORREL

Wood sorrel is a plant of long-established broadleaved woods. Its pale flowers are finely patterned with a tracery of lines, and both blooms and leaves add a subtle beauty to the woodland show of new plant life in spring and early summer.

SCOTLAND'S NATURE AND WILDLIFE

Northern Highlands

Nowhere else in Scotland are there mountains with such distinctive, individual characters as in the North Highlands. To the south, there are places where you can be spoilt for choice, where the ridges, summits and lines of glens run like waves in a sea of stone to the boundaries of vision. Not here, where the uplands stand in sharp relief against tens of kilometres of plain.

Morvern and its neighbours set the tone. No great heights here – Morvern is a mere 706 metres – but the effect of their contrast with the flatlands to the north, beyond Berriedale Water, is superb. The same principle holds, though with variations in the lowland setting, as you move north-west and west. There is Ben Hope and Ben Loyal, looking to the Pentland Firth, Ben Kilbreck and Ben Hee, then the huge, multi-armed mass of Ben More Assynt – a rocky leviathan, but still clearly drawn as a single mountain, standing apart from its surrounds.

Over the line of the Moine Thrust – that major geological boundary that marks the collision of long-vanished continents – and the mountains that look west to the Minch make individuality an art form. Foinaven, Arkle, Ben Stack, Quinag, Canisp, Suilven, Cul Mor, Cul Beag, their shapes against the evening sky are a defining element of place.

With such magnificence of mountains on days when the view is long enough to take your bearings from this backdrop, the low ground gains extra sparkle. For here is always the thought of what lies beyond – across the distant ridge, over the far summit – as well as the focus on what is directly ahead or underfoot. Over great sweeps of inland Caithness and Sutherland, that immediate surrounding will be big on bog.

Curlew

The North Highlands is a centre of global bog excellence, an area that does the particular kind known as 'blanket bog' better than just about anywhere else on the planet. Seen from the air, the finest stretches glisten with a myriad small pools, known as dubh lochans. Close to, it's the colours of the 'Sphagnum' bog mosses that amaze, this intensity of their tones and wildness of their mixtures – acid green with cherry red, yellow with claret and many more colours besides – blending in a water-swelled carpet spread and fitted over every hummock and hollow.

Getting a taste of the big bogs, and the communities that live there, will often be a high priority for wildlife-savvy travellers in the North Highlands. But there are many other aspects to savour here, such as the variety of freshwaters, from the large lochs and countless dubh lochans in the interior to the smaller lochs and numerous lochans towards the wet coast.

Along both western and northern fringes, there is scope to encounter a different blend of wildlife, with many kinds of hardy plants growing down close to sea level, seabirds on some coastal stretches and offshore, and the chance to see a dolphin or whale as you watch from a likely headland.

SCOTLAND'S NATURE AND WILDLIFE

BLACK-THROATED DIVER
The patterns of lines and flecks on a black-throated diver's plumage seem to suggest glints of light and ripples on water. Some reckon this could help the bird to be less obvious to the small fish it chases and eats underwater. Others just appreciate its elegance of black, grey and white.

The country that sits north of an imagined line from the Cromarty Firth in the east to Loch Broom in the west holds perhaps the greatest expanses of truly wild ground in the whole of Scotland. Soft low-lying coastlands snuggle into its fringe in the south-east, around places like Tain, Dornoch, Golspie and Brora.

But for the most part, this is an area of vast bogs, spectacular mountains, glens that see few visitors and coasts as rugged and beautiful as anywhere else in the country. The cliffs of Cape Wrath, the bonny woods of Assynt, the splendid, sodden Flows, a wealth of peaks and ridges, quiet beaches and the wave-pounded shores of the Pentland Firth all fall within the sweep of the north Scottish mainland.

Part of the excitement of the area lies in its sheer scale and the relative inaccessibility of big parts of it – you need to walk and walk to get a feel for some of its fastnesses. Yet there are also places here that are much easier to sample, including wildlife refuges which rank among some of Scotland's finest.

LEDMORE AND MIGDALE WOODS

One of these is at the southern fringe of the area, close to the scenic Dornoch Firth and not far into Sutherland – the land that, to the Vikings, lay below their North Isles domains and hence was southernland. At Ledmore and Migdale Woods (WT), there is native tree cover

NORTHERN HIGHLANDS

on a grand scale. No tiny remnants here struggling to make it against the odds of grazing and felling over recent generations, but a system of vigorously regenerating woods.

Some of the finest birchwood cover in the north, the northernmost substantial oakwood in Britain, an old pinewood around a small crag and a healthy chunk of bog sits close to the tiny hamlet of Spinningdale. There are several ways into these walks, offering contrasting trails, views and wildlife. A good place to get your bearings is in Spinningdale, from where you can walk back, with care, along the A949 towards Bonar Bridge to get an entry point to coniferous woodland flanking the old oakwood, and to paths which go alongside Spinningdale Bog and out onto the heather moor.

Another way is to go along an unclassified road that runs north-west from Spinningdale, towards Bonar Bridge, entering the wood by an obvious track to the left about 3 kilometres from the hamlet (with very limited car parking just beyond). From here, a trail runs along through the pines to Loch Migdale, with a branch to the left to the bog and moorland area.

The vigour of tree regeneration in this clutch of woods is tremendous, with small seedlings and taller saplings pushing the boundaries out over hill and along the dale, while the old trees at the core gather moss and lichen. At first glance, it's hard to see any signs of human action here, but the area has been used for thousands of years. Neolithic chambered cairns – one of which sits beside a high track along the northern slope of the woods, high above the unclassified road – are among dozens of ancient sites now nestled among the trees. Remains of an old watermill, eighteenth-century farming settlements and old field systems are all here.

But the wildlife of the place suggests that chunks of the ground also have a

> **DID YOU KNOW?**
>
> Dry bog moss, which can include many different species of Sphagnum, is hugely absorbent and has some antiseptic properties. It was used by some people in the past as nappy lining, and widely called into service for wound dressing.

REGIONAL HIGHLIGHT: LEDMORE AND MIGDALE

DESIGNATION:
Woodland Trust Reserve.

LANDSCAPE:
Oakwood, birchwood, pinewood, bog and loch.

HIGHLIGHTS:
A huge variety of trees including downy and silver birch, oaks, Scots pines, willows, blackthorn, ash and aspens, plus juniper. This, in turn, supports a diverse insect fauna, including slave-making ants and many kinds of sawflies, plus birds such as the great spotted woodpecker, redstart, siskin and crossbills. Pine martens, otters, wildcats, three species of deer and red squirrels also inhabit the area.

BEST TIME:
From late spring to autumn for birds, plants, insects and tree colours.

FACILITIES:
Limited car park, open all year round.

ADMISSION:
Free.

DIRECTIONS:
Oakwood off A949, E of Bonar Bridge. Pinewood, birchwood and bog off minor road from Spinningdale (on A949) to Migdale.

CONTACT:
www.woodland-trust.org.uk

SCOTLAND'S NATURE AND WILDLIFE

> **DID YOU KNOW?**
> You can tell the difference between the sexes of adult great spotted woodpeckers by looking at the feathers on the back of their heads. Males have a patch of crimson feathers, females don't. Youngsters have a red cap.

long history of woodland cover. Insects and other small creatures give one clue, with their variety indicating a degree of stability. More than 300 kinds of small beasties, mostly insects, have been found on woody plants here. Add to those upwards of 30 in dead wood and 137 on woodland fungi, and you begin to get an impression of Ledmore and Migdale's richness.

Stars among the insect cast are mostly species known only by their scientific names and identifiable by experts, but it can be intriguing to know that they're here, nevertheless. One of these is a tiny mite, *Eriophses populi*, which lives on aspen trees, where its larvae grow in hard-coated galls. Discovered in Deeside in the 1870s, it was not seen there or anywhere else in Britain until a local entomologist found it on aspens in these woods. Another intriguing insect is the so-called blood red slave-making ant – *Formica sanguinea* to those in the know – found only in old pinewoods in Scotland. This particular species raids the nests of other ant species, carrying off larvae and rearing them as slaves to work in its own nests. It could be happening among the pines below the crag here right now!

The spread of juniper at Ledmore and Migdale is better than anywhere else north of Inverness. Buds and needles, in turn, support their own insect fauna, including several kinds of saw fly. The birch trees here have a great range of shapes and forms.

Both downy birch (*Betula pubescens*) and silver birch (*Betula pendula*) with paler bark and some beautifully cascading drapes of stems and twigs grow here, plus some hybrids between the two. In addition to the oaks, Scots pines and aspens, the range of native trees includes rowan, bird cherry, ash, willows, hawthorn, holly and blackthorn, plus some rock whitebeam.

Woodland birds include crossbills, siskins and great spotted woodpeckers in the pine areas, wood warbler and redstart in the oakwood, and willow

REGIONAL HIGHLIGHT: LOCH FLEET NATIONAL NATURE RESERVE

DESIGNATION:
SNH/SWT.

LANDSCAPE:
Pinewoods, dunes and tidal basin.

HIGHLIGHTS:
A popular spot for birds such as greenshank, redshank, ospreys, greylag and pink-footed geese, eiders, Scottish crossbills and wigeon. Also of interest are common seals, and a range of flora including creeping lady's tresses orchid and St Olaf's candlesticks.

BEST TIME:
Spring and autumn for greenshank, redshank and pink-footed geese; greylag geese in August; summer for flowers.

FACILITIES:
Car parks (open all year round), and organised walks in the summer months.

ADMISSION:
Free.

DIRECTIONS:
On the A9, two miles S of Golspie.

CONTACT:
www.snh.org.uk
www.nnr-scotland.co.uk

NORTHERN HIGHLANDS

warbler among the birches. Pine martens use the trails as fast routes through the trees, often feeding on rowan and blaeberries in autumn. Roe deer live in the woods and red and sika deer use both the tree-covered ground and the moorland beyond; the red stags add a roar and the sika a high-pitched whistle to the autumn air. Otters hunt along both the bog and the loch shore, and there are red squirrels and wildcats in the woods. So this is a great place to look for signs of some classic Scottish wildlife, even if seeing the creatures is a lot harder.

The rich flora here includes creeping ladies tresses orchid among the pines, rockrose on a band of chalky rock on the crag at Migdale and bogbean, common reed and a wealth of bog mosses in Spinningdale Bog. Ledmore oakwood has an unusual ground cover, with much heather and bracken in its lower part, masses of blaeberry in its upper part and along the moorland fringe, where the oaks meet some birches and Scots pines. This blaeberry cover could be a boon for the local black grouse.

LOCH FLEET NATIONAL NATURE RESERVE

Where the A9 runs across the River Fleet, a few kilometres west of Golspie, a mix of estuary and planted woods stretches towards the sea. This is the Loch Fleet National Nature Reserve (SNH, Sutherland Estates, SWT), which includes a great range of wildlife on both land and water. One place to stop and get a general impression of both the estuary and the system of pools and alderwoods that lie to the west of it is in a large lay-by at the northern end of the Mound Causeway – the route taken by the main road. This gives a good vantage over the Mound Pool, used by many kinds of wading birds, including greenshank and redshank on passage in spring and autumn, by fishing ospreys, wintering pink-footed geese and other wildfowl throughout the year.

The alder swamp beyond the pool stems in large measure from the building of the causeway. Work on this began in 1814, and was eventually completed in 1816 under the guidance of the famous engineer, Thomas Telford. Sluice gates installed in the causeway to stop the flood tide flowing further upstream along

PINE MARTEN

Once pushed to near extinction in Scotland through persecution in the 19th and 20th centuries, pine martens are on the rebound. Now reoccupying some of their old woodland haunts, they are nowhere numerous. Martens have huge ranges and can live fairly solitary lives. Relatives, such as the beech marten and sable, are part of the boreal fauna in forests east of the Pacific.

SCOTLAND'S NATURE AND WILDLIFE

CURLEW

The curlew should be instantly recognisable from its very long, down-curved beak. If it calls, saying its 'curlew' name in rich flutey tones, the identification is also clear. Males use special song flights – rising steeply above moors and rough pasture then gliding down with bubbling calls.

the Fleet are still in place. Looking down above them, you might catch a glimpse of a migrating sea trout pressing home to reach its spawning beds.

There are two good places to get views across the main part of the estuary within the National Nature Reserve and the narrows where the Fleet joins the sea. One is beside a car park alongside the southern shore of the estuary, beside a minor road that runs the length of this enclosed basin and close to the unstable ruins of Skelbo Castle. From here, you can see big areas of mud, sand and musselbeds exposed at low tide – probing and sifting grounds for oystercatcher, redshank and shelduck in summer, and for curlew, bar-tailed godwits and knot in winter.

Redshank breed in small numbers along the coast here, their piping calls very much part of the summer scene. Loch Fleet is an important stop-over and roosting area for pink-footed geese, both when flocks head north enroute to Iceland in late April and early May and when the return passage happens in September and October. There is also a big influx of hundreds of greylag geese from Iceland in late August – a handful of greylag geese breed near the Mound.

Other wintering wildfowl include a thousand or more wigeon, whose whistles ring across the tidal flats, hundreds of teals and mallards and large flocks of eiders. Dozens of eiders breed in the reserve, mainly around the loch shore. Their ranks are swelled by birds from other areas in the moulting period – which for males starts in summer. Until the early 1980s, Loch Fleet and the nearby coast was also the winter heartland of many thousands of long-tailed ducks. You can still see long-tailed ducks here, especially in the narrows, but often in ones and twos rather than large gangs.

The other good starting point for viewing and exploring the Loch Fleet fringe is beside the cluster of houses at Littleferry, on the north shore of the Firth, which is accessible down a minor road past Golspie golf course. From a car park with interpretation boards, you can walk to the loch mouth – getting close views of eiders and gulls in the channel on most days – and along the coastal grassland or 'links', where autumn gentian grows abundantly in some places.

NORTHERN HIGHLANDS

In the Balblair pinewood, just to the south of the golf course and accessible along a path off the road to Littleferry, there is a choice range of pinewood flora, including the largest population of St Olav's candlesticks (or one-flowered wintergreen) in the country and numerous spikes of creeping lady's tresses orchid.

Scottish crossbills breed in the woods, but their identification is complicated outside the summer months by visiting common crossbills. Chaffinches and wrens are common breeders, plus small numbers of redstarts. Buzzard and sparrowhawk nest locally. Occasional otters hunt the burn gullies and loch margins, but the most obvious mammals are the common seals that haul out on mudbanks in the estuary, or ride the currents in the narrows.

The 'Flow Country' peatlands that form the huge, waterlogged core of Caithness and Sutherland are the finest bogland of their kind on the planet. This area gained notoriety in the 1980s from the inappropriate planting of conifer blocks out on the deep peat, to the detriment of the choice mix of breeding birds and other bog wildlife. Now, the Flows are gaining fame again for their natural assets and for the far-sighted work to undo some of the damage caused by the tax-break forestry schemes of the late-twentieth century.

FORSINARD

The RSPB is at the forefront of this work to restore damaged bogland and to cherish and understand what remains intact. To experience some of the wildlife and scenery and learn more about what is now recognised as a world-class wildlife site, the RSPB's Forsinard reserve is the best stopping place. A visitor centre in the station at the village of Forsinard (accessible by train from Inverness to Wick and Thurso, and by the A897 single track road) is open from April to October. A train journey along the line to and from Forsinard is itself a great way to get an impression of the sheer scale of these peat-rich flatlands, arguably one of the strangest landscapes in Scotland.

From the Forsinard Centre, a 1.5 kilometre flagstone path leads through a cluster of dubh lochans – Gaelic for 'black pools' – set in the wider bogland, rich in water-retaining Sphagnum mosses. The breeding birds at

> **BUZZARD**
> *(Buteo buteo)*
>
> It's the most widespread medium-sized bird of prey across Scotland and, at some angles, can look quite large. So it's not too surprising that many visitors to uplands and islands who think they've seen an eagle have actually had an eyeful of buzzard.
>
> Things to watch for (in case you're now worried) are the roundness of buzzard wings – eagle wings look much more rectangular in comparison – and size, if you can gauge it. A crow trying to chase a buzzard won't look that small beside it, but will seem fairly puny alongside a golden eagle and even smaller beside a sea eagle.
>
> Buzzards can nest in many different situations. Trees are popular, but they can also use cliff ledges or even nest on the ground. Listen too for their far-carrying calls and look for the soaring flights they use to advertise territories in early spring.

Birdsfoot Trefoil

SCOTLAND'S NATURE AND WILDLIFE

RED GROUSE
(Lagopus lagopus)

No other bird in the world makes such heavy use of heather. It's both food and home for the red grouse. So no wonder the bird is so linked to Scotland – as symbolic of the uplands as the thistle is of the wider nation.

Red grouse are territorial, with males defending a patch of heathland and hoping to woo a single mate. There's a flurry of territorial action in autumn, as males make 'song' flights (strange music to human ears) and lay claim to their native heath. Territories are often abandoned in winter, when grouse group together in coveys, but spring brings a new flush of action.

The upshot of all of this is, if you want to see grouse easily, both the autumn and spring are good times. And you don't need to visit a large grouse moor to get lucky. Red grouse can breed on much smaller heathy patches, even among the bogs of the west and north. So don't be put off by the 'go-back' call – just home-in and appreciate the icon.

DID YOU KNOW?

Only female Scottish biting midges feed on blood. A female is ready for a blood meal within 24 hours of emerging as a winged adult, and mates one to two days later.

Forsinard include many of the species for which the wider Flow Country is now famous including black-throated diver, common scoter, wigeon, hen harrier, golden plover, dunlin and greenshank. Merlins (sometimes viewable by CCTV link to the nest on the reserve) and buzzards also hunt the area, and curlews, lapwing and oystercatchers (as well as golden plover and dunlin) feed and breed near the river.

The insect fauna of the Flows is rich, including rare water beetles. However, dragonflies such as black darter and common hawker, and damselflies, such as common blue, are easier to see and identify, as is the large emperor moth. Both butterflies and the emperor moths can be prey for the mossland merlins. Aside from the many kinds of bog mosses, the frothy flowers of bogbean grace some pools, with the weirder-looking bladderworts setting traps for swimming insects underwater. For these, and for the stickily glistening sundews on the bogs, trapped insects give a mineral boost in a land where such plant food is scarce. Otters hunt the bog for frogs and newts, or look for small fish and other food along the river. The road from Forsinard to Helmsdale is also a good place from which to see herds of red deer in spring.

DUNNET BAY

At Dunnet Bay, beside the village of the same name along the A836 between Thurso and John o'Groats, a great sweep of sandy bay is backed by dunes, gripped by tough marram grass. Inland is the grassland (on blown sand) of the Dunnet Links National Nature Reserve. This is a great area for flowering plants, including different species of orchids and that gem of the Caithness and Orkney grasslands and heaths – the Scots primrose. Meadow brown, common blue and dark green fritillary butterflies feed some of the flowering plants.

Out at Dunnet Head – the northernmost point on the Scottish mainland – the pale blue flowers of spring squill give a pastel wash to the clifftop sward in early summer. Roseroot, Scots lovage and alpine saw-wort grow between the cliffs and there is a seabird colony (with puffins) below the lighthouse. Views from here stretch south over the peatlands, north over to Orkney and west along the rest of the north mainland. There is information on local wildlife in a small visitor centre and ranger base housed beside the Dunnet Bay caravan site, from where guided

NORTHERN HIGHLANDS

walks are led out to the headland and into the National Nature Reserve.

DURNESS

At the fringes of Balnakeil Bay, off the A838 by Durness near Cape Wrath, there are some impressive little plants in the low grassland fringing the coast between Balnakeil and Faraid Head, where there is a puffin colony. Several species more often found in lime-rich areas of Scottish mountains grow near sea level here, benefiting from the lime in blown shell sand and able to cope with exposure to the ferocity of wind and salt spray. These include mountain avens, alpine bistort, yellow saxifrage and hoary whitlow grass. Scots primrose is another bonny bloom in parts of the Durness summer turf.

HANDA ISLAND

Accessible from mid-April to mid-September by ferries that run to and fro across the narrow sound at Tarbet (signed down a minor road off the A894, roughly 5 kilometres north of Scourie) Handa Island (SWT) is the finest seabird colony in the whole of the north mainland. More guillemots breed here than anywhere else in Britain and Ireland – in excess of 100,000 birds, at the last count, are packed shoulder-to-shoulder on ledges along the Torridonian sandstone cliffs and on the offshore stacks. Finest of these is the Great Stack, thronged with guillemots, razorbills and kittiwakes and with a small colony of puffins at the top. All these are visible at fairly close range from across a chasm separating the stack from the main island. In recent years, puffins have begun to spread on the Handa mainland, responding to the relaxation of predation pressure on eggs and young after the removal of brown rats from the island in the late 1990s.

Day visitors to Handa are restricted to a path and boardwalk on journeys across and around the island. But since the route takes you through some excellent boggy moorland – busy with breeding great skuas and Arctic skuas in summer and with excellent views back to the hills and coast of the north-west mainland – this is a boon on a short trip, rather than a hardship.

Heath-spotted orchids, lousewort and butterwort grow among the ling and bog

HANDA ISLAND

Large sea cliffs close to good fishing grounds, such as these at the Minch side of Handa Island in Sutherland, can make excellent platforms for breeding seabirds. Characteristic cliff-breeding seabirds in Scotland include guillemot, razorbill and fulmar.

SCOTLAND'S NATURE AND WILDLIFE

WILDCAT
(Felis sylvestris)

Some call it the 'Scottish tiger', but this thick-coated, stripey-tailed cat once lived far beyond the Scottish border. Loss of the woodlands that are its home of choice, hunting for its fur and persecution as an unwelcome predator around human settlements pushed it off the map in England and Wales.

By the late 1800s, Scotland was the only place where Britain's one native feline still had a claw-hold. Now it's expanded its range again, helped by the cover of forestry plantations. But the southern edge of the Highlands is around the limit of its spread.

Solitary by nature, this is one of the hardest Scottish mammals to see. So look instead for its signs, especially droppings stuffed with bird and small mammal remains away from where domestic cats usually go. Wildcats do interbreed with domestics, and look a bit like big, blunt-tailed tabbies themselves. But there are still enough differences to convince scientists that the real McCat is alive and out there, prowling the Highland woods.

WILDCAT
The Scottish wildcat is Britain's only remaining native cat; (lynx were also part of the Scottish fauna beyond the last Ice Age). Long guard hairs can give the wildcat a fairly fluffy appearance and the tail is short and has thick, dark rings. Wildcats prefer to stay well clear of people and are among the hardest Scottish animals to see in the wild.

mosses near the boardwalk. Along the cliffs, scurvy grass, roseroot and sea campion (all boosted by the rain of bird droppings) can be lush in sheltered gullies, and Scots lovage pokes through the turf in places. Out west, over the sea beyond the cliffs, great seabird flocks throng the water in summer, and it is always worth checking for signs of sea mammals, especially the small dorsal fin and large back of a passing minke whale, the sleek forms of white-beaked dolphins or the big heads of grey seals breaking the surface.

Few main roads run through Caithness and Sutherland. All of them are scenic, whether crossing the flatlands of deep peat country, running along the northern coast between John o'Groats and Durness, or past isolated mountains and down the Atlantic coast. Cycling is one of the best ways to appreciate the changes of view, air and wildlife, not least because you can listen to the bird sounds around you. If you're driving, remember that the single track roads that are common here need extra consideration over what might be approaching and in having the courtesy to use passing places to allow others to overtake.

That said, travel in this part of Scotland can be more relaxed than just about anywhere else in the country. Good places to stop and enjoy the wildlife are many, in addition to those already described here. But a brief mention of some others may sprinkle possibilities in mind for travellers in the north mainland.

KNOCKAN CLIFF

At Knockan Cliff (SNH) (part of the Inverpolly National Nature Reserve), beside the A835, 24 kilometres north of Ullapool, a visitor centre gives an insight into the geology of the area. Deciphering the meaning of the 'MoineThrust' – the major feature that runs down near the coast here – was an important step in the development of geology (part of it has to do with collision of continents, in case you're wondering). Rocks apart, there is plenty of botanical interest here, thanks to lime-rich outcrops on the cliffs. Plants along the trail that runs from the Knockan Centre include alpine bistort, alpine lady's mantle, yellow saxifrage, mountain avens, stone bramble and the lovely autumn gentian, with the sparky green of tiny crowberry leaves as a contrast to floral displays. This is also golden eagle country, so it can be worth looking up from time to time to check the sky for broad-winged silhouettes.

NORTHERN HIGHLANDS

SCOTLAND'S NATURE AND WILDLIFE

Hebrides

The north-to-south reach of the Hebrides is enormous, forming a broken, multi-level, beautiful wall to the west of much of the rest of Scotland. Only the North Isles and the Borders sit clear of this Hebridean fringe (although Orkney has Hebridean outliers far out from its Atlantic side).

The southern tip is at the Mull of Oa on Islay, on a parallel with central Ayrshire around Irvine and Kilmarnock, but far closer to the hills of Antrim in Northern Ireland than to the farmlands of Kyle. From here, the Butt of Lewis (across the Minch from the stretch of north-west coast that leads to Cape Wrath) is more than 330 kilometres distant. Stretch the Hebridean definition further and you can include North Rona (that green, isolated outlier to the north of Lewis) and neighbouring Sula Sgeir, and there's at least a 400 kilometre span – as far as from Cape Wrath to Northumberland.

Manx Shearwaters

Add to this geographical spread the variety of islands, from tiny and low-lying to huge and mountainous, and the true scale of the Hebrides becomes apparent. A basic division between Inner and Outer Hebrides recognises two principal clusters within the bigger picture, though (as always with groups of islands) once you start to explore from sea or land, the diversity of scene at much smaller scales suggests a wealth of other ways of understanding the Hebrides.

Lewissian gneiss, the oldest type of rock in Britain, makes up much of the Outer Hebrides, where mountain ground is mostly confined to the southern part of Lewis, West Harris and the eastern side of the Uists. Heather is very widespread inland on these isles, giving feeding opportunities for birds of prey such as merlin, and there are large areas of blanket bog, used by golden plover and other breeding waders.

Top billing for wildlife enthusiasts in both the Outer Hebrides and Tiree and Coll in the Inner Hebrides should go to the 'machair' systems of flower-rich grassland on wind-blown shell sand. The finest machair in the world is here, with an array of clovers, vetches, daisies, buttercups, cranesbills and more that feeds many kinds of insects and where wading birds can breed at some of the highest densities in Europe.

The Inner Hebrides are generally more mountainous than the outer isles, in part a legacy of volcanic activity linked to the birth of the Atlantic tens of millions of years ago. As on the outer islands, small scale, low intensity agriculture, including crofting, has both nurtured and maintained a variety of wildlife now largely absent from farmland on the Scottish mainland.

The icon of the wildlife that benefits from Hebridean farming methods is the corncrake, but there are many other species that gain, such as the pearl-bordered fritillary butterfly and chough on Islay, orchids on Eigg and bees on Tiree. Even the much overlooked starling, now struggling in many a mainland place, still thrives on the islands. So travel here and it's more than just the wild coasts that will delight.

SCOTLAND'S NATURE AND WILDLIFE

CORNCRAKE
(Crex crex)

It's got something of the look of a sleek free-range chicken, and can certainly be a match for any early-crowing cockerel through the insistence of its far-carrying calls. A hundred years ago and more, its distinctive sound was a feature of many rural areas, even figuring in the chorus of an Ayrshire-based song.

Even more amazing to modern ears is Lord Cockburn's account of the break-up of fields near Edinburgh in the early nineteenth century, in which he describes how: 'I have stood in Queen Street, or the opening at the north-west corner of Charlotte Square, and listened to the ceaseless rural corn-craiks, nestling happily in the dewy grass.'

Now the corncrake has all but gone from the mainland, although a few still come to Caithness and Sutherland. Long-term shifts in farming practices – especially the mechanised mowing of hay and silage and the development of early maturing grass types, have been the main cause of corncrake decline.

Thanks to low-intensity farming methods in crofting areas and on some other small farms, coupled with corncrake-friendly mowing methods (cutting from the centre of the fields outwards) the Hebrides and Orkney are now European strongholds for the species. It's a great advert for the merits of small-scale agriculture, whatever your view on the sound-track.

Flying straight as a gannet's dive, some 330 kilometres separate the Butt of Lewis at the north end of Lewis, from the Mull of Oa at the south end of Islay. That's more than the distance from Glasgow to Cape Wrath, or Dumfries to Inverness. So it's no great surprise that the many islands of the Hebrides hold a great deal of wildlife, scenic and social variety in their wave-washed bonds.

Even a simple measure like the one given above understates the diversity, for beyond the main island groups lie the Hebridean outliers. Beyond all of these again is the rocky lump of Rockall, the last outpost of British land, far out in the Atlantic and so exposed to its forces that huge waves can cover the whole thing.

Rockall aside (which few other than visiting eco-warriors, RAF pilots on reconnaissance missions and deep-water fishermen ever see), the Hebrides hold so much in the way of natural beauty, clean water and relatively undisturbed wildlife as to be a must-see. Like most parts of Scotland, the weather can sometimes be disappointing, but if you are prepared to sit-out the worst of it, the Hebrides can deliver the best in huge measure. It's no exaggeration to say that the quality of light here can be astonishing. When the sun bursts through after a shower, places from Gigha to Iona, to Berneray and beyond seem truly blessed. Small wonder that so many early Celtic monks reckoned that hermithood on a chunk of the Hebrides gave a fast track to communing with the power behind Creation.

A good practical step you can take to get a first-hand impression of the Hebridean wilds is to get a good map of the area you're keen to explore. This advice is true for the whole of Scotland, but in the Hebrides, where wee strips of shell sand beach can be tucked out of wider sight beyond a lump of headland, where the burn and its waterfall could be muffled by a screen of moorland, and where tracks, let alone roads, can be very scarce, a decent map is a must.

The basic division in these isles is between the Outer and Inner Hebrides, the waters of the Minches (Little and North) giving the split between the two. Beyond that, there are several groups of large islands which form something of a unity in terms of where they sit

HEBRIDES

in the sea. Islay, Jura, Colonsay and Oronsay to the south; Tiree, Coll and Mull; the Small Isles and Skye; the Uists and Barra; Lewis and Harris. But don't be fooled by the simple geography of map groupings at this scale. Each of the separate isles in these groups (or not separate at all, in the case of Lewis and Harris, or the Uists) is very different in character from its neighbours. So an exploration of one gives little in the way of insight into another, even a fairly close neighbour.

A good area to bring home the sheer scale and diversity of these isles is around the Small Isles and Skye. Rum, Eigg, Muck and Canna: collectively this bunch of names makes a strange-sounding mix, but together they hold some excellent wildlife.

EIGG

Perhaps the best known of this group in recent years is Eigg (Isle of Eigg Heritage Trust, the Highland Council, SWT). The island made world news when the islanders, working in partnership with the regional government and the Scottish Wildlife Trust, purchased it after a high profile fund raising campaign. Central to that campaign was the idea that the natural heritage of Eigg was a key asset for the people living here,

and that a healthy community could nurture the island's wildlife in ways that would benefit all. Years on, the sense of optimism engendered by that reform of land ownership in the 1990s is still here, and places on the island – especially the woodlands – have benefited from community involvement.

Access to Eigg is by ferry from the fishing port of Mallaig at the end of the A830 'Road to the Isles' (all year round) or from Arisaig during the summer. A scenic rail route runs along to both these places from Fort William. Once ashore, there are several options for walking (pretty much the only transport available to visitors). The area around the bay at Kildonan, close to the pier, has tidal muds sifted by shelduck and waders and used from time to time by otters.

Close behind, mixed woodlands have a variety of trees and ground flora, including ramsons and wood avens. As everywhere in these isles and in the west mainland, tree stems and branches are

CORNCRAKE

The sound of a corncrake, like this one calling in the Outer Hebrides in May, used to be common in Scottish farmland – even within earshot of central Edinburgh. Now the bulk of the population lives in the Hebrides, where the birds benefit from the low-intensity cultivation of in-bye land of crofting townships.

SCOTLAND'S NATURE AND WILDLIFE

COMMON SEAL

Also known as the harbour seal, you can tell a common seal apart from its larger relative – the grey seal – by the arrangement of its nostrils. Common seals have V-shaped nostrils and short muzzles. Grey seal nostrils are parallel slits and their heads tend to be longer – although take care when trying to identify short-headed youngsters of both species.

often plastered with so much lichen and moss that you can't see the wood beneath for the plants that cling to it. Eigg is a good place for birds of prey, with the buzzards that breed in the trees between Galmisdale and Kildonan usually the most obvious.

For people keen on a hike, the walk up the Sgurr of Eigg (the island's most prominent landmark) gives an opportunity to see some striking columnar basalt rock formations, views to surrounding islands and perhaps the chance
of an eagle soaring in the distance. The Sgurr is the largest lump of exposed pitchstone (a volcanic outpouring) in Europe, and its rocks can shelter a number of plants.

The croftlands of Cleadale snuggle up to the gentle curve of Laig Bay in the north-west of the island. In the early summer, the growth of orchids along the roadside here and in low-lying meadows can be superb, with fragrant, northern marsh and butterfly orchids and others, including the occasional frog orchid. The old woods that skirt the lower slopes of Beinn Bhuide (eastern rampart to Cleadale) are thick with hazel and can shelter primroses, bluebells, wood sorrel, wood anemone and ramsons. At the edge of the crags above there is a small colony of manx shearwaters (tiny in comparison to the mega-colony in Rum, but enough to add some good howls to the night air here).

At Camus Sgotaig (the Singing

Sands) just beyond Cleadale, the small beach is well known for its covering of squeaky quartz grains. Shimmy your shoes here and you can play a tune as you scan the shore for signs of otters.

RUM

The waters of the Sound between here and the Rum National Nature Reserve (SNH) can be a great place for roving bands of common dolphins in mid-to-late summer, the time when minke whales also like to feed and travel around these islands. Rum is, at first glance, a great fortress of a place (some reckon that its crags were an inspiration for Tolkien's creation of Mordor). A cluster of peaks, often cloud-swept, takes up most of the southern third of the island.

The usual access point to Rum – Loch Scresort and the tiny scatter of houses at Kinloch – is much softer in aspect, the sharp edges smoothed by planted woods, both native and exotic. This is a good place to guddle among shallow sea loch seaweeds, such as egg wrack, at the low tide and watch for red-throated divers out in the sheltered water. Stones near the shore can be patterned with rock-hugging lichens such as map lichens, and the woods have a variety of small breeding birds (including chaffinch, wren, robin, dunnock, tits and goldcrest).

Out on the more open ground beyond Kinloch Castle (a fading monument to Edwardian excess), ravens tumble between crags and over moorland used by moths like emperor and northern eggar.

A herd of ponies roams the hills, beyond major native woodland restoration areas where young Scots pine, birch, rowan, oak, alder and other trees are gradually transforming the slopes of Kinloch Glen and the promontories beyond.

The red deer on Rum belong to what must be the most intensively studied population of these animals in the world. Over many decades, scientists have built up an intimate picture of the life of this – the largest British land mammal – in one of its strongholds. One of Rum's other claims to fame is as the launch-pad for reintroduction of the white-tailed eagle, beginning with the rearing of young Norwegian sea eagles on the island in 1975. So the island is still a good place to scan the skies for a glimpse of a flying sea eagle, likened by some to a

---

LAPWING
(Vanellus vanellus)

This is a bird with many names, including 'green plover', 'peesie', 'teuchit' and 'peewit' – the last perhaps the most evocative of its call. When several of these glossy-winged waders are nesting in a field, there's no mistaking that high-pitched rise and fall of voice.

The aerial antics match the sound. In courtship, a displaying lapwing rises from the ground, makes some sudden swerves and swoops, then soars up before twisting and plunging down to the ground again. Add in some wilder variations of the usual call, and it's a bravura piece of stunt flying and soundtrack.

Lapwings nest on the ground, mostly in spring-sown crops and in grassland. Some also nest on damp or abandoned pastures, grazed moorland and hayfield, with the flower-rich machair grasslands of the Uists and Benbecula having a strong population. Even an old cowpat can be put to good use as a shelter for the clutch of four eggs!

In Scotland, the main farmland areas occupied by them are in the Borders, Lothians, Tayside and the north-east lowlands. Changing farming practices have led to a decline in numbers in recent decades.

DID YOU KNOW?

Glasswort, a strange-looking but attractive saltmarsh plant, contains sodium salts that were once useful in glass manufacture (hence its name). It also puts on a show of autumn colour, shifting from yellow-greens to reds as the weather chills.

SCOTLAND'S NATURE AND WILDLIFE

> **GREAT YELLOW BUMBLE-BEE**
> *(Bombus distinguendus)*
>
> With their mass of summer-flowering plants, the machair grasslands of the Hebrides are a nectar-and pollen-rich haven for many kinds of butterflies and bees. Among these is the great yellow bumble-bee, a rare bee for which machair is now a stronghold.
>
> Bumble-bees tend to have preferences for different kinds of flowers, based on the length of their own tongue. The great yellow bumble-bee has a long tongue, and so it likes long-tubed flowers where it can get access to nectar that some other species can't reach.
>
> Ideal conditions for it are where an area of machair has been grazed in winter, but not in spring and summer when the livestock could eat away vegetation protecting underground nests and prevent plants from flowering. Winter-grazed machair with good stands of red clover and common knapweed seems to suit the great yellow, but even there, it's thin on the ground, with only one or two nests per square kilometre.

'flying barn door' because of the sheer size of its wings.

Best known of Rum's other breeding birds is the manx shearwater. Thousands breed high on the mountain slopes, nesting in burrows. But the best chance of seeing them for most visitors is when flocks gather offshore in the evening before swarming in to the mountain fastnesses.

CANNA

To get good views of a larger variety of seabirds in the small Isles, Canna (NTS) is the best of the bunch. Cliff-girt for much of its rim (though with tranquil, low-lying sweeps of tidal mudflats and gentle shore between the harbour area and the neighbouring island of Sanday), Canna has breeding puffins, razorbills, guillemots, tysties, kittiwakes and common terns, plus its own slice of the Small Isles shearwater action. Mixed woodlands near the harbour hold speckled wood butterflies.

MUCK

The tiny island of Muck, southernmost of the group, may take its name from the Gaelic for harbour porpoises 'MucMara', and the waters around it are still a good area to scan for these and other cetaceans, including minke whales. The Muck breeding bird community also includes a good range of seabirds (similar to Canna, but in smaller numbers), lots of nesting eider ducks and oystercatchers and a group of breeding greylag geese on Horse Island.

Insects are many and varied here, including belted beauty moth (whose caterpillars munch the leaves of yellow flags), transparent burnet moths on wild thyme and darter dragonflies over lochans. Some alpine plants grow fairly close to sea level on Muck (away from sheep bite), including dwarf juniper, crowberry, roseroot, mountain catspaw and pyramidal bugle.

SKYE

North beyond the Small Isles sits Skye, famed for the 'Far Cuillins' of its mountainous south and now reachable by a controversial (and pricey) toll bridge overlooking the old ferry route from Kyle of Lochalsh and Kyleakin. At more than 165,000 hectares, Skye is a Hebridean giant. Add to the fact that it is also big on major peninsulas – Sleat in the south, the trident prongs of Minginish, Waternish and Trotternish to the north

> **DID YOU KNOW?**
>
> *Oakwoods in the West Highlands are a type of temperate rainforest, with an amazing variety and abundance of mosses and liverworts (which rely on water to reproduce) and lush growth of lichens and ferns on the trees.*

– and the length of coast starts to get mind-boggling.

EILEAN BAN AND KYLERHEA

Close to the Skye bridge itself, Eilean Ban (Eilean Ban Trust) – the White Island – and its associated shore-based visitor centre in Kyleakin are great places to learn more about the naturalist and writer, Gavin Maxwell, and about otters, the creatures which were a focus for so much passion and creative zeal in his life and work. At Kylerhea (FC) at the eastern end of a small steep road through Glen Arroch (off the A850, about 6 kilometres beyond Kyleakin) an 'Otter Haven' has a car park with views across the Kylerhea narrows. A nearby viewing hide, open all year in daylight hours, offers a chance to see otters in action.

SCONSER, TORRIN AND STRATHAIRD

Straddling Skye in a saddle from Sligachan south to the tip of the Elgol peninsula is a major chunk of mountain ground and its crofted fringes, now under the care of the John Muir Trust. This includes the estates of Sconser, Torrin and Strathaird. Much of the Red Cuillin is within the Sconser ground, where dwarf juniper grows up to more than 800 metres above sea level. Torrin, accessible along the A881 south-west from Broadford, is in something of a geological layer cake, with granite, limestone, old Jurassic sediments and other rock lineages running through it and down to the shores of Loch Slapin.

This variety is reflected in the range of different habitats around the crofting township. Limestone grassland, acid heath and moorland, broadleaved woodland, freshwater loch, salt marsh and sandy and rocky shores are all here. Globeflowers can make a good show in summer, and some Arctic-alpine plants grow close to the road near the innermost end of the sea loch. Beyond, Bla Bheinn in the adjacent Strathaird ground (overlooking the sublimely situated Loch na Creitheach) has limestone cliffs in Coire Uaigneach with rich growths of tall flowering plants. From a path leading just north of the forestry plantations beside the A881 across the loch from Torrin township, the near-vertical damp limestone faces are visible up in the corrie. Here, yellow saxifrage can form almost pure banks together with the much earlier-flowering purple saxifrage, alpine meadow rue and a salmon-pink coloured moss. Roseroot, alpine saw-wort (which looks like a spineless thistle) and globeflower are among the other plants that thrive in ungrazed areas here.

SEA EAGLE

The sea eagle is a massive bird – big beak, big wings, big legs – that can make a golden eagle look small in comparison. But this is a very different bird, more closely related to vultures than to the golden eagle. It can snatch fish from the surface or just under it and eat carrion and mammals.

SCOTLAND'S NATURE AND WILDLIFE

BARNACLE GEESE

Two different groups of barnacle geese come to Scotland to spend the autumn and winter here. Along parts of the west coast and islands, including Islay, the barnacle geese come from Greenland. The entire breeding population from Spitsbergen (Svalbard) in the high Arctic visits the inner Solway Firth each year.

An outcrop of Durness limestone gives botanical zing to the Suardal area, south of Broadford and near the A881. The limestone here forms both small cliffs and large areas of limestone pavement. Cleft by fissures that run through its smoothed, flat surfaces, limestone pavement is very scarce in Scotland. It supports some excellent plants, including abundant mountain avens with its five-petalled white flowers. Woodland plants such as sanicle, common twayblade and dark red helleborine grow in deeper fissures.

The far-famed Cuillins are fairly sparse on plant cover at their higher levels. The best area for mountain vegetation is away to the north of them, along the Trotternish ridge – a massive feature that dominates the scene inland from the A855 for most of the way between north of Portree to Flodigarry. Access to sample part of this can be gained from the unclassified road that runs up and over the high spine of the peninsula between the Staffin area on the east side and Uig on the west. From a car park by a cemetery you can walk among the rocky peaks of the Quirang. Grasslands here can be rich in alpine lady's mantle. Yellow saxifrage is another feature of Trotternish, with the possibility of a scattering of choice plants such as mossy cyphel and moonwort. Summit areas along the ridge include large stretches of woolly fringe moss and stiff sedge heath – the sort of plant cover you might otherwise see more commonly in the high Cairngorms. Ravens and buzzards can add year round aerial action to the area, with a sprinkling of wheatears and meadow pipits in summer.

ISLAY

Within the Inner Hebrides, some other islands are a focus for visiting naturalists. Islay (accessible by ferry from North Kennacraig to Port Ellen or Port Askaig, or by air from Glasgow) is a favourite destination for many. Lush and wooded in places (helped by the Atlantic-Drift-boosted climate), but with everything from huge beaches, big bogs and moors, breezy headlands and craggy tops, Islay has some greatly contrasting places within its 61,000-hectare-and-then-some spread.

Foremost in the minds of many with a love of wildlife is Islay's position as the best single island for number and variety of breeding birds, with more than 100 recorded. Among the breeders is the chough, that electric-voiced, red-legged, curve-beaked tumbler of the crow family, now reduced to a pale shadow of its former distribution in Britain.

RINNS

Islay is a great place to see choughs, especially in and around old buildings on the Rinns peninsula and on its west side at the major dune systems at Machir Bay (beside Kilchoman) and Ardnave, at the mouth of Loch Gruinart. Such is the significance of the Rinns for wildlife that the bulk of it has been included within a network of Sites of Special Scientific Interest. One way to sample some of the Rinns scene is to travel from Port Charlotte along the A847 to Portnahaven, then north in a loop to return to Portnahaven by an unclassified road via Kilchiaran. On the way, you could have a chance of seeing hen harrier and short-eared owl near forested areas, hear corncrakes and see choughs in fields, black guillemots offshore on the west side (with Kittiwakes around the Frenchman's Rocks off Portnahaven – a prime sea-watching locality) and greenland white-fronted geese in winter.

LOCH GRUINART

The prime spot for goose watching is at the RSPB's Loch Gruinart reserve. The reserve is about 5 kilometres from Bridgend, signed from the A847 and along a minor road that runs to Gruinart, near the head of the loch, or along the B8017. Around 30,000 barnacle geese can arrive on Islay each autumn, with the first arrivals in late September and early October. Together with thousands of Greenland white-fronts, these birds make particular use of the fields and foreshore around both Loch Gruinart and Loch Indaal, just to the south.

One advantage of the fairly flat fields here is that you can use a car as a hide to birdwatch at different places along the roads near both lochs. A live video

REGIONAL HIGHLIGHT: LOCH GRUINART, ISLAY

DESIGNATION:
RSPB Reserve.

LANDSCAPE:
Loch with sandflats.

HIGHLIGHTS:
A host of wildfowl and waders including barnacle geese, Greenland white-fronts, dunlin, scaup, eiders and whooper and mute swans.

BEST TIME:
Waders, hen harriers and corncrakes in the spring and summer; white-fronted geese, ducks and waders during the winter.

FACILITIES:
Visitor centre (open all year round) with an exhibition and live video link; car park, picnic area and toilet.

ADMISSION:
Free.

DIRECTIONS:
N side of Islay, off A848 on B8017.

CONTACT:
Tel: 01496 850505   www.rspb.org.uk

link to the visitor centre at the Loch Gruinart reserve gives close-ups of the flock action.

In spring, the road close to the shore also gives great opportunities for seeing other wildfowl and waders in the tidal sandflats and shallow water at the head of the loch. Curlew, oystercatcher, bar-tailed godwit and dunlin feed here in their hundreds, plus a scattering of other waders, and one of the largest flocks of scaup in Britain winters offshore. Also on site are slavonian grebes, divers, large flocks of eiders and other ducks, and whooper and mute swans.

JURA, MULL AND THE TRESHNISH ISLANDS

Nearby Jura is the wildest of the inner isles. It's a place of red deer, high peaks (the 'Paps'), adders and huge, relatively untravelled shores. Snuggling against the tail end of Morvern and not so far from the mainland at Oban (and accessible by ferry from both Oban and Lochaline), Mull and its surrounds have many wildlife-watching opportunities both on its mainland and offshore. The Treshnish Islands, accessible by day trip from Ulva Ferry at the west of Mull, hold some of the best seabird colonies in the Inner Hebrides, including some of the most easily viewed puffins anywhere in Scotland, on Lunga. Shags, kittiwakes, guillemots, tysties, razorbill, herring and greater black-backed gulls are among the other seabirds on this cluster of islands. These waters are also well used by minke whales and porpoises, with trips available to watch them and other cetaceans through the Hebridean Whale and Dolphin Trust.

Mull has a good population of otters along its several hundred kilometres of coastline, with the shores of Loch na Keal in the west and Loch Spelve in the south well worth a close look. Inland there are herds of red deer, plus fallow deer in the woodlands around Knock and Gruline and a variety of birds of prey including both golden and white-tailed eagles. Other breeding birds of prey include widespread buzzard, sparrowhawk, hen harrier, kestrel, merlin and peregrine.

CROTAL

More than forty different kinds of lichen were once used in Scotland to make dyes, especially for wool. Lichens that encrusted rocks were particularly favoured. Several different species were given variations on the name 'crotal' in Gaelic – whether unadorned or with adjectival colour – such as *crotal buidh* for *Parmelia parietina* (the yellow wall lichen) or *crotal geal* for *Lecanora pallescens* (white crotal).

Readily available, the lichens could also be soaked in another easily obtained substance – urine – to prepare them before boiling with wool hanks or whole fleeces. It was also thought courteous for island guests to do their bit for the 'pee-tub' contents before making their way home. Different lichens scraped from stones could be used after such treatment to yield various scarlet, red, brown and yellow colours.

Robert Atkinson's description of Finlay McQueen (a famous St Kilda cragsman) and Mrs Gillies (another native islander) gathering crotal on a brief summer visit to their old home, several years after evacuation of the village on Hirta, is particularly striking: 'He and Mrs Gillies were both nearer 80 than 70,' says Atkinson, 'they climbed 1000 feet from the village, spent all day at the crotal, descended and thought nothing of it.' Seems they knew the recipe for more than just dyestuffs, these old-timers.

HEBRIDES

TIRE AND COLL

Out to the west of Mull, the islands of Tiree and Coll (accessible from Oban and Mull) hold a wealth of interesting flora and breeding birds. Tiree has the largest and most varied expanse of machair – that flower-rich grassland on windblown sand at the edge of the Atlantic fringe of Ireland and Scotland, beyond the Outer Hebrides. A long history of seasonal grazing here, coupled with an absence of rabbits, has added to the machair's interest. To travel in June and July along the roads through the flatlands that cover much of the island is to encounter a proverbial sea of flowers in the croft grazings alongside, with swathes of daisies, clovers and buttercups setting some of the colour notes. Around the old airfield at The Reef, many waders breed, including ringed plover and redshank.

Coll, in contrast, is rockier, with farmed fields set among stony outcrops and beyond huge dunes. The island is something of a powerhouse for corncrakes, especially in ground managed as an RSPB reserve, where breeding numbers have been increasing. Among the big dunes, a floral highlight is bloody cranesbill, whose wine-soaked tints splash crimson against the pale sands.

HARRIS

Harris is part of the same large island (the Long Island) as Lewis, but utterly different in character. It majors on bare rock and hills, wrinkled and heaved in ancient corrugations (just look at the contours on an Ordnance Survey map and you'll get the picture). Among the glories of Harris – aside from the glints of light on grey stone, lochs and lochans – are the huge, sandy strands along parts of the west side.

At Northton, where it's worth listening for corncrakes among the yellow iris to the north of the village, there is a particularly fine grazed saltmarsh close to the houses and a beach and dune system that stretches several kilometres north-east to Scarista. Largest dunes of all are at the Taransay end of Luskentyre. Look out to sea and you're likely to notice some of the gannets from the outlying islands at most times of year. On the sand, keep and eye out for otter tracks, and inland be on the alert for red deer or a golden eagle overhead.

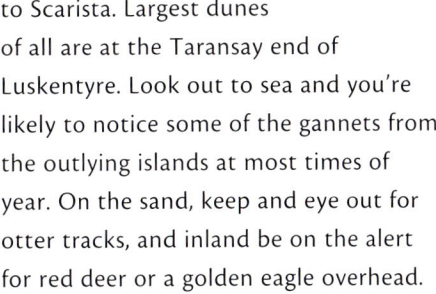

Red-Throated Diver

LEWIS

Lewis is dominated by the massive peatlands that cover much of its interior. Second only to the Caithness and Sutherland peatlands in overall extent, the Lewis bogs can rival the best in the Flow Country for sheer unbroken extent in places. The A858 road from Stornoway to Calanais (surely the most beautiful Neolithic monument surviving in Scotland) marks a major divide in the Lewis peatlands and can give a bit of an overview of the bogs beyond.

To the south is a 'cnoc and lochan' terrain of hillocks and many small waters – a good place to look out for black-throated divers and greenshank. To the north, the landscape is much, much flatter, with more inland colonies

DID YOU KNOW?

The record fishload captured by a puffin in Britain and Ireland is 61 small fry in one beakful, recorded on St Kilda in 1976. The world record is now held by a puffin from Arctic Norway that held 80 capelin larvae and two tiny sandeels in its beak in July 2001.

199

SCOTLAND'S NATURE AND WILDLIFE

OYSTERCATCHER
With its striking plumage, orange-red bill, piping call and diligent approach to defending its territory, the oystercatcher is a noticeable bird in many coastal areas. Oystercatchers, like several other kinds of wading birds, can enjoy good breeding success on the islands. The machair grasslands of the Outer Hebrides hold good numbers of them.

of gulls and skuas and bigger numbers of red-throated divers and dunlin. As ever in big bog country, the variety of colours and species of Sphagnum bog mosses under-wellie is superb.

BARRA

Barra, southernmost major island in the Outer Hebrides, has a glorious mix of high and low ground. From the summit of Heaval (383m + statue) above Castlebay you can look north towards Eriskay and South Uist and south to the final islands in the Outer Isles chain, culminating in Mingulay (NTS) and Barra Head. The former is well worth a day trip to see its dizzying cliffs, deserted village and breeding seabirds, including puffins, if you get the weather for it.

Part girdled by rocky shore, part by sand, Barra has some excellent machair along its west and north coasts. The Eoligary peninsula (one of several traditional crofting areas on the island) is excellent for flora, and the Barra show of primroses in May can rival Scotland's best. Another, much rarer, plant that grows here is Irish Lady's-tresses orchid. Despite its name, this species is most widespread in North America.

Traigh Mhor – the Cockle Strand – is in a bay that provides one of the most unusual landing places in the world at low tide. Step off a plane here and you can immediately get to grips with the natural scene as you walk away with cockle fragments on your footwear.

NORTH UIST, BENBECULA AND SOUTH UIST

For sheer floral exuberance, the machair in the Outer Hebrides, especially along the west side of North Uist, Benbecula and South Uist, is superb. Nowhere else in the world has such an expanse of this flower-rich ground. It's the scented bonus from the fragments of countless millions of shells, blown inland from Atlantic shores by the prevailing westerly winds. There are many places along the western fringe of these islands where you can get a taste of machair, including the wider systems of beach, dunes, wetlands and peaty 'blackland' which interlock with the grassland to form a complex whole.

The mix of flowers varies from place to place or even field to field. In one area, such as Berneray in the Sound of Harris for example, wild carrot, meadow cranesbill and lesser meadow rue hold sway in late summer. In another, such as Baleshare in North Uist, you can be dazzled by fence-to-fence daisies, or a golden-yellow wash of buttercups. In terms of plants, machair has few rarities associated with it although there are scarce Hebridean subspecies of early marsh orchid here. It is the sheer extent of the massed displays which is superb.

The principle that applies to machair plants – few rarities but impressive extent and number – can also hold true for breeding birds, especially the community of wading birds. Quite simply, machair in the Uists and Tiree has densities of breeding waders unsurpassed in Europe. Dunlin, ringed plover, redshank, snipe, oystercatcher and lapwing are the main species in this blend. Around one-quarter of the dunlin in the UK breed in the Uists, at densities higher than anywhere else in the world.

Various bumble-bees feed on the machair. These nectar-rich grasslands also have good numbers of butterflies, including common blue, small tortoiseshell, meadow brown and grayling.

BALRANALD

North Uist has very extensive areas of wet and dry machair.
A good place to get an idea of the wider machair system here is Balranald (RSPB). Access is off the A865, 5 kilometres north of Ceann a' Bhaigh (Bayhead), turning west down a minor road to Hogha Ghearraidh (Hougharry). Bear left after 1.5 kilometres and park near the RSPB visitor centre.

The shallow Loch na Feithean is at the heart of the reserve. Here, beds of sedges, amphibious bistort, bogbean and mare's-tail, coloured by marsh marigold and yellow iris, give shelter to breeding ducks – mostly mallard and teal, but also including shoveler, gadwall, wigeon and tufted duck.

The machair between the loch and the coastal dunes has corn marigolds and poppies, green alkanet, tufted vetch and many other flowering plants, including sea sandwort, frog orchid and wild pansy. Breeding waders on the croftland include

DID YOU KNOW?
Badgers that live in rockier, acid-soiled parts of the West Highlands are more solitary than those in the more fertile ground of other mainland areas. So for them, the east and the lowlands are their true clan strongholds.

Grey Seal

SCOTLAND'S NATURE AND WILDLIFE

hundreds of pairs of lapwing, scores of redshank, oystercatcher, ringed plover and dunlin. The best time to hear and see the waders, and the corncrakes that still breed here, is in late May, with late June and early July best for the machair flower show.

LOCH DRUIDIBEG

The same timing and a similar blend of species applies in South Uist, where Loch Druidibeg (SNH) is a superb place to see a big range of Hebridean habitats and their wildlife. The reserve covers a large area ranging from moorland and blanket bog in the east through lochs, freshwater marsh, coastal dunes and rocky shore. Loch Druidibeg, whose name means 'little starling' in Gaelic, is at the core of all this variety. A good way to experience some of its richness is to walk along a trail that leads from Stilligarry (close to the public telephone box) on the A865, out over the crazily shaped chunk of land that spreads across the middle of the loch, to the B890 and back in a circuit via Loch a' Mhachair.

Loch Druidibeg is best known for its colony of greylag geese. Islands in the loch have scrubby woodland, with birch, rowan and juniper and some are fringed with royal fern. To the east, heather moorland and rough grass stretch up the hills, red grouse and golden plover are not uncommon, and recently introduced red deer roam.

The machair is to the west of the reserve area, and is part of the most wide-reaching system in Scotland, running along the whole length of South Uist and stretching up to two kilometres inland. Red and white clover kidney, vetch, tufted vetch, eyebright, lady's bedstraw, lesser meadow-rue and red bartsia are widespread, their floral tones drawn from a large palette of pastel, but intense, colours. Near Loch Druidibeg, as in many other places in the Hebrides, the mix of plants, and breeding waders that nest among them, depends in large measure on the work of local crofters. Grazing by cattle, the use of seaweed gathered from nearby strands as fertiliser

---

REGIONAL HIGHLIGHT: LOCH DRUIDIBEG

DESIGNATION:
Nature Reserve (SNH).

LANDSCAPE:
Loch with sandflats.

HIGHLIGHTS:
The machair area to the west of the island offers a range of plants such as eyebrights, tufted vetch, kidney vetch and red bartsia. Also of interest are greylag geese, red grouse, corncrake and golden plover, plus red deer.

BEST TIME:
Spring and summer for vegetation; early summer for breeding waders and wildfowl.

FACILITIES:
Car park.

ADMISSION:
Free.

DIRECTIONS:
On A865, centre of South Uist.

CONTACT:
SNH, 135 Stilligarry,
South Uist HS8 5RS
Tel: 01870 620238
www.snh.org.uk

and the growing of fodder crops on the machair ground are all part of the secret of its success.

ST KILDA

On a clear day, you can look west from the Uists and see the shapes of large islands rearing up against the far horizon. The shapes are St Kilda National Nature Reserve (NTS) – an archipelago tens of kilometres clear of the other islands in the Outer Hebrides that holds the finest concentration of seabird colonies and underwater wildlife in the whole of North-West Europe.

For many, the closest approach to St Kilda will be to read about it in a book. Others may look longingly, from the Uists; others make the crossing only to be beaten by the weather. But that can be the way of it with outlying islands – a mixture of challenge, mystery and not infrequent frustration, punctuated by the possibility that one day, with luck and a fair wind, you might make it.

Most people who get to St Kilda as visitors do so either as members of a work party organised by the National Trust for Scotland, or through a trip with a specialist boat charter firm. Once there, the island of Hirta is the principal focus for life and exploration. But each of the four principal islands in the group has its own attractions, more usually (apart from Hirta) seen from a boat looking up or across than from ashore.

Hirta is the site of the village, evacuated in 1930, which was home to St Kilda's former inhabitants. Contrary to widespread belief, these people did not have an unbroken ancestry on the islands stretching back into prehistory, although people have lived on St Kilda off and on for over 2000 years. Their roots were as much on Skye, home of St Kilda's former laird, than on the outer isles. Hirta is now used as a tracking station operated on behalf of the army.

The old fields around the village, bounded on the hillslopes behind by a head dyke, are a great place to see Soay sheep – an ancient breed unique to these islands – at close range. The sheep graze the rough grasslands and damp meadows near the old houses, often to

LOCH DRUIDIBEG

The Loch Druidibeg National Nature Reserve on South Uist has a great range of different wildlife-rich and scenic areas within it. These include sandy beaches and flowery machair grassland on its Atlantic side, several lochs, and moorland along the skirts of hills to the east. Native Scottish greylag geese breed here.

SCOTLAND'S NATURE AND WILDLIFE

GANNET
With its huge span of white wings, you can literally see a gannet, not just a mile off, but many kilometres away. Forward-pointing eyes and an ability to swivel the wings around to fold them behind its body help a gannet to locate and dive down on fish just below the sea surface.

ATLANTIC PUFFIN
(opposite)

the accompaniment of snipe drumming or a wren (of the St Kilda subspecies) belting out a high energy burst of song from among the stoneworks. Beyond the village, just about every direction seems to demand an uphill walk. Rewards for the exertion can include a peek over the rim of Conachair, where the highest sea cliffs in Britain have a massive colony of fulmars (and the occasional cluster of puffins) scattered across sheer faces and dizzyingly perched patches of greenery. To the north lies Boreray, separated from Hirta by the several kilometres of ocean that fill the cauldron of the old volcano that once blew its top here.

Boreray and its flanking sea stacs hold the largest colony of North Atlantic gannets in the world and a free-ranging flock of black-faced sheep untended for decades. Like the other main islands in the group, puffins thrive on the greensward, sharing part of their home turf with Leach's petrels (at their major British outpost) and storm petrels.

Close to Hirta, and flanking Village Bay, the island of Dun swarms with puffins around its summit slope and has magnificent banks of sea pink and sea campion beside lush beds of sorrel and scentless mayweed in summer. Over the other side of Hirta, close to Glen Bay, sits the island of Soay, original home of the sheep that bear its name, huge and seldom visited. A place of sheer cliffs, steep slopes, low clouds and many seabirds including fulmars, puffins, manx shearwaters, great skuas and great black backed gulls, Soay seems near to Hirta and yet is largely out of reach; perhaps the ultimate outlier in all the Hebrides, secure – with luck – in its splendid isolation.

HEBRIDES

Scotland's Nature and Wildlife

Northern Isles

Fly north-east, straight as a speeding skua, from John o' Groats on the northern rim of the Scottish mainland. First there is the Pentland Firth to cross – a wild frontier of strong currents and powerful tides, as befits a narrow channel where the ocean to the west meets the North Sea to the east.

Skirt the edge of Orkney and its scatter of 70 islands, sculpted from sediments of old red sandstone laid down in a vast and vanished lake. Fly on past Fair Isle, sitting alone in the broad channel to the north of Orkney, distinctive with its prow of rock at Sheep Craig. Nearly 150 kilometres clear of Caithness, you'll reach Sumburgh Head at the southern tip of Shetland.

Beyond is an amazing archipelago of over 100 islands, stretching for some 100 kilometres to the Out Stack of Muckle Flugga, northernmost point of Britain and as far from the Scottish mainland as Inverness is from England. Hard, ancient rocks, formed in the roots of the Caledonian mountain belt between 600 and 400 million years ago, are to the fore in Shetland, with more acidic soils than on the richer sediments of Orkney.

Contrasting with each other, and both contrasting with the mainland, Orkney and Shetland should be high on the list of must-visit places for anyone keen to experience the breadth of wildlife and landscapes within Scotland. Some familiar elements from the south, such as woodland, are so scarce in the North Isles as to seem almost non-existent. The wildlife mix on the isles is thin on butterflies and some other insects. But it's big on species whose lives are bound to the sea, or which can cope with the worst that salt-laden spray can throw at them.

Seabirds, seals, whales, marine fish, seaweeds and a host of smaller saltwater dwellers are part of the distinctive wildlife tang here, as are the many otters thriving around the thousands of kilometres of North Isles coastline. Colonies of seabirds, both on cliffs and flatter expanses of island moor, are likely to feature strongly on any spring and summer visit to Orkney and Shetland.

Close to one quarter of the high cliffs in Scotland are in the North Isles; Shetland alone hosts arguably the most spectacular array of breeding seabirds in Europe, with over a million birds of 22 different species – one-tenth of the total British seabird population. For those with an eye for plants, the maritime heaths on Orkney are rich in dwarf shrubs and home to the Scots primrose. The unusual plant communities on outcropping serpentine in Shetland can be botanical highlights here.

But the glory of these islands can't be pinned down in lists of species and habitats. It's born of the close interweaving of sea, land and sky, with the lives of people and of wildlife set within this blend of the solid and the shifting.

Edmonston's Chickweed

ORKNEY

Take a large-scale map of Orkney – any part of Orkney – and look at the names on it. Now savour a few in mind or on the tongue. The rhythms, the strangeness, the glints of meaning that are almost, but not quite, understood. All these speak volumes about the layers of human involvement in these islands.

On Hoy, say, move from the Glifters of Lyrawa, over the Dwarfie Hamars across to the Howes of Quoyawa, then glide west to the Too of the Head and over, nearly back where you started, beneath the Knap of Trowieglen at the head of the burn called 'Summer of Hoy'. So many possibilities, images and sounds – and that's before you've even begun to explore the ground that underpins the names, on the isles that have supported Orkney folk for some 5000 years.

Like many island groups, you're spoilt for choice here, with some 70 islands in total; more than two dozen of them are more than 40 hectares in size and around 20 are still inhabited. Many of the islands are low-lying, their surface a weave of pasture (big on dairy cattle) with heathland beyond – including the finest maritime heaths, rich in salt-spray-shaped plants, that you'll find anywhere in Scotland.

The presence of the sea is all pervading here. Even when you can't see it, which is seldom, you'll smell it in the air, feel it as the time-shaper and rhythm-keeper of the islands. That, and the presence of the past. Nowhere else in Britain are there so many ancient sites visible, side by side with such rich areas for breeding birds and other wildlife.

ROUSAY

The island of Rousay is a prime example of this heady blend of sea coast, antiquity and wildlife. Accessible by ferry from Tingwall (off the A966) in the north-east of Orkney Mainland, Rousay has a fairly high rise, for an Orkney isle, to the 250 metre high summit of Blotchnie Fiold. Moorland punctuated by lochs takes up most of the interior, with more fertile ground out around the fringes.

Just above the ferry terminal is an orientation centre where you can find out more about Rousay and its smaller

---

DID YOU KNOW?

Owl pellets, which are coughed-up and contain indigestible material from prey, can hold a great deal of information about other wildlife. Vole bones, teeth and skulls, bits of beetle wing case and mouse fur are some of the pellet contents that could point to creatures that live within the owl's hunting range, largely unseen by people.

REGIONAL HIGHLIGHT: ROUSAY, TRUMLAND

DESIGNATION:
RSPB Reserve.

LANDSCAPE:
Loch with sandflats.

HIGHLIGHTS:
The reserve is home to a host of birds including curlew, golden plover, hen harrier, short-eared owls, Arctic terns and skuas, plus guillemots, fulmars and razorbills on the coast.

BEST TIME: Early summer for seabirds.

FACILITIES:
Visitor centre (all year round) with exhibition, toilet and picnic area.

ADMISSION:
Free.

DIRECTIONS:
Travel by ferry from Tingwall, Orkney Mainland.

CONTACT:
Tel: 01856 821395
www.rspb.org.uk

neighbours, Egilsay and Wyre. A large chunk of Rousay is run as an RSPB reserve, but before homing-in on the wildlife, you can get an idea of the islands' other riches, and appreciate the views over Eynhallow Sound, along the Westside Walk. Described by some as 'the most important archaeological mile in Scotland', the walk runs north-west from the Bay of Westness. There is evidence of settlements from the Stone Age, Iron Age, Viking Age, the time of the medieval Orkney Earls and later crofting eras here. The crowning glory is Midhowe – largest excavated Stone Age cairn in Orkney – with the Midhowe Broch, a fortified dwelling from the Bronze and Iron Ages, below it on the shore.

Up on the moors, above Trumland House in the RSPB's Trumland reserve, hen harriers, curlews and golden plover breed, plus red-throated divers over to the north-west. The Orkney voles on the island also provide food for short-eared owls, while the local merlins have plenty of meadow pipits to chase.

The west side of Rousay has cliffs which hold large numbers of seabirds, including fulmars, kittiwakes, guillemots and razorbills, and the maritime heath, both here and in the Quendale and Brings Heathlands in the north-west, has Scots primrose growing among its tougher-stemmed, shrubby plants. Quendale and Brings hold large numbers of breeding Arctic terns, up to 100 pairs of Arctic skuas and a smaller number of great skuas.

HOY

Highest of all the Orkney islands is Hoy – the name literally means 'High Island' in old Norse. You can get to this by means of a passenger ferry that links Moaness near Hoy village with Stromness, or by car ferry from Houton to Lyness or Longhope. Hoy is best known for its distinctive rock pillar – the Old Man of Hoy. This 137 metre sandstone pinnacle must have been a landmark, or seamark, for sailors from the earliest days of Orkney's colonisation onwards.

It's still a source of excitement for travellers on the ferry *en route* from the north coast of Scotland to Stromness – a sign that Orkney waters have been well and truly gained as you sail past. Once on Hoy, it's a pointer to an excellent area for wildlife along the nearby coast and inland moors.

The RSPB's North Hoy reserve

BLACK GUILLEMOT

The black guillemot, or 'tystie' as it is called in Shetland dialect, nests singly or in small colonies. This sets it apart from the other Scottish representatives of the auk family – puffin, common guillemot and razorbill – all of which are colonial and sometimes breed in the company of tens of thousands of their kind.

SCOTLAND'S NATURE AND WILDLIFE

RED-THROATED DIVER
As grebe chicks also do, young divers (like these red-throated divers) can hitch a ride on the back of a willing adult. After clambering aboard, they can snuggle between the wings to get an easy ride. As adults, they will slip silently beneath cool waters, both fresh and salt, to hunt small fish.

includes thousands of hectares of moor and coast at the north-west of the island around the Old Man. One way to walk the moorland here is to take the footpath that leads through the glen in the pass between Culags and Ward Hill. This begins close to Sandy Loch, around 1.5 kilometres east of the B9047 at Hoy village and goes several kilometres south-west to Rackwick. This would be a whole-day expedition for most people, needing perhaps seven hours for the return journey. A shorter route along the coast to the Old Man runs from Rackwick along a broad, peaty path under the hill called Moor Fea. This runs close to the cliffs part of the way, then cuts inland to the moor.

Hoy is home to one of the largest concentrations of breeding great skuas in Scotland, so you'll usually have an excellent chance of seeing one of these 'bonxies' in the air – big, bulky, dark-bodied birds that can knock most other seabirds for six if they choose. The Arctic skuas are scarcer, more dapper in looks and speedier in actions.

Red grouse, golden plover, dunlin, snipe and curlew breed on the Hoy moors, as do small numbers of hen harrier, peregrine, merlin and short-eared owls. Cliff nesters include large numbers of fulmars, guillemots and kittiwakes and smaller numbers of razorbills and shags, with a sprinkling of clifftop puffins, herring gulls and great black-backed gulls – a major black-back colony lies several kilometres away near the coast in the central portion of the island. Ravens nest on both sea cliffs and inland crags and mountain hares thrive in the hills here.

Bearberry, alpine bearberry, mountain everlasting and heath spotted orchid grow beside the path to the Old Man, with red and sea campion, primrose, spring squill and roseroot on the cliffs overlooking the rock pillar. Inland, plants such as least willow and yellow mountain saxifrage are among the Arctic alpines that grow at fairly low altitude on Hoy.

BERRIEDALE

At Berriedale, on glen sides a couple of kilometres north of Rackwick, is the northernmost native woodland in Britain. A mere couple of hectares in size at the moment, it is set to gradually expand, thanks to the work of the Orkney Islands Native Tree Restoration Project. About 100 downy birches, two stands of aspen, and a mix of rowan, eared willow, grey willow and some tea-leaved willow grow here, with wild rose and honeysuckle in the shrubbery below and a ground cover of ferns, rushes and flowering plants. Small it may be, but Hoy's native wood is big on both atmosphere and future potential.

MAINLAND

Mainland Orkney is a big place. Some 40 kilometres at its widest, girdled by a complex coast that holds mudflats, cliffs, low rocky shores and more in its many ins and outs. With large lochs and heathy hills in its interior, Mainland has much to explore. Kirkwall – the island's capital – has an otter crossing sign on one of its approach roads to whet the appetite for wildlife-watching. Only a few kilometres to the west of the town is the RSPB's Hobbister reserve. Access is to the part which lies between the A964 and the sea, with a good entry point via a minor road at the east of Waulkmill Bay – a good place to watch for waders on passage.

The waters of Scapa Flow – site of the scuttling of the German fleet in 1919 – lap the southern shore of the reserve, and are worth scanning for wildfowl, including eiders and shelduck that breed here in summer and long-tailed ducks and velvet scoter in winter. Ravens, jackdaws and rock doves breed on the cliffs, while the moorland areas inland (breeding ground for snipe and redshank) are hunted by hen harrier, kestrel, merlin and

ARCTIC TERN
(Sterna paradisea)

It's famous as the life form that sees more daylight than any other creature on the planet. Each year, arctic terns leave the Southern Ocean (where they've fed at sea during the southern summer) to fly north and breed during the northern summer. That done, they head for the south again.

So the round-trip could easily cover 30,000 kilometres in a single twelve-month period, much of it during days with reduced hours of darkness. In its lifetime, an arctic tern could cover hundreds of thousands of kilometres, mainly flying over the open sea.

The great majority of British-breeding Arctic terns are in western and northern Scotland and the majority of those are concentrated in the North Isles, scattered across more than 800 colonies (more than 500 of which are in Shetland). These 'tirricks', as they are known in Shetland, return in early May, laying a two-egg clutch in the second half of the month. Shortage of sandeels – one of the major foods of North Isles terns – caused large declines in their numbers and breeding success in the late 1980s and early 1990s. The situation has improved since then, but like all terns, the breeding success of arctics can vary hugely from one year to the next.

DID YOU KNOW?

Scotland is probably the world stronghold for the river jelly lichen. This grows on submerged rocks in shady parts of fast-flowing burns.

SCOTLAND'S NATURE AND WILDLIFE

ORKNEY VOLE
(Microtus arvalis)

Like the field voles (*Microtus agrestis*) which are among the commonest rodents on the Scottish mainland, Orkney voles are an important food for birds of prey and owls on the islands. Many an Orcadian hen harrier and short-eared owl benefits from a vole takeaway grabbed at a grassy field edge or from among the heather of a patch of moor. But there's an aura of mystery about these chunky wee nibblers, whose presence is usually evident more from signs such as holes and runways through the vegetation, than from seeing the creatures themselves.

The only other part of Britain occupied by the Orkney vole is Guernsey – a good 1000 kilometres away from Orkney. Yet the Guernsey voles are more similar to members of the same species in northern Germany than they are to their North Isles cousins. The closest relatives to Orkney voles (on the basis of skull measurements) are in former Yugoslavia.

So how did Balkan-type voles come here? Perhaps they jumped ship from an early settler's boat (they were here at Skara Brae some 4000 years ago). No one knows. What is certain is that these are special creatures in more ways than one, and worthy of special help at a time when numbers are falling.

---

short-eared owls.

West Mainland, from Stromness up to Brough Head and including the area a few kilometres inland from the wild coast, is excellent for number and variety of birds and plants. Maritime heath, with its mix of dwarf shrubs such as crowberry and some colonies of Scots primrose, can be seen in coastal situations from close to Stromness out to near the famous Neolithic settlements at Skara Brae. A great concentration of good wildlife sites lies to the north of Skara Brae.

Marwick Head (RSPB) is one of the finest Orcadian seabird colonies. Accessible from either the end of a minor road off the B9056 to Marwick Bay, or from a car park at Cumlaquoy off the B9056, the reserve has beautiful sandstone cliff ledges, built up like layers in some monumental cake. These are thronged with thousands of breeding guillemots and kittiwakes in summer, with small numbers of fulmars, razorbills and a few puffins. Rock doves and ravens also use the cliff area, and the clifftop has summer displays of sea campion, thrift and spring squill.

Only a short distance inland from Marwick Head, marshland at The Loons (RSPB) is viewable from a hide. The marsh gives nesting cover for ducks and waders. These include wigeon, teal, mallard, pintail, tufted ducks, snipe and redshank. Common gulls also breed in the reserve, kittiwakes from Marwick Head come across to wash here – a real communal bathing event – and there is a small colony of Arctic terns. In winter, wildfowl include whooper swans, greylag geese and several scores of Greenland white-fronted geese.

Another RSPB hide worth visiting on Mainland Orkney is at Lowrie's Water within the Birsay Moors reserve and on the flank of Burgar Hill. The moorland, home for hen harriers, short-eared owls and Arctic skuas, and a year-round base for Orkney voles, lies to either side of the B9057 between Dounby and Evie. Access to the hide area is off the A966, 1.6 kilometres north of Evie, along peat cutters' tracks. From it, you've a good chance in summer of watching breeding red-throated divers at a good close range without disturbing them.

For people with an inkling to travel beyond Mainland Orkney and its two hilly neighbours, there's plenty of wildlife interest in the other inhabited islands in the group. Inter-island ferries and

NORTHERN ISLES

air services make access to these other islands fairly straightforward, although you'll often need to plan to spend at least a night there – a good plan for island-goers in any case.

NORTH RONALDSAY, WESTRAY & PAPA WESTRAY

Strong tips for three contrasting islands would be North Ronaldsay with its bird observatory and seaweed-eating sheep; Westray, for maritime heath and nearby Papa Westray, accessible from Westray by the world's shortest scheduled air route.

On Papay, as it is known locally, North Hill (RSPB) has excellent maritime heath near the coast, with patches of mountain everlasting, grass-of-Parnassus, Scots primrose and alpine meadow rue, and a huge breeding population of thousands of Arctic terns. Cliffs at the eastern rim were one of the last refuges of the now-extinct great auk.

Beyond here, Scotland stops. There's nothing else beyond the Out Stack, which represents the farthest-north chunk of sea rock in the country, a giant's stone-fling from the lighthouse at Muckle Flugga. Yet although the many isles of Shetland are part of Scotland in terms of government, they also seem a world apart. Some 100 isles make up the group, many more if you count the offshore skerries, stacks and holms that break the

GREAT SKUA

The great skua, or 'bonxie', is the most powerful predator and food pirate among Scotland's seabirds. It is strong enough to knock a bird as large as a gannet out of the air, and agile enough to intercept an incoming auk and get it to drop its beakload of fish. This one is calling and displaying with raised wings on its island territory.

SCOTLAND'S NATURE AND WILDLIFE

SHETLAND

OTTER

Otter cubs, born blind in winter, spend the first few weeks of life sleeping in the warmth of a holt and suckling their mother's milk. At ten or eleven weeks old (and now well able to see the wider world) they start to follow their mother on feeding trips. Coastal otters eat a variety of fish (such as lumpsucker and butterfish), crabs and starfish.

surface beyond their larger neighbours. Unravel the coast here, and you could stretch the edge of Shetland to reach in a straight line from its northernmost tip to just south of Paris.

And what a line that would be, trailing seaweeds, barnacle-encrusted rocks, gannet guano, otter prints and the breath of great whales in its wake. For Shetland, at its core as well as its edge, is a place of the sea. People on the islands have, for millennia, been sustained by the sea and influenced by it, whether in the different colonists, from Neolithic times onwards, in the fishermen who still harvest the rich waters around here, or in the simple everyday business of inhaling the tang of it, even among the buildings of its largest town.

Fourteen of the islands are inhabited now, including Fair Isle. Although it sits at something of a halfway anchorage between Orkney and Mainland Shetland, Fair Isle fits, in its rocks, wildlife and community, with this northern group of islands.

The great bulk of the population lives on Mainland – largest of all the Shetland Isles, with a fair proportion in the capital, Lerwick. The upshot is that Shetland has enormous areas where you won't be jostling for space with other people. There is quiet moor and shore aplenty here, with the fingers of sea, known locally as 'voes', making their salty inroads not far away, wherever you choose to go.

NOSS

Certain places within the many isles stand out as offering even more than the pleasures of quiet shore rambles and breezy heathland walks for visitors. A prime example is the Noss National Nature Reserve (SNH), where a spectacular, seabird-thronged cliff system borders moorland rich in flowers. One way to fully appreciate the cliffs – where old red sandstone has been layered in ledges and blasted by wind and spray into a honeycomb of cavities – is to go on a boat trip from Lerwick harbour. That's a way of seeing the rocky southern skirts of neighbouring Bressay and having a chance of close encounters with flocks of auks on the water as you head for Noss.

Another way is to take the regular ferry service from Lerwick to Bressay, go about 5 kilometres across the island to Noss Sound and travel on an inflatable boat operated by Scottish Natural Heritage to the nature reserve isle. This service runs during the summer until the end of August, except on Mondays and Thursdays.

Once ashore, Noss is a pleasant place to walk, thanks to its sedge- and grass-rich moorland. Lousewort, heath spotted orchid, chickweed wintergreen and tormentil grow among the heather, and the moor is summer home to hundreds of great skuas – known as 'bonxies' – and a handful of pairs of the smaller Arctic skuas. Bonxie fortunes have been on the up in Shetland in recent years. These big, swashbuckling food pirates and predators first arrived on Noss in 1914, and now some 400 pairs breed here. Arctic skua fortunes have been on the wane, with a local decline. At the top of the cliffs, spring squill and thrift grow towards the edge, with roseroot, sea campion, red campion, Scots lovage and scurvy grass on the cliffs themselves.

The crowning glory of this dizzy edge is the Noup – a 181 metre high point. Seabirds with a breeding hold below include more than 45,000 guillemots, 7000 pairs of gannets and 6000 pairs of fulmars. A few thousand kittiwakes and smaller numbers of razorbills share the cliffs, with shags, black guillemots ('tysties') and herring gulls down towards the shore. A colony of great black-backed gulls is located on Cradle Holm, a small offshore stack. Puffins burrow close to the clifftop and in cracks in the high cliffs, especially around the Noup.

> ### TYSTIE
> #### (*Cepphus grylle*)
>
> 'Black guillemot' somehow doesn't roll off the tongue in the right way to suit the looks of this dapper seabird. Perhaps that's why many birdwatchers prefer to use the Shetland name 'tystie' instead. It's a straight shot of Norse, brought across here in Viking times, so it seems highly appropriate for a bird that is particularly widespread and abundant around the shores of the North Isles.
>
> Even in these island tystie havens, you're unlikely to see more than a handful of the birds together at one time. But what they lack in the force of numbers that their auk relatives – such as puffins and common guillemots – can muster, tysties more than balance with their sheer elegance.
>
> Watch closely, if you can, when a small group gathers on a rock close to the sea. Take in the chocolate sheen on dark feathers, the dramatic white wing flashes, and the vermilion lining to bill and gape. See the complex movements as the birds interact – high-stepping to emphasise foot colours, tail-cocking, and flaring wings, to flash white linings. Then you'll see that the tystie has something special – a balletic poise and elegance amidst the rolling surge and rough rocks of its chosen environment.

MOUSA

For something a bit different in island experiences, a trip to the small isle of Mousa comes highly recommended. It's a bonny place to visit by day, with hundreds of Arctic terns, lots of black guillemots, bonxies and Arctic skuas on the moor, eiders nesting and riding the water, and a haul-out for common seals. Sea campion, thrift, Scots lovage and Danish scurvy grass grow on low cliffs and there are some clumps of moss campion.

Mousa comes into a league of its own on a still summer's night. At this

> *DID YOU KNOW?*
>
> *Dragonflies and damselflies can spend years as wingless, water-dwelling larvae before taking flight for a few weeks as winged adults.*

SCOTLAND'S NATURE AND WILDLIFE

SILVER Y MOTH
(Autographa gamma)

The Silver Y is a medium-sized moth, named for the pale squiggle on each forewing. This is shaped like the letter 'Y', and also looks like the Greek character gamma – hence the second part of its scientific name.

Its autograph is intriguing, but its mass movements can be amazing. The Silver Y is common in North Africa and around the Mediterranean in winter. In summer, a first wave of sexually mature migrant moths moves north, crossing the Channel and arriving in southern England around the end of May before dispersing more widely.

This first influx is followed by a second, larger influx of non-breeding moths from the end of July until September. Some Silver Y moths can get as far north as Shetland and, in a few years, their swarms can be enormous. In August 1996, for example, Shetland lepidopterists (as moth and butterfly enthusiasts are known) reckoned that tens, if not hundreds, of millions of Silver Y moths were on the islands. As elsewhere in Britain, not one of these would have been able to overwinter, since they would not have been able to cope with the seasonal temperature drop.

latitude, although the sun does set below the horizon in summer, the afterglow can give a gentle brightness that never completely dulls to dark. This is the 'Simmer Dim', and the hours when it works its Shetland spell are the times when storm petrels are active at their breeding place.

One of these petrel colonies is Mousa, where chinks in the island's stonework can shelter the little ocean-rovers, their eggs and chicks. Drystane dykes are one thing, but the Pictish broch, for which Mousa is renowned, is something else – a palace for petrels, reeking of their musk by day, echoing with their calls by night. You can travel to Mousa by tour boat from Sandwick to take the night air, and if you time your visit right, you'll have a chance to marvel at one of the most accessible, yet strange, petrel colonies anywhere in Scotland.

UNST

The island of Unst is the northernmost populated island in Britain. Within it are two very different National Nature Reserves, one with an exceptional array

REGIONAL HIGHLIGHT: NOSS NATIONAL NATURE RESERVE

DESIGNATION:
National Nature Reserve (SNH).

LANDSCAPE:
Loch with sandflats.

HIGHLIGHTS:
Vegetation on the moor includes heath spotted orchid, chickweed wintergreen and tormentil, with sea campion, Scots lovage and thrift on the clifftops. Great and Arctic skuas can be seen on the moorland, while the cliffs hold huge numbers of seabirds such as gannets, guillemots, shags and puffins.

BEST TIME:
Early summer for skuas.

FACILITIES:
Visitor centre with exhibition.

ADMISSION:
Free.

DIRECTIONS:
Accessible by ferry from Lerwick to Bressay, travel three miles by car, then take an inflatable boat for a three-minute crossing (dinghy runs from late May to August).

CONTACT:
SNH, Ground Floor, Stewart Building, Alexandra Wharf, Lerwick, Shetland ZE1 0LL
Tel 01595 693345 www.snh.org.uk
www.nnr-scotland.org.uk

of plants, the other a major league seabird breeding station. The Keen of Hamar is the plant place and as weird a landscape as you'll find anywhere in Scotland.

Accessible from the minor road to Littlehamar, off the A968 just east of Baltasound, the reserve is on a low hill, where serpentine rock has shattered and weathered in an unusual way over large areas to form one of the biggest expanses of its kind in Europe. There's a feel of the extraterrestrial about these strange hectares of broken stone, as if the surface of another planet has lodged here, with some Earth plants colonising the rocky barrens.

Serpentine is loaded with heavy metals and poor in phosphate (a good plant booster), so the vegetation that grows here, as in some other, smaller serpentine areas in places like Caenlochan in Angus, includes some special plants, able to survive this challenge and the general dryness of the site. A number of species which have a very restricted distribution in Britain grow here, including northern rockcress, hoary whitlow grass and Norwegian sandwort. Rarest of all is the Shetland mouse-ear. Also known as Edmondston's chickweed, this grows nowhere else in the world but on Unst.

This white petalled beauty was discovered in 1837 by 11-year-old Thomas Edmonston of Buness. He later became a Professor of Botany at the Anderson University of Glasgow. Commoner plants that share the wind-blasted debris with the rare mouse-ear include thrift, sea plantain, kidney vetch, sea campion and thyme, plus the frog orchid, moss campion and stone bramble.

REDSHANK

Redshank breed in damp pastures and rough grassland on the Scottish mainland, although numbers here have fallen due to drainage and other changes in such areas. The biggest concentrations are now in the Hebrides. In winter, birds from Iceland join Scottish-bred redshank on estuaries.

HERMANESS

Only a few kilometres to the north-west of the Keen of Hamar, the Hermaness National Nature Reserve (SNH) has a huge spread of steep moorland, rising to a couple of hundred metres at the top of Hermaness Hill and bordered by steep seaward banks and cliffs. The offshore is packed with stacks, the inshore holed with natural arches and inlets, from the south-western fringe of the reserve at the headland of Tonga – a world away in weather from the Pacific isle of the same name – round by Looswick to overlook

> **DID YOU KNOW?**
> Horse chestnuts have sticky buds. This is a good way to identify them, even in late winter. For the tree, the stickiness helps to deter nibbling insects and birds that could damage or destroy the growing bud.

the waters of Burra Firth.

Access is along a waymarked route from a parking area at the end of a minor road which continues from the end of the B9086. The trail runs for several kilometres over the moor by way of Burn of Winnaswarta to the cliff edge (where it becomes unmarked) and back by way of Hermaness Hill – so there's a good deal of hiking involved. Reward for the effort comes in close views of moorland-breeding bonxies in what is now one of the largest colonies of these birds in the world. Once persecuted by collectors of eggs and bird skins, bonxies have been protected at Hermaness since the 1830s. Many hundreds of them, and smaller numbers of Arctic skuas, now breed here, among the ling, crowberry, blaeberry and orchids, sharing the moor and coastal grasslands with breeding snipe, golden plover and dunlin. Red-throated divers also use the area, flying over to feed at sea and returning to nests in inland waters.

Along the clifftops, angelica, Scots lovage, red campion and sea campion, thrift and spring squill add washes of white and pastel shades, seen to even better advantage when a pair of bright orange puffin feet is walking nearby. Hermaness is a major puffinry, with some 25,000 pairs burrowing at the clifftop and on grassy seaward slopes. The whole seabird throng here holds more than 100,000 breeders, including over 12,000 gannets in different areas. These are best viewed around the Neap and Saito and in the Humla Stack area close to the 'Ness' of Hermaness itself

Arctic Tern

– also a good place for puffins.

Tens of thousands of guillemots, a much smaller number of razorbills and a bevvy of black guillemots add to the puffins to make up the full house of British breeding auks here. Fulmars, kittiwakes, herring gulls, great black-backed gulls and shags add yet more seabird diversity, with the noise of the raucous seabird calls and cackles, sometimes punctured by a burst of wren song or the electric zing of twite over the moor and cliff edge.

FETLAR

More seabird variety again is found on the island of Fetlar, where, in addition to many of the birds found at Hermaness (except gannets), there is a small colony of manx shearwaters. These birds can be seen gathering at Tresta Bay on summer evenings. An honorary seabird that lives here is the red-necked phalarope – a bonny little wader that spends much of its year on the ocean wave.
A hide within the RSPB reserve at Loch of Funzie gives the best chance in Scotland of watching it in action. Fetlar became famous for a while from 1967 onwards for its breeding snowy owls, but no snowy owls live here any more.

FAIR ISLE

Away to the south-west of the Shetland mainland, Fair Isle (NTS) is another fine seabird breeding place, the bird colonies set close to a now-thriving community of island residents famous for their distinctive way with knitwear. Access is by the *Good Shepherd* mailboat from Grutness on the south Shetland mainland (three times a week in summer) or by air from Tingwall airport west of Lerwick.

The island is also famous for its bird observatory, established more than half a century ago. Thanks to generations of birdwatchers who have made their pilgrimage to this northern Mecca, a mind-boggling array of bird species has been recorded here. These include birds which are thousands of kilometres away from their normal migration route – some blown here by storms, others just seriously confused.

A stone wall – the Hill Dyke – divides the northern, heathery part of the island (where the observatory buildings sit down towards the pier at North Have) from the fertile southern part (where most of the inhabitants live and work their crofts). The distinctive shape of Sheep Craig, rising like the prow of an enormous, green-decked ship to the east, and the deeply indented wider coast, from the Sheep Rock round to the Nizz and back to Bu Ness, are the wilder setting for the gentler grazings, fields and moor. Many of the rarer migrants that turn up on Fair Isle make use of the food and cover in the small croft fields and along the dykes and ditches.

But it's the much commoner breeding birds on Fair isle that are guaranteed to catch the eye, whether you can tell a rustic bunting from a reed bunting or not. There are more than 40,000 individual puffins here, roughly that number of fulmar nest sites, and nearly as many individual guillemots. That's a cool 160,000-plus from these species alone, not counting their youngsters. Add another 14 breeding seabirds, including small gannet and storm petrel colonies and both Arctic and great skuas on the moor, and you have a seabird island of huge importance – and great scenic beauty.

ATLANTIC PUFFIN
Hundreds of thousands of puffins make Scotland their summer home. Their continued health depends on how people use and cherish the life-rich waters of the surrounding seas.

Useful Contacts

If you're interested in wildlife, there's no shortage of organisations that can help you to take your interest further. Some of these will offer the chance to participate in 'field' meetings, where you can get first-hand advice from experts and develop your own skills.

Specialist society publications, such as magazines and newsletters, are another excellent way to get regular refreshment of enthusiasm for a particular kind of wildlife. These days, if you have Internet access, you'll also enjoy a high success rate in finding information about anything from ladybirds to whales on websites dedicated to sharing the page creator's passion for that group of creatures.

The details given here include web addresses, although these can change as people shift service providers. But a tip for quickly locating information of this kind is to use a reliable search engine, then simply enter the organisation name or words that best apply to the information you are seeking. Type 'pine marten', for example, and you'll get relevant web links at the head of your search list. Type 'hebridean whale and dolphin' and the Hebridean Whale and Dolphin Trust also comes out top of the list.

Slight confusion can arise from sites with very similar names, such as the two groups called 'Trees for Life' (one Scottish-based, the other North American), but the minor hassle of going to the wrong web destination (at least in this case) is balanced by the good content you'll find on both these sites.

Listings here are bunched according to major species groups, followed by details of national conservation organisations. But first, a couple of contacts for associations that provide a broad range of training opportunities and information for naturalists.

GENERAL NATURAL HISTORY

The Scottish Field Studies Association provides children and adults with the opportunity to study a wide range of countryside subjects through residential courses at its base at Kindrogan in rural Perthshire:
Scottish Field Studies Association, Kindrogan Field Centre, Enochdhu, Blairgowrie PH10 7PG.
www.field-studies-council.org/kindrogan

The British Naturalists' Association, the national body for naturalists, is one of the country's oldest Natural History organisations, founded in 1905. It is the only national body which promotes the study of all branches of natural history. Nationally the Association organises study days, field weeks and weekends, lectures and exhibitions. BNA's magazine Country-Side is sent to members twice a year and covers all aspects of natural history, catering for both adults and youngsters.
www.bna-naturalists.org

INSECTS AND OTHER INVERTEBRATES

Dragons and damsels
The British Dragonfly Society promotes and encourages the study and conservation of dragonflies, damselflies and their habitats. It organises field trips in different parts of Britain and publishes a journal and newsletter.
www.dragonflysoc.org.uk

SLUGS AND SNAILS

The Conchological Society is one of the oldest societies devoted to the study of Mollusca (molluscs). The Society promotes the study of Mollusca in its widest aspects through its publications, meetings and census schemes. It publishes papers on the shells, anatomy, distribution, nomenclature of British and worldwide molluscs, and holds meetings in London, field meetings and workshops on mollusc identification.
www.conchsoc.org

BUTTERFLIES

The alarming decline of many butterflies in the mid twentieth century led a small group of dedicated naturalists, headed by Sir Peter Scott, to form Butterfly Conservation in 1968. Since that time Butterfly Conservation has grown steadily to become the largest insect conservation organisation in Europe. It now has over 30 regional branches covering the whole of the UK, which carry out the vital local conservation tasks, and offices in Scotland, England and Wales. Members get a colour magazine three times a year, regular newsletters and the chance to take part in field trips and practical conservation tasks.
www.butterfly-conservation.org

USEFUL CONTACTS

SPIDERS, PSEUDOSCORPIONS AND HARVESTMEN
The British Arachnological Society is open to any individual interested in the study of spiders and other arachnids. Membership privileges include a bulletin and newsletter published thrice yearly.
www.britishspiders.org.uk

REPTILES AND AMPHIBIANS
The British Herpetological Society publishes a newsletter and journal and has meetings in Scotland and England.
www.thebhs.org

BIRDS
The Scottish Ornithologists' Club (SOC) was established more than 65 years ago. The network of 14 branches organises field meetings, a winter programme of talks and social events. Its headquarters, at Aberlady from summer 2005, houses the largest library of bird literature in Scotland: SOC, Scottish Birdwatching Resource Centre, Waterston House,
Aberlady, East Lothian EH32 6PY
www.the-soc.org.uk

The British Trust for Ornithology has existed since 1933 as an independent, scientific research trust, investigating the populations, movements and ecology of wild birds in the British Isles. BTO Scotland started operation in 2000. Members receive *BTO News* and have the option of a journal: BTO Scotland.
www.bto.org/national-offices/scotland

The Royal Society for the Protection of Birds has the largest membership of any wildlife conservation body in Europe and runs many open access reserves in Scotland, from Shetland to the Solway. There are members' groups that hold indoor and field meetings in different parts of the country and a network of regional offices. Members receive *Birds* magazine quarterly:RSPB Scotland.
www.rspb.org.uk/scotland

The Wildfowl and Wetlands Trust aims to conserve and protect the world's wetlands and waterfowl. Members receive a quarterly magazine and an annual journal: WWT Caerlaverock Wetland Centre, Eastpark Farm, Caerlaverock, Dumfries-shire DG1 4RS
www.wwt.org.uk/visit/caerlaverock

MAMMALS
The Mammal Society works to protect British mammals, halt the decline of threatened species, and advise on all issues affecting British mammals. It encourages the study of mammals, works to identify the problems they face and promotes conservation and other policies based on sound science. Members receive a newsletter and other publications.
www.mammal.org.uk

BATS
The Bat Conservation Trust is the UK's only organisation solely devoted to the conservation of bats and their habitats. It supports a network of batworkers' groups, runs a national helpline and a bat monitoring programme.
www.bats.org.uk

BADGERS
The National Federation of Badger Groups promotes the conservation, welfare and protection of badgers, their setts and habitats. It supports 80 local voluntary badger groups, gives expert advice on all badger issues and works closely with MPs, the police and other conservation and welfare organisations. The NFBG uses all lawful means to campaign for the improved protection of badgers and the Federation is a member of the Partnership for Action Against Wildlife Crime (PAW).
www.nfbg.org.uk

WHALES, DOLPHINS AND PORPOISES
The Hebridean Whale and Dolphin Trust has pioneered the study of the whales, dolphins and porpoises found in the waters of the Hebrides. This helps to provide useful information for cetacean conservation and materials for work in environmental education.
The Hebridean Whale and Dolphin Trust,
28 Main Street, Tobermory, Isle of Mull,
Argyll PA75 6NU
Tel: 01688 302620
www.hwdt.org

WDCS (The Whale and Dolphin Conservation Society) is the world's most active charity dedicated to the conservation and welfare of all whales, dolphins and porpoises. It supports research on bottlenose dolphins and other cetaceans in Scottish waters and runs an 'Adopt-a-dolphin' scheme to help this work.
www.wdcs.org

GENERAL MARINE WILDLIFE
The Marine Conservation Society is the UK's national charity for the marine environment and its wildlife.
www.mcsuk.org

PLANTS
Plantlife acts directly to stop common wild plants becoming rare in the wild, to rescue wild plants on the brink of extinction, and to protect sites of exceptional botanical importance. The charity carries out practical conservation work, influences relevant policy and legislation, and collaborates widely to promote the cause of wild plant conservation:
Plantlife – The Wild-Plant Conservation Charity,
www.plantlife.org.uk/scotland

MOSSES AND LIVERWORTS
The British Bryological Society provides tuition, organises meetings, facilitates research and aids measures for moss and liverwort conservation.
www.britishbryologicalsociety.org.uk

The British Lichen Society was formed in 1958 to stimulate and advance interest in all branches of lichenology. The first society in the world entirely devoted to the study of lichens, it has many overseas as well as British members. It publishes *The Lichenologist* six times a year and a bulletin.
www.thebls.org.uk
www.britishlichensociety.org.uk

TREES
Reforesting Scotland promotes awareness of the deforestation of Scotland and is committed to helping ecological restoration and community development through reforestation.
www.reforestingscotland.org

Trees for Life is a Scottish conservation charity dedicated to the regeneration and restoration of the Caledonian Forest in the Highlands. Members receive a newsletter and have the opportunity to help with practical conservation projects:
www.treesforlife.org.uk

The Woodland Trust is the UK's leading charity dedicated to protection of our native woodland heritage. Members receive a regular large-format colour newsletter and directory of trust woods.
www.woodland-trust.org.uk

The Forestry Commission Headquarters are in Edinburgh:
Forestry Commission, Silvan House, 231 Corstorphine Road, Edinburgh EH12 7AT
www.forestry.gov.uk

NATIONAL CONSERVATION AND ENVIRONMENTAL GROUPS
Friends of the Earth Scotland:
Thorn House, 5 Rose Street, Edinburgh, EH2 2PR
www.foe-scotland.org.uk

The Scottish Wildlife Trust has branches throughout mainland Scotland and many reserves, from the North Isles to the Borders. Members receive a magazine and local newsletter. Junior membership is catered for by Watch Scotland, which produces its own newsletter and supports local environmental education events.
www.swt.org.uk

The John Muir Trust, named after the pioneering Scottish-born conservationist who played a key part in setting up the US National Parks System, owns several large estates in Scotland and aims to 'conserve and protect wild places with their indigenous animals, plants and soils for the benefit of present and future generations'.
www.jmt.org
www.johnmuirtrust.org

WWF Scotland promotes the conservation of nature and natural processes by protecting biodiversity, sustainable use of resources and reduction of pollution and waste.
www.wwf.org.uk/scotland

The National Trust for Scotland is a broad-ranging conservation charity that promotes Scotland's natural and cultural heritage.
www.nts.org.uk

Scottish Natural Heritage is the government conservation agency whose mission is to work with Scotland's people to care for our natural heritage.
www.snh.org.uk

USEFUL CONTACTS

NATIONAL PARKS & NATURE RESERVES

Scotland's National Nature Reserves the National Nature Reserve (NNR) accolade applies to the best wildlife sites in Scotland so everyone can appreciate and be proud of Scotland's wonderful nature. Most reserves have habitats and species that are nationally or internationally important so the wildlife is managed very carefully.
www.nnr-scotland.org.uk

Scotland's National Parks
Both of Scotland's National Parks, Loch Lomond and The Trossachs and the Cairngorms, are central to rural economic development and recreation, sustainability, and the conservation of their diverse natural habitats.
www.cairngorms.co.uk
www.lochlomond-trossacs.org

DR KENNY TAYLOR has had a passion for wildlife since the age of five. Birds, lizards, butterflies and flowers close to a burn in Kirkintilloch set him on the trail of learning more about Scotland's natural richness.

Now based on the Black Isle, Kenny is a respected writer and broadcaster on natural history, environmental issues and popular science. Author of several books, his articles appear regularly in BBC Wildlife Magazine and many other publications and he has travelled widely on TV, radio and magazine assignments for the BBC and for National Geographic Magazine.

Kenny has given more than two hundred talks on Scottish wildlife at venues from the North Isles to the Borders. For the thousands of people who have heard him speak about wildlife and for many more besides, this book will be a widely welcomed account of his knowledge of Scotland's natural scene.

Index entries in **BOLD** indicate photographs

Aberdeen 15, 26, 111, 118, 120, 122-3
Aberfeldy 136
Aberlady Bay 106, 107
Abernethy Forest Reserve 152
Abriachan Forest 160
Abriachan Woodlands 161
Adder 8, 35, 38, 39, 70, **98**, 99
Ant, Wood 14, **44**, 56, 133, 140
Arctic Tern 102, 115, **115**, 122, 123, 125, 208, 209, 211, 212, 213, 216
Ariundle 173, 174
Arnhall Moss 123
Arran 92, 93
Ayr Gorge Woodlands 92
Badger 32, 33, 52, 86, 88-9, **91**, 111, 201, 222
Balmacaan Woods 159
Balranald 201
Barnyards Marsh 103
Barra 118, 190, 200
Bass Rock 94, 108, **109**
Bat 28, 29, 54, 55, 58, 105, 221
 Pipistrelle 25, 28
Bawsinch 106
Beauly Firth 112
Bee 42, 53, 85, 194, 201
Beinn Eighe 169, 170, 171
Ben Lawers 9, 130, **131**, 132
Ben Lomond 94, 95, 96
Ben Nevis 16, 173
Benbecula 201
Berriedale 211
Birches **50**, 61, 85, 136, **144**, 149, 156-7
Birsay Moors 212
Black Wood of Rannoch 133
Bluebell 54, 67, 79, **80**, 81, 83, 88, 89, 92, 105
Bog Asphodel **97**
Bullers of Buchan 118
Buttercup 138, 189
Butterfly, Chequered Skipper 174
 Orange Tip 88, 95, 154, 159
 Peacock 95
 Red Admiral 38, 56, 95
 Scotch Argus **56**, 83, 137, 138
 Small Heath 88, 122, 133
 Small Pearl-Bordered **43**, 122, 175
 Small Tortoiseshell 38, 53, 56, 90, 133
 Speckled Wood 161, 175
Buzzard 95, 96, **165**, 171, 183, 184
Caenlochan 154, 155, 217
Caerlaverock 9, **76**, 77
Cairnsmore of Fleet 67
Canna 191, 194
Capercaillie **18**, 133, 144, **149**, 152
Carrifran 68, 69
Carstramon Wood 81
Cashel Farm 95
Chaffinch 79, 104, 114, 123
Clatteringshaws 82
Clyde Valley Woodlands 89
Colinton Dell 105
Coll 118, 189, 190, 198, 199
Corncrake 189, 190, **191**, 199
Cottongrass 90
Countryside Code 65
Crab 45, **47**
Craigellachie 148, 149
Craigleith 108
Creag Meagaidh 156, 157
Crinan Wood 174
Cromarty Firth 113
Crossbill, Scottish 35, 133, 136, 140, 144, **160**, 183
Culbin 113, 114
Culbin Bar 114
Curlew 62, 78, 96, 103, 107, 109, 113, 182, **182**, 198
Dee Marshes 79
Deer, Red **1**, **34**, 35, 48, 82, 93, **132**, 140, 142, 156-7, 181, 184, 193, 198
 Roe 35, **88**, 99, 118, 181
 Sika 35, 181
Diver, Black-Throated 14, 54, 165, 172, **178**, 184, 199
 Red-Throated **49**, 150, 162, 200, **210**, 218

Dolphin, Bottlenose **3**, 26, 56, **112**, 118, 123
Donmouth 123
Dotterel 27, 54, 155, **159**
Dragonfly, Golden-Ringed 41, 160, **171**
Duck, Eider 52, 100, 102, **120**, 167
Duddingston Loch 106
Dunlin **36**, 62, 78, 100-1, 113, 184, 198, 201
Dunnet Bay 184
Durness 185
Eagle, Golden **6**, 81, 93, **143**, 155, 169, 186
 Sea 16, 81, 193, **195**, 198
Eden Estuary 100
Eigg 191-2
Eyemouth 74, 75
Eyemouth Marine Reserve 75
Fair Isle 207, 219
Falcon, Peregrine 62, 68, **69**, 78, 82, 88, 97
Falls of Clyde 86, 87, 88
Fetlar 218, 219
Findhorn Bay 114
Flanders Moss 97
Fly Agaric 74
Fowlsheugh 124, 125
Fox, Red **30**, 31
Fraserburgh Harbour 117
Frog 39, **40**, 53, 62, 184
Fulmar 75, **75**, 102, 116, 118, 138, 204, 215
Galloway Forest Park 81
Gannet 94, **109**, 116, 199, 204, **204**, 215, 218
Glasswort 113, 193
Glen Affric 164
Glen Cannich 164
Glen Muick 142
Glen Nevis 173
Glen Strathfarrar 163
Glen Tanar 143, 148
Glenmore Forest Park 140, 142, 151
Goat 67, **168**
Godwit, Bar-Tailed 100, 101, 107, 109, 114, 121, **127**, 182, 198
Goose, Barnacle 54, 61, 77, 79, 117, **196**, 197
 Bean 104, 123
 Brent 104
 Grey 59, 117, 123, 126
 Greylag 54, 78, 79, 104, 106, 117, **119**, 123, 145, 182
 Pink-Footed 78, 99, 104, 117, 123, 182
 Snow 104
 White-Fronted 61, 80, 104, 123, 212
Gordon Moss 70
Gorse 123
Grebe, Black-Necked 90
 Great Crested 80, 90, 91, 139
 Slavonian 160, 162, **163**
Greenshank 14, 54, 103, 113, 199
Grey Mare's Tail 68
Grouse, Black 95-6, **141**, 144, 152, 165
 Red **9**, **58**, 59, 67, 133, 148, 184, 211
Guillemot 53, 55, **73**, 74, 108, 124, **209**, 215
Handa Island 124, 185, **185**
Hare, Brown 18, 30, 53
 Mountain **7**, 18, 30, 63, **63**, 157
Harris 13, 189, 190, 191, 199
Heather 55, 58, 67, 148, 157, 170, 189
Hedgehog 55, 61, **87**, 92
Hen Harrier 78, 82, 99, 162
Hermaness 218
Hirsel Country Park 72
Hobbister 211
Hogganfield Park 90
Hoy 209, 210, 211
Inchcailloch 95
Insh Marshes 145, **145**, 146
Inverewe Gardens 172
Inverness 15, 26, 112
Inversnaid 96

Islay 123, 197
Isle of May 85, 101, 102, **102**
John Muir Country Park 108
Jura 198
Keen of Hamar 217
Kessock, North 112
 South 112
Killiecrankie 137
Kingfisher 74, 90, 92, **93**, 112
Kite, Red **37**, 121
Knapdale 174
Knockan Cliff 186
Kylerhea 194, 195
Ladybird 106
Lake of Menteith 99
Lammermuir Hills **17**
Lapwing 57, 78, 103, 117, 121, **139**, 193, 201, 202
Ledmore 178, 179, 180
Lewis 13, 199
Liathach 168
Lily, White Water 22
 Yellow Water 139, 147
Limpet 42, 62
Lizard 38, 39, 58
 Common 12, **39**
 Slow-Worm 12, 38, 39, 161
Loch an Eilein 150
Loch Druidibeg 202, 203, **203**
Loch Faskally 138
Loch Fleet 180, 181, 182
Loch Garten Osprey Centre 152
Loch Gruinart 197, 198
Loch Ken 79
Loch Leven 103
Loch Lomond 13, 15, 94, 95
Loch Maree 170, 172
Loch Ness 13, 158, 162
Loch of Strathbeg 117
Loch of the Lowes 138, 139
Loch Ruthven 162
Loch Tay 130
Lochnagar 141, 142, 143
Lochwinnoch 91
Longhaven Cliffs 118
Loons, The 212
Marwick Head 212
Merlin 62, 78, **83**, 97, 189
Mersehead 78
Midge, Highland 14, 170, 184
Migdale 178, 179, 180, 181
Minnow 88, 100, 147
Montrose Basin 126
Morrone Birkwood 140
Moth, Emperor 43, **82**, 122, 142
 Fox Moth 122, 133
 Northern Eggar 133, 142, 193
 Puss **24**
 Silver Y 216
Mousa 216, 217
Muir of Dinnet 144
Mull 198
Newt, Palmate 40
Nigg 113
North Hill 213
North Ronaldsay 213
Noss 215, 216
Orchid, Heath-Spotted **135**, 157, 186
 Purple 74, **78**, 79
Orkney Mainland 13, 208
Orkney Vole 209, 212
Osprey **13**, 53, 57, 115, 139, 146, 150, 152, **153**
Otter 31, 32, **33**, 83, 195, 198, 207, 211, **214**
Owl, Barn 78, 83
 Tawny **20**, 88, 89, 159
Oystercatcher 62, 78, 101, 107, 109, 114, 121, **200**, 201
Papa Westray 213
Pass of Ryvoan 151
Pine Marten 8, 14, 52, 133, 157, 170, **181**
Pitlochry Dam 138
Pollock Country Park 90
Possil Marsh 89
Ptarmigan 47, 59, 93, 96, 157, 171, **172**
Puffin 35, 36, 55, 56, **57**, 101, 102,

119, 185, 198, 199, **205**, 218, **219**
Purple Saxifrage 88, **131**
Queen Elizabeth Forest Park 96
Rabbit **29**, 30, 55
Rannoch Moor 134
Redshank 62, 115, **217**
Reindeer 52, **150**, 151
River Spey 115, 147, 156
River Tweed 68, 70, **71**
River Ythan 119
Rosebay Willowherb 85
Roseisle 113
Rothiemurchus Estate 150
Rousay 208, 209
Rowan 48, 89, 161
Rum 17, 191, 193
Salmon, Atlantic **137**, 148
Sandpiper, Purple 62, **116**, 117
Sands of Forvie 121
Schiehallion 135
Sconser 195
Scots Pine **10**, 12, 95, 111, 133, 143, 148, 170
Scots Primrose 45, 184, 207, 209
Scotstoun Moor 122, 123
Scottish Seabird Centre 108
Seal, Common 27, 55, **94**, 113, 192, 216
 Grey **23**, 27, 61, 85, **102**, 113, 116, 151
Sea Thrift **53**
Seaton Cliffs 127
Seaweed, Brown 15, 167
Shag 53, 75, 102, 118, **125**
Shelduck 78, **101**, 120, 121, 122
Sitka Spruce 96, 113, 151
Skye 13, 17, 194
Snow Bunting 114, 122, 155, **157**
Solway 75, 76, 77
Southwick Coast 78, 79
Sparrowhawk 52, 62, 88, 152, 198
Spey Bay 115
Spider, Garden Cross 28, 45
Squirrel, Grey 30, 104, 133
 Red **4**, 31, 59, 67, 93, 133, **161**
St Abb's Head 74
St Cyrus 124, 125, 126
St Kilda 25, 199, 203, 204
Starling 79
Strathaird 195
Sundew, Common **122**
Swan, Bewick 61, 77
 Mute 71, 72, 90, 106, 109, 121
 Whooper **54**, 61, 72, 77, 99, 104, 109, 118, 212
Tay Estuary 140
Taynish 175
Tentsmuir Forest / Point 99
Thistle 56, 59, 114
Threave Wildlife Refuge 79
Tiree 189, 198
Tit, Crested 114, 140, 152, **155**, 164
Torridon 168, 169
Torrin 195
Treshnish Isles, The **11**
Troup Head 116
Trout, Brown 70, 103, 106, 158
 Sea 70, 95, 126, 158
Trumland 208, 209
Tummel Shingle Islands 138
Twinflower 14, 138, 142, **146**, 165
Udale 113
Uist, North 201
 South 201, 202, 203
Unst 217
Urquhart Bay Woods 158, 159
Vane Farm 103
Water of Leith 105
Westray 213
Whale, Minke 25, **26**, 56, 193, 194, 198
Wigeon 78, 80, **104**, 118, 126, 182
Wigtown Bay 83
Wildcat 8, 52, 61, 157, 161, 186, **187**
Wood of Cree 83
Wood Sorrel 81, 89, 96, **175**, 192
Woodpecker, Great spotted **60**, 74, 88, 95, 137
 Green 74, 106

PLEASE NOTE THE FOLLOWING ABBREVIATIONS USED THROUGHOUT THIS BOOK:
FC: Forestry Commission **JMT**: John Muir Trust **LNR**: Local Nature Reserve **NNR**: National Nature Reserve **NTS**: National Trust for Scotland **RSPB**: Royal Society for the Protection of Birds **SNH**: Scottish National Heritage **SWT**: Scottish Wildlife Trust **WWT**: Wildfowl and Wetland Trust